THE KINGDOMS OF AFRICA

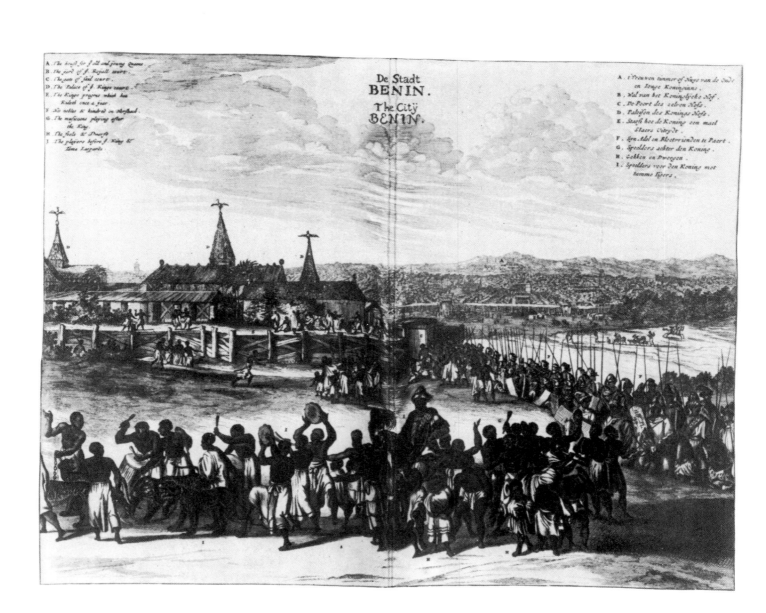

The Making of the Past

The Kingdoms of Africa

Peter Garlake

Peter Bedrick Books
New York

Sir John Boardman
Lincoln Professor of Classical Art and Archaeology,
University of Oxford

Basil Gray
Former Keeper of Oriental Antiquities, British Museum

David Oates
Emeritus Professor of Western Asiatic Archaeology,
Institute of Archaeology, University of London

Frontispiece: the Oba of Benin processes past his palace and city, from a 17th-century engraving by a Dutch artist.

AN EQUINOX BOOK
First American edition published in 1990 by
Peter Bedrick Books
2112 Broadway
New York NY 10023

First edition © 1978 Elsevier Publishing Projects SA, Lausanne
Second edition © 1990 Equinox (Oxford) Ltd

Library of Congress Cataloging-in-Publication Data
Garlake, Peter S.
    The kingdoms of Africa / by Peter Garlake. - - 1st American ed.
        p.   cm. - - (The Making of the past)
    "A Equinox book" - - CIP t.p. verso.
    Includes index.
    ISBN 0-87226-305-3 (hard)
    ISBN 0-87226-234-0 (pbk.)
    1. Africa - - Civilization.   2. Africa - - Antiquities.   I. Title.
    II. Series: Making of the past (New York, N.Y.)
DT14.G38   1990
960'.2 - - dc20   90-37778
                                                            CIP

Printed in Portugal
5 4 3 2 1

Contents

Maps

Preface to the series

This book is a volume in the Making of the Past, a series describing the early history of the world as revealed by archaeology and related disciplines. The series is written by experts under the guidance of a distinguished panel of advisers and is designed for the layman, for young people, the student, the armchair traveler and the tourist. Its subject is a new history – the making of a new past, uncovered and reconstructed in recent years by skilled specialists. Since many of the authors of these volumes are themselves practicing archaeologists, leaders in a rapidly changing field, the series is completely authoritative and up-to-date. Each volume covers a specific period and region of the world and combines a detailed survey of the modern archaeology and sites of the area with an account of the early explorers, travelers, and archaeologists concerned with it. Later chapters of each book are devoted to a reconstruction in text and pictures of the newly revealed cultures and civilizations that make up the new history of the area.

Preface

The kingdoms of Africa, with their many different forms, are difficult to categorize in conventional western terms. They have their own characteristics. People were always more important than land. Order was frequently ensured by spiritual and magical forces, as much as through military strength. Power did not always rest with a single authority. A diverse range of institutions – such as age sets and secret societies – cut across family, clan and lineage loyalties that survived from earlier times. They met the need to integrate people who shared no ties of blood into a single community.

African kingdoms show great continuity with the past. Their roots lie deep in prehistory, in the first villages on the continent. Many lineages retained the prestige and power that they had gained in early village communities and formed the hierarchies of the new kingdoms. Institutions developed in response to many different strains or incentives within a given society. Often they would soon be adapted to new circumstances or abandoned. No kingdom was unchanging. Thus, there is no polarity between states and stateless societies in Africa. In the same way, there is no gulf between "primary" and "secondary" states. Such terms have little significance.

Kingdoms came into being in many different ways. Some groups gained power because they had acted as mediators between conflicting elements. They were judges in disputes; brokers in dealings with foreign traders; arbiters between farmer and herder or miner and merchant. Some kingdoms prospered through their control of long-distance trade: the early empires of Ghana and Mali, in the West African savanna, were intermediaries between the miners of the forest and the merchants of North Africa. The states around the Great Lakes of East Africa reflect various means of reconciling the conflicting interests of cattle herders and cereal farmers. Many groups rose to power through their ownership or control of cattle herds. Among the Chewa people of Malawi and the Mbundu people of Angola, the process by which religious specialists became political leaders can be traced. The Kongo kingdom in northern Angola grew up as a redistribution center where the products of the tropical forest could be exchanged with those of the grasslands. It grew powerful on the wealth and specializations generated by its internal trade.

In an attempt to trace some of these themes through time, concentrating particularly on the evidence from archaeology, some kingdoms have had to be omitted. Egypt has already been the subject of a separate book in this series. Meroë, the kingdom on the Upper Nile, had its origins in pharaonic Egypt. Egyptian influence was central and all pervasive. Its African content is visible only in some stylistic elements of the architecture and ceramics. The extent of its technological and political influence on the rest of Africa, manifested by the spread of ironworking or particular forms of kingship, is still debated. Aksum, in the northern Ethiopian highlands, inherited Meroë's power. Its origins lay outside Africa – in southern Arabia – and its influence on the lands to the south was negligible. The monuments of Meroë and Aksum are too dramatic to go unillustrated here, but their role in the development of the kingdoms of the rest of the continent was probably peripheral.

This study concentrates on information derived from archaeology. Some states are therefore not discussed simply because no archaeological work has ever been undertaken in their territories. Around the southern edges of the equatorial forests were the Kongo kingdom, the Mbundu, Lubu and Lunda states and, in the east, Rwanda and Burundi. No site of theirs has yet been excavated. In West Africa, the kingdoms of Oyo, Dahomey and Asante and the Islamic city-states to the north of them are equally untouched.

The contribution of archaeology to an understanding of the growth of African kingdoms has been largely indirect. Studies concerned with the origin of man and with the Stone Age in Africa have made headlines throughout the world. Work on the later periods has been much more isolated and fragmented.

Most archaeologists in Africa have yet to recognize the complexities and richness of the societies they are studying or to design programs of research that will elucidate the disparate elements within a society and the way in which these interacted to mold the economy and its development. For it is most frequently in the inner workings of a society that changes are generated. Reflecting this realization, historians of Africa are now turning their attention to studies of social and economic process, in order to seek an understanding of the origins of many of Africa's problems – such as those of underdevelopment and rural poverty. These new perspectives will greatly stimulate archaeological research, for these are concerns with which archaeology can, in fact, come to grips most readily. Sadly, much of the rich mass of archaeological data now available from African kingdoms was gathered in excavations by archaeologists with very different concerns. It is, therefore, frequently difficult to place it or to interpret it in new frameworks. Often it has little relevance to the new problems. This then is a report from a discipline that it only just starting to seek new directions and focus on new interests. The process of developing methods to realize these new aims has barely commenced. Certainly, the best is yet to come.

Chronological Table

Timeline (BC / AD) with events on the left margin:

- 7000 BC
- 6500
- 6000
- 5500
- 5000
- Sheep and pottery in Cyrenaica
- 4500
- 4000 — Food production in lower Egypt
- 3500
- 3000
- 2500
- 2000 — Saharan desiccation far advanced
- 1500
- 1000
- 500 — Carthage founded
- 400
- 300
- 200
- 100 — Rome conquers Carthage
- 0 — Camel introduced into Sahara
- 100
- 200
- 300
- 400
- 500
- 600
- 700 — Death of Muhammad / Muslim conquest of N Africa
- 800 — Muslim expedition to Mauritania
- 900 — Zanj revolt in Iraq
- 1000
- 1100 — Almoravids capture Awdaghust / Seljuk dynasty in SW Asia
- 1200 — Mongols unify Asia
- 1300 — Mamluk dynasty in Egypt / Europe adopts gold standard
- 1400
- 1500 — Portuguese enter Gulf of Guinea / Vasco da Gama reaches India
- 1600 — Dutch, English enter Gulf of Guinea (1593) / Morocco conquers Songhay (1591)
- 1700
- 1800
- 1900 AD

Entries / cultures plotted across the chart (approximate positions, left to right):

- Cape sheep herders
- Transvaal
- E Transvaal
- Natal
- Leopard's Kopje
- Manekweni
- Khami/Rozvi
- Great Zimbabwe
- Rhodesia
- Munhu Mutapa
- Urungwe
- Zambia
- Zambia transitional industries
- Zambian copper
- Malawi
- Zambia
- Manda
- Mogadishu
- Kilwa
- Bigo
- Aksum
- Igbo Ukwu
- Ife
- Luo
- Benin
- Ghana
- Mali
- Songhay
- Begho
- Asante
- Turkana
- Sudan "dotted wavy line" ware
- Sahara potters
- Sahara herders
- Tassili
- Karkarichinkat
- Kintampo
- Dhar Tichitt
- Mauritanian copper
- Senegambian megaliths
- Nok
- North Horr pottery
- East African pastoralists
- Kantsyore
- Meroe
- Uganda
- Kenya
- Sanhaja confederation

Sources / chroniclers (right margin):

- Herodotus
- Periplus of Erythraean Sea
- Claudius Ptolemy
- al Fazari
- al Yakubi
- al Masudi
- al Bakri
- al Idrisi
- al Omari
- Ibn Battuta
- Catalan Atlas
- Joao d'Aveiro
- (1512) Leo Africanus
- (post 1520) Kilwa Chronicle
- Vicente Pegado
- Olfert Dapper
- van Nyendael

Introduction

In looking at the most significant archaeological advances in Africa over the period since this book was first published, one unifying impulse becomes apparent. It is the increasing recognition of the autonomy, creativity and innovative dynamism of indigenous local societies. These qualities emerge at every technological, economic and social level as societies have recognized and responded, through conscious rational choices and decisions, to the challenges and opportunities of new lands, resources, products and technologies, and to changing patterns of rainfall, vegetation and fauna. This has been made apparent by archaeologists who have designed their research programs and strategies on the level of whole ecological regions and tried to study all the people, resources and settlements in these regions rather than concentrating exclusively on a single site, however important. The old implicit assumptions that Africans through the ages were the passive recipients of new products and technologies, that developments were imposed on societies by external agents and agencies, have almost gone. The changes represent a general shift of outlook, a new way of thinking about the past and about society. It was foreshadowed in this book but the ways in which it would work its way through every aspect of the study of prehistory could not then be predicted.

The shift is evident in studies of every region and period: in studies of Late Stone Age hunters or foragers throughout the continent through to intensive studies of contemporary San groups in the Kalahari; of the first pastoralists of the Sahara and Sahel by Fred Wendorf and Andrew Smith; of the first farmers in eastern Africa by Stanley Ambrose and Peter Robertshaw and in the eastern coastlands of southern Africa by Tim Maggs and Martin Hall; of the settlement and rapid rise to prosperity of new settlers on the harsh fringes of the Kalahari Desert in Botswana by Jim Denbow; of the settlement of the high interior grasslands of South Africa by Tim Maggs; and of the internal economic and political dynamics of the states in Zimbabwe and Mozambique by Graeme Barker and myself. Roderick and Susan McIntosh have investigated the great and virtually newly discovered ancient West African city of Jenne-Jeno and its many dependent settlements in the floodplain of the inner Niger delta and have revolutionized our understanding of the rise and nature of cities not only in western Africa but world-wide. Historians have followed suit and come to explore the autonomous internal dynamics that developed and sustained Saharan cities such as Awdaghust. Along the East African coast, studies and excavations of settlements by Mark Horton and Thomas Wilson have given a firm base to their origins in local African society and shown that they were flourishing concerns with widespread trading contacts long before they felt the impact of Islam.

Studies of technological innovations have progressed less dramatically but our understanding of their implications for development and their consequences has deepened. There is increased recognition that almost all the fundamental developments probably took place within the continent. A new and convincing relationship has been suggested between ironworking and the development of agriculture, establishing the need to have metal cutting tools to reap cereals and domesticate grains such as sorghum.

Prehistorians are now much more aware of how important to an understanding of the past are studies of the internal dynamics, structures, institutions and beliefs that led to wealth and power becoming concentrated in the hands of the few, of the ways that control or coercion were exercised to maintain the stability and permanency of the state. However, much of the work in this field remains on the level of speculative generalization and is based on the imposition of externally generated models, often neo-Marxist, with little detailed evidence to support it.

There has, nevertheless, been a much wider recognition of the role, emphasized in the following pages, that control over increasing herds of cattle played throughout southern Africa in the rise of lineages, chiefs and kings and in the growth of states such as Great Zimbabwe and its many neighbors in Zimbabwe, Mozambique, the Limpopo valley, Botswana and the southern highveld. Cattle are now recognized as a primary means of expressing and mediating transactions of ownership and property, patronage, clientage, inheritance, marriage, tribute and sacrifice, and law. But how precisely this worked is still only dimly discerned, and dangerous overreliance is still placed on recent anthropological analogues.

As detailed knowledge of many more sites accumulates and recognition of the creative responses of any community to their situation grows, many of the old sharp distinctions fade in significance and blur. Categories such as the Late Stone Age, Early and Later Iron Age lose their separate identities and much of their meaning. They may remain useful as descriptive shorthand or serviceable maps, but can become restrictive as concepts. Groups based on common forms of ceramics no longer have the same sharp definition and many seem arbitrary. Distinctions between hunter, pastoralist, farmer and craftsman also often become difficult to sustain. The hunter becomes a fisher, builds semipermanent villages by lakes and rivers and collects wild cereals habitually and intensively. The pastoralist plants grain after good rain and hunts when his herd diminishes with disease or drought. Cultivators shift their energies to cattle raising in new environments.

Villages and farmers. The concept of a pan-Saharan "aquatic civilization," based on the widespread occurrence of a distinctive method of decorating pottery and on the presence of bone harpoons, was already judged misleading in the first edition of this volume. It is perhaps the best example of "the folly of excessively generalized statements" that has bedeviled African prehistory and is now emphatically discarded. This is especially true in East Africa where the Saharan "aquatic" connections rested on particularly slender evidence of isolated potsherds.

What seemed one of the most convincing demonstrations of the fundamental changes arising from the development of agriculture in the Sahara, the Dhar Tichitt sequence of changing locations and types of settlement in the last two millennia BC, has also now been generally rejected. The various settlements are now seen as contemporary and reflecting seasonal changes in the single subsistence system of the same predominantly pastoralist group, who herded and hunted in dry season camps on the plains and moved to permanent stone dwellings on the plateau edge and grew millet during the wet season.

On the edges of the rain forests of what is now Ghana, a firm continuity between later Stone Age groups and the first cultivators, rather than the intrusion of new people, has been established in Ann Stahl's re-investigation of Kintampo. Actual evidence of domesticated stock or crops may look less certain but it is clear how, from 1600 BC, people made progressive economic adjustments to the opportunities of agriculture. The forest was gradually cleared – as shown by the new animal species attracted to the clearings. People settled down; the quantity and variety of their possessions, particularly pottery, increased; systems of local exchange were established; and dwellings were made more substantial and durable.

The search for correlations between ceramics and language groups in the central Rift Valley of East Africa in the first millennium BC and the search to establish ethnic and racial identities have been abandoned in preference for detailed ecological analyses of small areas. As one consequence, a convincing resolution of the confusion over the many different assemblages of stone tools and pottery types of this period in Kenya has been constructed by Stanley Ambrose. It is based not on seeking a single evolutionary sequence but on a consideration of the way that different people exploited the diverse habitats of the dry and lightly wooded floor of the Rift Valley, the forested valley sides and mountains and the open grasslands of the highlands. This variety permitted peoples with very different life-styles and economies to coexist in close proximity for many centuries. Interactions between them then took many different forms and illustrate traditional archaeological concepts such as migration, diffusion, assimilation and economic transformation.

People who were predominantly foragers, making a complex of stone tools now named Eburran, settled the valley floor and margins and adapted their hunting strategies to the different habitats. The makers of distinctive Elmenteitan obsidian blade tools were predominantly goat herders living in rock shelters on the sides of the valley and in large settlements in the highlands. The grasslands were grazed by the cattle of "pastoral Neolithic" peoples, of which there were at least five different groups, to judge by their pottery, often living together on the same site or occupying it successively. Some were nomadic; others settled near permanent waterholes.

All relied on stone for their tools and weapons; all made pottery; and all had domestic stock, although the emphasis they placed on this varied from the few goats associated with Eburran sites, to the large herds of goats of the Elmenteitens and the often complete reliance on cattle of some pastoral peoples. The forebears of the pastoralists lived in northern Kenya throughout the second millennium BC and had their ultimate origins on the Ethiopian highlands. Pastoralism is presented by Peter Robertshaw as above all an ideological system in which the cultural bias toward herding exceeds the functional value of that way of life, and herding defines identity.

The origins and initial development of ironworking in Africa remain unclear. The prediction when this book was written that studies of technology were the most promising strategy for advance in this field has proved correct. So have the doubts expressed over Meroë as a source for East African iron technology. The designs of furnaces and the smelting processes in the two places are now recognized as too different for there to be any connection. Studies of the development of smelting around Akjoujt and Agades, deep in the Sahara, have made them exciting candidates for an indigenous source of metal technology. In both, native copper was smelted during the second millennium BC by Saharan pastoralists. Copper ores were smelted by 800 BC and iron ores by 500 BC. It is suggested that this represents a progressive local mastery and extension of the same basic technology. However, though considerable effort was made to obtain ore – the nearest sources were at least 35 miles from the furnace sites – the scale of Saharan copper production was minuscule: no more than 37.5 lb of metal was produced in a year – enough only for the tiniest tools, such as needles or awls.

In the East African interior, on the eastern Buhaya shores of Lake Victoria and in Rwanda and Burundi, Peter Schmidt and others have found considerable evidence of intensive iron smelting industries from 600 BC, employing a sophisticated technology and firmly set within the Early Iron Age cultures of the region. The tuyeres (pipes) through which air was introduced into the furnaces were set within the furnaces for most of their length, ensuring that the air entering was already at a high temperature before it met the furnace charge. The furnaces thus reached high temperatures much more efficiently and easily: a technological innovation that was not developed outside Africa until centuries later. Iron production west of Lake Victoria was early, technologically sophisticated, extensive, specialized and almost industrial. The environmental impact of metal production on this scale, the amount of mature hardwood that had to be felled and burnt to produce the charcoal, and the devastation that this caused, have been emphasized in many different areas. This may have had some positive effects as it turned forests into pasturage that allowed cattle herds to multiply, but it also forced communities into frequent movement.

The most significant work over the last 15 years on Early Iron Age farming has taken place in South Africa. It too has been based on intensive surveys and close analysis of complete ecological units. On the coast of Natal in the 3rd and 4th centuries AD small ephemeral villages were established in the strips of open grassland at the foot of the long, narrow cordon of ancient dunes, then covered in dense forest. Evidence of ironworking or agriculture is extremely slight and there is no indication that these settlers had domesticated animals. Shellfish was their sole source of protein. In this, as in social organization and quality of life, there is very little to distinguish the first southern farmers from their Stone Age contemporaries. Their ceramics, however, leave no doubt about their archaeological classification.

Over 150 villages of the 7th century, some housing several hundred people, have been found in Natal. In marked contrast to the first settlements, they are all inland – on deep fertile soils along the deeply incised river valleys in the foothills of the interior high plateau: good evidence that they were predominantly farmers. Goats or sheep were now the main source of meat. Only in the 9th century had sufficient land been cleared to open substantial grazing lands and allow cattle to be kept in significant numbers.

The increasing maturity of African prehistory is best illustrated in reassessments of the role of external migrations in the establishment of the Early Iron Age in eastern, central and southern Africa. The last generation of prehistorians was preoccupied with the origin and diffusion of the Iron Age, conceived as a pre-assembled package of traits including race, language, distinctive pottery forms, metalworking, domesticated sheep, goats, cattle and crops. It therefore necessarily represented a migration of peoples from a particular region at a particular time. Phillipson's scheme of a succession of distinct streams of migrants, described in the chapters that follow, was the culmination of this approach. It has since been slightly refined, while alternative interpretations of the routes the migrants took have been presented by Thomas Huffman.

It is now possible to argue that no migrations on this scale ever took place. Certainly the nature of the movements, if any, is now seen much more realistically and no one would any longer suggest that the Iron Age was introduced with a single "vast, fast colonization". Rather, it represents the almost random seepage of tiny groups, unconsciously extending the frontiers of farming as they sought the few small pockets of new land that their fragile and uncertain technology and economy could bring to production to supplement the older and more certain life of the forager.

Almost all the concepts that underlie the migration theories have now been brought into question. As the package is disentangled and its components are examined singly, their contemporaneity becomes questionable. Race is no longer seen as a useful category and certainly not one to which the bones of isolated individuals can be assigned. Interest now is in gene pools and interbreeding populations. Language relationships are no longer envisaged as the results of an evolutionary sequence of progressive differentiation but as a complex, changing and possibly impenetrable network of relationships marked by convergences as much as divergences. Ethnic divisions are recognized as often recent, arbitrary, even colonial inventions with little historical meaning or significance. Ceramic forms are no longer taken to equate simply with tribal cultures. Changes in these forms correlate as well or better with changes in craft organization, degrees of specialization, intensity of production, and shifts from, for instance, specialized production for exchange to intermittent production in the home for purely domestic consumption. Changes in economic emphases, even the growth of cattle herds, can and do reflect changes in social organization, systems of kinship and inheritance, and concepts of ownership and property. Archaeologists have now lost interest in the sweeping generalizations that underpin migration theories. They now seek to understand their own material more fully and in its own right rather than to make glib correlations with poorly understood concepts of linguists or physical anthropologists.

The origins of the Early Iron Age require a lot more, and more sophisticated, investigation; the debate about the nature of the discontinuity that it represents continues. On the other hand, local continuities between it and the later Iron Age are now so many, strong and various, that very few archaeologists indeed continue to seek distant origins for the latter or to explain any of it in terms of population movements.

Mines and courts of the south. When this book was first published, the earliest development of complex hierarchical societies, living in large towns under centralized control of a wealthy minority with cattle playing an important role in economic, social and political relations, was placed in the dry grazing lands of Matabeleland, in southwestern Zimbabwe, in the 11th century. Today the ways that such societies developed can be traced in convincing detail in what looked then a most improbable area: northeastern Botswana.

Along the eastern edges of the Kalahari Desert, the monotonous, flat, open country, covered in thorn scrub and grass and broken by isolated flat-topped sandstone hills, has even less rain and sparser vegetation than its western neighbor, Matabeleland, the cattle country of Zimbabwe. Cultivation, even of drought-resistant and quick-maturing indigenous grain crops, is hazardous. Today it is the heartland of traditional Tswana cattle owners and their almost feudal economy with client herders guarding their cattle, for much of the year at cattle posts far from the vast traditional towns where the owners live. In the 1970s, so little was known of the prehistory of this part of the subcontinent that it was assumed that until very recently it had only been the hunting grounds of nomadic San foragers. Now, one research program has discovered over 250 Iron Age settlements occupied between AD 600 and 1300, the homes of a single society, whose pottery establishes their close cultural links with their contemporary small-scale Early Iron Age farmers throughout Zimbabwe.

Settlements centered round cattle pens. The manure of the pens, hardened and burnt over the centuries, encourages so distinctive a grass cover that sites can be identified from aerial photographs. The settlements vary considerably in size, depth of occupation deposits and length of occupation, and fall into four distinct categories. The largest were substantial hilltop towns, sited for defense and taking little account of distance from water or agricultural land. Large villages, though little more than a tenth of the size of the towns, were built on smaller hilltops around the towns. In the plains below were hamlets and homesteads comparable in size to contemporary Tswana cattle posts and occupied for two generations at most. They differed from the villages and towns in being located near water courses and within reach of both heavy and light soils: crops planted on one or other of the soils would survive whatever the rains brought.

By the 9th century, there were three hilltop towns, some 60 miles apart from each other. Villages clustered at some distance from them and the lesser settlements in turn clustered round the villages: a distinctive pattern and hierarchy of settlements indicative of three independent, self-sufficient and competing city-states in control of their own territories, each with its own infrastructure of agricultural villages and cattle posts. Their control over their populations was strong enough for them to extract cattle, presumably in the form of tribute, to sustain the towns. The pattern of culling shows that the townsfolk subsisted on the meat of cattle killed at their prime, while in the lesser settlements only young bulls and animals past reproduction were killed: the characteristic pattern of ranchers seeking to maintain and increase herd growth.

In these Toutswe settlements we can trace the earliest example in southern Africa of the growth of wealth, inequalities, a ruling group, sustained political control over wide territories, considerable populations and rich herds. This took place in the far interior, at the farthest point from any foreign trade contacts, in an area without the gold of Zimbabwe and far less attractive for farmers or ranchers. Although external contacts certainly existed and glass beads and seashells reached the Toutswe settlements, the real trade infrastructure was an internal one, with cattle and grain passing between the settlements and skins, hides, ivory and probably salt being exchanged with San hunting groups beyond the Toutswe territories.

About 12 miles east of Toutswe, Mapungubwe, in the Limpopo valley, was a much larger contemporary hilltop town. In the 1970s knowledge of Mapungubwe was still limited to the rough excavations and even cruder analyses of the 1930s. Extensive re-excavation by the University of Pretoria, the owners of the site, has provided much closer dating and a great deal of material, though most remains unpublished and interpretations of it by the excavators continue to equate all change with successive incursions by different tribes. A re-entrant valley near the hill was settled in the 8th century by people with ceramics matching those of contemporary groups in Matabeleland. It rapidly drew to enormous proportions until the debris of the huge central cattle pens drowned it. In the late 11th century, people moved to the foot of the hill and a ruling elite established itself in stone-walled enclosures on the hilltop soon after.

Some continue to attribute the prosperity of Mapungubwe to trade in ivory from the valley and gold from the Matabeleland goldfields with the Indian Ocean coast, supported by the introduction of cotton weaving, glass beads and shells from the coast. There are as good or better reasons to see both ivory and gold as absorbed within the settlement as court luxuries; most of the ivory was in a uniform design of bracelet, suggesting the work of specialized court craftsmen and certainly not designed for export.

Mapungubwe was abandoned after less than a century. At much the same time Great Zimbabwe became the capital city of a state. The assumption that there was a causal connection, that perhaps foreign trade routes shifted north, is unproven and unnecessary. Rather, one is witnessing a further manifestation of the widespread development of similar new forms of society and economy. When writing this book, I was also engaged in the excavation of the most outlying *zimbabwe*, Manekweni, in the lowlands of coastal Mozambique. Studies of the bones recovered and of the local ecology by Graeme Barker demonstrated that the local environment could only sustain cattle herds for a small part of the year, that

An artist's reconstruction of how part of the king's residence at Great Zimbabwe would have looked in the 1400s. Near the Conical Tower – probably a store for grain – the buttressed walls (5m thick at their base) were decorated with a chevron (zig-zag) pattern. The outer wall was 250m long and 9.75m in height. The expertly cut and laid stones (no mortar was used) showed the skill of the builders.

the herds were kept a considerable distance away from the *zimbabwe* for most of the time and that, when they were at the *zimbabwe*, animals in their prime were slaughtered and their meat was eaten only by the elite who lived within the stone enclosure. The rest of the population got their meat almost entirely from goats and game. Manekweni provided the first evidence of an economy based on cattle that were moved seasonally (transhumance) under the control and for the benefit of a small ruling group.

A re-examination of the siting of the many *zimbabwe* in the interior suggested that this was a general pattern, that herds grazed in the agricultural lands of the highveld for part of the year and were moved to the lowveld for the winter, when the grass there was nutritious, browsing was also possible and the fly-borne diseases prevalent during the summer were absent. Vast quantities of cattle bones thrown down the slopes from the hill enclosures at Great Zimbabwe show that here also prime animals exclusively were culled for and consumed by the inhabitants of the enclosures. This review of the distribution of *zimbabwe* also suggested that there were some ten major capitals, regularly spaced some 60 miles apart round the edge of the plateau, that these were thus best interpreted, like Manekweni, as the capitals of autonomous and competing states, that Great Zimbabwe exerted little more than a cultural hegemony over the plateau, and that its political or economic control over these states was at best slight, transient and insignificant. The patterns deduced for the high plateau found confirmation in the subsequent studies in Botswana.

Throughout Zimbabwe and across its borders into Botswana, Mozambique and the Transvaal, from at least the 9th century until and even beyond the disruptions initiated by the Portuguese from the 16th century, there were several prosperous, stable, long-lived, self-contained states which fall into at least three culturally distinct groups. Each was master of its own predominantly pastoral economy. The role of foreign trade in creating and sustaining them, as the most important agent of change or as the way of placing control of wealth in the hands of a small elite, is greatly diminished and, I would claim, peripheral and insignificant. Their rulers were not the compradors of Arab or Portuguese masters, passive beneficiaries of foreign aid, though they may in the end have been bribed by small quantities of foreign luxuries to squander their resources and labour.

Cities on the East African coast. The pages that follow insist that the cities of the Indian Ocean coast of Africa also were not "foreign transplants" or "the passive recipients of foreign initiatives". Since they were written, extensive excavations in the ruined towns of Manda and Shanga in the Lamu archipelago of northern Kenya have provided much more detailed confirmation of this. The dates of their foundation have been pushed back even earlier than the 8th century, by which time they were already flourishing concerns, importing foreign ceramics – whose dating is now considerably more precise and certain through excavations of the kilns in the Near East and China in which they were manufactured. However, 95 percent of the pottery on all these sites was of local African design and manufacture. Sharply distinct from contemporary Early Iron Age wares and remarkably uniform over an astonishing area, it has been found some distance inland in settlements along the Tana river and into the Usambara mountains and along the length of the coast, as far south as central Mozambique not far from Manekweni. This distribution points to a wide-ranging coastal and maritime trading culture comparable and probably ancestral to that of the Swahili.

The first settlements were modest and unsophisticated villages of wattle and daub huts covering about an acre of land close to the beach but also close to deepwater channels. They already showed evidence of local craft activity. By the 10th century, building in coral blocks had started and with it the long local evolution of the distinctive domestic architecture. The towns that now grew up were set farther back from the sea. They covered 10–50 acres and showed some evidence of formal planning and layout. African features, shared with contemporary inland African towns, included walled central meeting places. The first foreign traders, from the Muslim ports of Persia, were visitors to these already long-established towns. They made up a small and insignificant sector of the population, living in limited enclaves within the town. The first and only mosque in Shanga, for example, can have housed no more than 25 worshipers though the population as a whole was some 500. Only in the 11th century were the people of these cities as a whole converted to Islam.

Chance finds of hoards of ancient gold and silver coins are sometimes made along the coast. They always excite the imagination and often also constitute revealing "time-capsules". In 1984, a hoard of tiny silver coins bearing dates from 1050 to 1066 was found in the ancient settlement of Mtambwe Mkuu on the island of Pemba, where they had remained hidden and untouched for some 900 years. They were certainly minted on the coast and point to a mint on the Lamu archipelago. Their designs and rhyming inscriptions are elements shared by the coinage of the Fatimid caliphs of Sicily. Some bear the name of the first sultan of Kilwa, Ali ibn al Hasan, and a date of 1050. This suggests that Kilwa may well have been founded by a family or clan from one of the Lamu cities in the 11th century, a particularly disturbed period in the archipelago.

Kingdoms of West Africa. In the main text of this book, the cities of the Sahel and northern savanna lands of West Africa are recognized as the capitals of kingdoms, in large part indigenous African in culture, architecture and population. But they are also seen in equally large part as creations and dependencies of the trans-Saharan caravan trade, initiated by Muslim traders after the Muslim invasion of Mauretania in 734. One of the most exciting programs of research, published after this book was written, has gone a long way to overturning this view.

The delta of the middle Niger, where the river splits into a changing, silting network of a myriad temporary channels, lakes and swamps, has at its head the city of Jenne. (Timbuktu stands at the lower end of the delta and Gao farther downstream where the course of the river swings south.) Above the flat and otherwise featureless floodplain round Jenne that is inundated to a considerable depth each year, project artificial mounds (tells) of ancient occupation. Roderick and Susan McIntosh have identified over 400 of these tells from aerial photographs – suggesting a population density ten times that of today. They have surveyed and collected artefacts from a random sample of 75, and dated them by comparing their pottery with that from excavations through the deep deposits of the largest tell, Jenne-Jeno ("ancient Jenne").

Jenne has not proved a center of indigenous domestication of cereals as had been predicted. Settlement came comparatively late. Only by 300 BC was the delta drying, were the areas of permanent lakes in it decreasing and the dangers of waterborne diseases diminishing. The first signs of permanent settlement, small hamlets of mixed agriculturalists, date from about 250 BC. Their inhabitants fished, hunted wild cattle and collected wild grasses but they also grew rice, sorghum and millet and herded goats and cattle. From the start, they also imported stone grindstones, stone beads and iron ore from beyond the floodplain.

Over the following five or six centuries the settlements remained predominantly rural but grew in numbers and size – by AD 150 Jenne probably covered more than 30 acres. Resources such as copper and gold were drawn from farther afield. Crafts diversified and some were clearly the products of at least part-time specialists.

By 500 several settlements had coalesced into a fully urban town. At the height of its prosperity, about 800, Jenne covered some 100 acres; many buildings were of brick and the town was surrounded by a massive wall. However, there is no evidence that it had a ruling group, any system of coercion or authoritarian control, palaces, temples or a citadel, and very little of luxury imports or wealth concentrated in the hands of a few – though the area excavated was limited and it is possible that the buildings of such a group have not yet been located. What is significant is rather the way specialized craftsmen in a variety of manufactures were organized into cohesive bodies, physically separated and living in their own settlements round the edge of the town, identified by separate neighboring mounds some 1,500 ft apart and

also clustered, with 3–15 villages forming a cluster, each in its way an independent manufacturing and social center. These units may have had an ethnic as well as a productive basis. Nevertheless, town, craft villages and country formed a single social and economic system. The ambiguities of personal and group identity within this system may well have been expressed and resolved through the proliferation of art and particularly terra-cotta statuary that is a feature of Jenne: symbols of the disparate, interacting and overlapping loyalties and unities of groups with different origins, ethnic loyalties, occupations, beliefs and values.

The floodplain settlements can be ranked in size and distinguished by location: 34 percent are on land suited for rice growing and 54 percent are located on waterways that give opportunities for travel and transporting goods. The intensity and reach of the regional trade through the delta is shown by the homogeneity of the material culture, particularly pottery, over a wide area, evidence either of the spread of objects from the urban manufacturing centers or of the way the high fashion of the city was everywhere emulated by local craftsmen.

Downstream, large grave mounds or tumuli built with ever-greater elaboration over wooden burial chambers, contain rich grave goods and Jenne pottery. They have now been dated to between the 8th and 11th centuries and are thus contemporary with Jenne's greatest prosperity. More than anything in the city, they do suggest that some people grew wealthy and powerful through control of the flow of trade goods through the delta.

North African, Arab and Islamic influences only appear at Jenne after 1000, with new rectangular house plans, trade beads and the introduction of cotton weaving. This is also a point at which the climate became wetter. The river floods were more extensive, higher and longer and rice growing had to be largely abandoned and with it many settlements. The population of the floodplain declined and the new settlements were on higher, lighter soils where millet could be grown. The climate then grew steadily drier and settlements reduced further to a cluster round Jenne itself. The end there came by 1400 and the town was abandoned.

The investigations of Jenne were concerned with understanding the dynamics of an autonomous process of urbanization and change over a whole region, seen as a single economic and social system, and of the changing relationships between the components of the system. Many of the other well-known towns of the savanna, Sahel and Sahara have also been investigated further since the 1970s but these inquiries are set more firmly in a descriptive, particularist and historical frame, and continue to seek correspondences between the architecture and layouts of the towns with early documentary descriptions of them by foreign visitors. Nevertheless, they have provided at least hints that they could have histories as long, as rich and as independent as that of Jenne.

Both Tegadaoust and Kumbi Saleh are built over deep deposits attesting to a long pre-urban local history of a development. Archaeologists have recognized, along the edge of the towns, quarters of specialized artisans working in glass, copper, iron and jewelry that were established in the 9th century.

Conclusion. In the last two decades, only South Africa has established its own body of highly productive and professional archaeologists. Otherwise it is a striking feature that all the work that has been described, all the conceptual advances and significant fieldwork, has been achieved by individuals and teams from outside Africa itself, particularly from universities in the United States of America.

It is puzzling how this situation has arisen. Every country in Africa is now an independent state and more than a generation has passed since the great movements for liberation bore their first fruits. Every new nation has claimed to recognize the important role of archaeology in recovering its authentic past, untainted by colonial historiography. Many have sent some of their best undergraduates abroad for further training in archaeology. Their impact on their subject has been minimal. Their problems are many. Many return inhibited by their inexperience of fieldwork in their local conditions. Many face problems of equipment, finance and transport: others are swept into purely administrative posts. Many countries continue to suffer from years of civil war: economies and infrastructures on which any research depends have been wrecked in these and many other countries. Yet even where there has been lavish foreign funding and support to enable the local archaeologists of several countries to cooperate in research into the origins of the states of the eastern seaboard and its hinterland, the results so far have been negligible.

The dominance of foreign researchers is certainly not a healthy situation. Local feeling that only indigenous peoples can or should investigate the past of their own cultures and that research by foreigners is in some sense theft, loss or removal of their own past, has often led to extreme, ignorant and unimaginative bureaucratic obstruction and cancellation of foreign research programs. The frustrations and costs in time and money can be immense. As a consequence, the desperately needed new commitments to new programs and new entries into the field of African archaeology diminish.

It has been claimed, with justification, that "it is presumptuous and dangerous for archaeologists to write the past for others . . . to discover a past . . . for any section of society . . . must necessarily involve an attempt to control and incorporate those segments of society, to change their attitudes and to appropriate and thus debilitate their social statement". Expatriate archaeologists perhaps have a particular duty "to encourage indigenous and alternative archaeologies". On the other hand, it is equally true that "archaeology is not the purveyor of satisfying pasts".

As one could expect, given its long and inglorious history of controversy. Great Zimbabwe has provided the most extreme example of the chauvinist and opportunist invention of a satisfying but purely fictitious past, pandering to current political forces and as outrageous in its distortion and neglect of history and archaeology as any of the old colonial propaganda. The first black Director of Museums and Monuments to take responsibility for conservation and research at the site, Dr Kenneth Mafuka, denounced all previous research. "Proven scholarship is intellectual imperialism . . . The bulk of European scholarship have (sic) conspired to deny us that which by right belongs to us". He substituted tales of a "glittering civilization . . . wealthy beyond imagination . . . its buildings create the most awe-inspiring effect ever witnessed by man". Though "it teemed with celibates . . . austere, non alcoholic and spatial (sic) couped (sic) up in their little perches", its people were also "capable of an infinite happiness, free, garrulous, intensely democratic . . . (providing) a heritage that should be the envy of the human race . . . a historic reflection in a somewhat idiosyncratic form of the socialism of the present government".

This represents an extreme example of the absurdities of a purely invented past. When this happens, it presents a serious obstacle to the progress of research in the sense that it is generally known. The chapters that follow in this book are optimistic about the new perspectives, new directions and new approaches that would be brought to bear on the African past with the political and economic evolution of a continent where autonomy was then in large part a new experience. Much of what they foresaw has been realized but the future is now obscure. The advances of the last two decades are still the work of a tiny number of dedicated and imaginative foreign researchers and they have provided what are still only glimpses into a few aspects of the very long past of a vast and ancient continent. And certainly at the moment, researchers like these are an endangered species, one whose time is drawing to a close.

Peter S. Garlake

1. The Character of Africa

The African environment. For most people, the image that Africa conjures up is of vast level plains, covered in grass and stretching to distant horizons, broken only by isolated trees and grazed by great herds of antelope. Savanna country like this extends from the Atlantic shores of Senegal through the Sudan to the mountains of Ethiopia. It also runs southwards through East Africa, Zambia and Rhodesia to the southern shores of South Africa. The better-watered, lower and hotter regions support a heavier vegetation of deciduous woodland. The savanna, throughout history, supported the bulk of Africa's population.

In the drier highland zones of East and South Africa, such as western Kenya, Uganda and the Orange Free State, the high grass gives way to open downland. This provides fine grazing, although the grasses are not the rich pasturage or sward of northern temperate countries but tough, tufted, tussocky growths that are only nutritious for short periods after rain. Pastoralists here are inevitably committed to a largely nomadic life.

In many dry lowland areas, like the *nyika* along the coast of East Africa, the valleys of great rivers such as the Zambezi and the Limpopo, and the desert fringes of the Sahel, the Kalahari and the Turkana plains, flat-topped acacia trees stand above thorny scrub. Here few cultivators can survive.

As rainfall increases, the savanna woodlands merge into tall, dense forests, like the Guinea forest and the forests along the shores of Lake Victoria and on the lower levels of the mountain ranges of East Africa. Here soils are often fertile but land clearance is a daunting task.

The tropical rain forest of the West African coast and the Congo basin provides another extremely powerful image of Africa – "the heart of darkness." Great trees shut out the light and sun, so knitted together by creepers, and their trunks so well buttressed, that they are nearly impossible to fell. Here it is always hot and humid. Rain falls heavily and very frequently. In some areas, such as the Ibo homelands in eastern Nigeria, the rain forest supports some of the densest populations in Africa. Tropical root crops and oil palms provide extremely high rewards to cultivators.

Climate and cultivation. These vegetation zones may look very different but they have much in common. Outside the forests, almost all the rain falls in a single short season, generally in violent thunderstorms. This produces a great deal of surface floodwater, eroding the soils and filling the rivers with alluvium. Rainfall may look adequate in annual statistics – 20 to 30 inches is the mean rainfall over very wide areas – but farmers very seldom get its full benefit. It is not only markedly seasonal but often unreliable and subject to very great fluctuations from year to year. A series of drought years can cause economic disaster. Abandoned lands, decimated herds and starvation take generations to repair. More often than not the search for surface water for livestock is difficult and troublesome for many months of the year.

Soils are generally poor and infertile. Heat oxidizes what little humus there is. High rainfall leaches vital minerals from the soils. When leaching is combined with impeded drainage, salts accumulate in the subsoil to form toxic layers or impermeable crusts. These "iron pans" or "ferricretes" destroy the fertility of many tropical soils.

The savanna once supported great herds of game. Antelope in huge numbers and enormous variety exploited every available habitat. This biomass was so rich that very few peoples in Africa were ever entirely dependent on their livestock or crops for food. Hunting

Previous page: Mt Kenya, from which Mogai – the Creator – first showed Gikuyu – Father of the Kikuyu people – the land he had prepared for them. Mt Kenya remains Mogai's resting place, symbol of a nation, center of its lands.

Opposite: the sites, vegetation and (inset) languages of Africa.

Below: the savanna has many faces. The Nhunguza Ruin, *below*, stands in deciduous woodland on the high, well-watered northern end of the Zambezian plateau. From the hilltop settlement of Mapela, *below left*, at the opposite end of the plateau, dry acacia scrub stretches past granite hills.

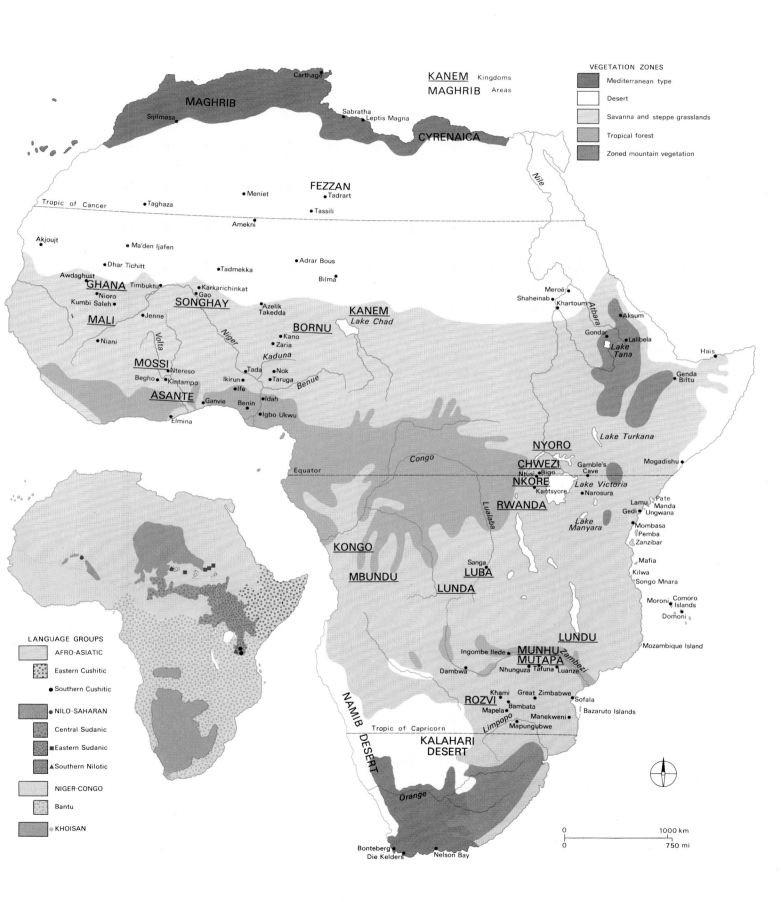

and wild game almost always supplemented the diet. One can well surmise that the incentives towards farming in Africa, in the remote past, were possibly never as great as they were in other continents.

Among agriculturalists, sheep and goats were ubiquitous. But socially and economically cattle were always much more important. They were not primarily sources of food. More significantly, they were the basis of many social relationships and exchanges. They symbolized and ratified many bonds and alliances. They have never been used as draft or transport animals. Until very recently the plow was only known in parts of Ethiopia. Disease limits the numbers and distribution of cattle.

The famous long-horned cattle of Nkore were introduced to western Uganda at the same time as institutions of kingship.

Above: the high mountainous plateau of Ethiopia provides an ideal environment for temperate cereal crops but in such a rugged landscape there is often little arable land.

Opposite above: tropical rain forest encourages the growth of many different plants and creepers beneath its canopy, but clearance is daunting.

Farmers, whose only tool for cultivation is a hoe, tend to seek out and cultivate light soils – fine sands rather than heavy, adhesive clays. These are precisely the soils that lose their fertility most rapidly. With no knowledge of how to harness animal power for plowing and no tradition of manuring, the soil, except in the most favored areas, rapidly becomes exhausted. Swidden, or shifting agriculture, in which new land has to be cleared every few years while the old lands are left to regenerate, often for a decade or more, can exhaust so much land that settlements are forced to move three or four times in a generation.

Cereal crops make the highest demands on soils. Compared with the wheats and barleys of the temperate zones, which germinate with winter rain, the African cereals are drought resistant and need only a short summer growing season. They give high yields with little attention. The staple African grains are sorghum and millet. Sorghum, like wheat, rice and maize, is one of the world's main cereals. It needs 16 inches of rain per year to bear a crop. *Pennisetum* (or bullrush) millet is the commonest of the various indigenous African millets. It can give a crop on half the rain needed for sorghum.

Natural resources. Africa has few resources that can be exploited commercially by simple, preindustrial technologies. Export crops were limited to kola nuts, a stimulant grown in the forests of West Africa and particularly popular in Islamic communities.

Salt is, of course, a vital element in diet. Everywhere in Africa it became an important item of trade. Lack of salt can have enormous economic consequences. Traditions frequently associate the decline of kingdoms with endemic shortages of salt. At a pinch, inferior substitutes for salt can be made by filtering and drying solutions of various ashes. This is a despised and temporary source. Salt distilled from the sea or from brine springs is much more desirable. Brine springs, like those at Ivuna and Uvinza in Tanzania, were the basis of a salt-making industry. Both sites were excavated in the 1960s and attest to centuries of use. But salt from brine is deliquescent and therefore deteriorates rapidly. Rock salt was the most sought-after form: being crystalline, it does not deteriorate. In West Africa cakes of rock salt were rare and valuable enough to become almost a currency and be exchanged, weight for weight, for gold.

Iron ores were widespread. The iron oxide concretions in most tropical soils – "bog iron" or "ironpan" – are rich enough to supply the ores for part-time smiths. Every village had its iron workers and there was generally little incentive to trade in iron. Only communities that lived near particularly rich and easily worked iron ores took the opportunity to become specialist smiths and traders.

Copper was scarce enough to form the foundation for regional trade networks. There are no workable copper ore bodies in the West African forests. There, copper must have been obtained from mines in the desert of Mauritania and Niger. The ores of southern Zaire and northern Zambia, supplemented by workings in the Urungwe district of Rhodesia, were part of a wide regional exchange network in southeast Africa, which may have extended as far as the East African coast. The metal was frequently cast

Left: the mines of Bilma in the great sand desert of the central Sahara have exported salt to Lake Chad and Hausaland since the 15th century.

Below: rock salt is cut from a deposit in the desert of Mauritania.

in rods and ingots, which are of sufficiently standardized weight to be interpreted as forms of currency. The traded metal was generally reworked as jewelry. Great quantities of copper wire weighed down the limbs of many women in several later Iron Age societies.

It was gold, however, which most attracted foreign traders to both West and East Africa. In the goldfields of Senegal and Ghana the metal occurs in pockets of alluvial gravel. In Rhodesia it occurs in narrow veins in granite rocks. In both regions the sources were diffuse and the yields quite unpredictable. Few villagers could depend on gold mining for a regular income. Mining was generally done by farmers in the agricultural slack season. Luck played a great part in the rewards of gold mining, and in these circumstances it was difficult to develop and control regular forms of production. This subject is described in more detail in Chapter 4.

Most animal products – other than food bones – do not survive in archaeological contexts. For an estimate of their economic importance one must examine early documents and traditions. Ivory was an export which in many places must have rivaled gold. Elephants could be hunted almost anywhere. They were a much more transient and uncertain commodity than gold. This would suggest that controlling elephant hunting was much more difficult than controlling gold mining. In fact, hunting elephants was dangerous and difficult. Many accounts suggest that it demanded communal efforts by the men of entire villages. Their need for charms, medicines or hunting magic provided a means for control. The importance of furs, skins and rhinoceros horns is difficult to estimate. Certainly they were traded but, to judge from documents, this was subsidiary to other exports.

Transport. A great deal of social and economic development is dependent on easy communications. When communities are readily in touch with each other, ideas can be exchanged, goods bartered and techniques and skills diffused. Self-sufficiency breaks down; markets grow up; individual and regional specializations are stimulated. Wealth and power tend to accumulate at nodal points in the communication network; larger political units can develop; coordination and government are easier. In Africa much of this was impossible.

The interior of Africa is virtually a single great plateau. The rolling plains present few physical barriers to travel. The great rift valleys of East Africa may be largely waterless and their scarps may appear to be formidable obstacles, when seen from a distance, but they could still be crossed without great difficulty. This does not mean that communication was easy. Distances are enormous and the population was always small. Consequently there were no roads. This lack of roads or transport animals meant that wheeled vehicles were useless: they were never developed. All goods had to be carried on human heads. The small, widely dispersed villages had none of the

Above: a brassworker in Benin finishes a casting beside his forge. Clay molds stand around the walls ready for heating to receive the molten metal.

Opposite: a Venda woman wears wire anklets identical to those worn for centuries in prosperous later Iron Age communities.

Below: a traditional iron-smelting furnace in operation in northern Ghana. Beside it lies the product of an earlier firing, ready for forging.

security provided by strong government. Therefore men needed very strong incentives to work as porters. This meant that commerce in bulky products was impossible: trading had to be limited to small, expensive items.

Much of black Africa was isolated from other continents by a forbidding coastline. There are few harbors. Africa's perimeter is so unbroken that, despite the continent's great area, its coastline measures only a tenth of that of Europe. In West Africa the waters are too cold for coral reefs to build up and protect the shore. Inshore currents and a large tidal range mean that beaches shelve steeply and are battered by surf. Entrance to every river is blocked by sand bars. Light, uncertain winds – the doldrums – are a hazard to vessels sailing to West Africa. What wind there is, blows against ships leaving the coast. As sailors said: "Beware the Bight of the Benin, where few come out, though many go in."

In contrast, the tropical waters of East Africa are protected from ocean swells by a continuous line of reefs. Inside these is a safe passage with secure havens for small craft. In East Africa monsoon winds facilitate a regular annual cycle of trading voyages, from India and Arabia to Africa and back. This part of the continent was able to participate for centuries in the trading economy of the Indian Ocean.

In West Africa access from the coast to the interior is impeded by continuous mangrove swamps and a network of shallow lagoons, 30 to 40 miles deep. (On the other hand, the lagoons encouraged regional canoe traffic to develop over a considerable distance from the Niger river into the Republic of Benin.) In most of East and South Africa scarps rise abruptly from the narrow coastal lowlands to the interior plateau. Consequently, few rivers are navigable for any distance before passage is barred by rapids and falls. Inland river traffic was limited to canoes. It was made difficult by seasonal flooding. After the rains the volume and flow of water can increase tenfold. In winter the rivers dry up and shifting sandbanks make channels temporary, tortuous and uncertain.

In the north the Sahara desert was a barrier to foreign contacts as daunting as any hostile sea. Caravans crossing the desert ran very much the same risks as oceangoing ships. There were similar problems of survival: caravans needed the same careful provisioning and organization; trading ventures had to attract the same high-risk capital; the same high return on investment was demanded. Towns bordering the desert had very much the same functions and atmosphere as ports. The same specialists – brokers, bankers, provision merchants, guides or pilots – used them as bases.

Disease. Diseases that are endemic to Africa probably impeded development more than any other single factor. Malaria is perhaps the most widespread and common disease of man in Africa. Worms and parasites – the

Copper manillas, the smith's raw material, surround the Portuguese trader who imported them, in this Benin plaque.

schistosomes of bilharzia, filaria, flukes and jiggers – cause chronic infections. These debilitate rather than kill. Because man is a host and carrier in every case, they particularly menace concentrated populations. Certainly they have restricted population increases.

The disease with the most significant effect on patterns of settlement was trypanosomiasis. This is carried by flies of the genus Glossina – the tsetse fly. Repeated or massive infection can cause "sleeping sickness" and death in man. More significantly, this parasite is invariably and rapidly lethal to cattle. Areas infested by the tsetse fly can fluctuate widely and rapidly. The fly prefers to live in a humid shady environment, but it can survive anywhere, except in completely open grassland. It normally feeds on wild game. The presence of suitable hosts is a crucial factor in its survival because it cannot fly far. Therefore, as agriculturalists clear land and drive game away, the fly is forced to retreat. Cattle can then be introduced. But if cattle herds increase or lands are no longer cleared, domestic animals are able to come into contact with wild game. The risks of infection then increase markedly. Once infection occurs, cattle herds are entirely destroyed.

People and land. We have looked at vegetation, climate, resources, agriculture and disease. All these factors have a common outcome. Compared to the rest of the world, Africa, in later prehistory, had very few inhabitants. This single factor has played a determining role in much of the course of human history in Africa. It is, of course, impossible to calculate the population of the continent

As it passes through the dry Sahel, the Niger river breaks into many streams – the "delta" – and irrigates a fertile flood plain, an island of very high agricultural production.

with any certainty before the colonial period. In 1962 the population of Africa was 269 million, in an area of 11,500,000 square miles. The average density was thus 23 people per square mile. In 1920 this figure was halved, at a time when densities in Europe averaged 130 people per square mile, and in Asia 75. An estimate of Africa's population in 1680 suggests a total of under five million. This is equivalent to less than one person in two square miles, much less than half the population density of Europe in the Dark Ages.

Overall density may mean little. Much of the continent is desert or forest, hostile to any settlement at all. Other parts, like the Nigerian forests today, have populations as

Only lagoons and the lower reaches of the greatest rivers, like the Congo, shown here, permit regular traffic and trade by canoe.

dense as any in the world. They may well have been densely settled for centuries. But these figures do give a clear indication that the demography of Africa was of a different order from that of the rest of the world.

With few people, land was freely available to any who sought to clear and work it. Cultivation was entirely dependent on human labor. With no system of enriching the soils or preventing their exhaustion, land could not be improved. The value of land diminished with its fertility. When its fertility was exhausted, men could only clear new lands. Because land had no absolute value, there was no means of investing in it or accumulating wealth or power from the ownership or control of it. Africa never had estates whose rent or produce would support men who held public office. Differentials, in the fertility or value of particular pieces of land or in the area of land controlled, could not produce inequalities of wealth.

The basic unit of agricultural production remained the family or kin group. Farming technology was too simple to provide a steady or reliable surplus. There was, in any case, no means of transporting food in bulk or storing it in large enough quantities to be economically significant or to give rise to redistribution or trade. Agricultural production could contribute little or nothing to the support of rulers, administrators, craftsmen or traders – the specialists who enable market towns or states to function. Without markets, there could be no regional agricultural specialization. There are few cases in Africa, even in historical times, of particular localities exploiting their own resources with a view to exchange in nearby regions, differently endowed. Nor could individuals devote all their time to the practice of a single occupation or craft. Everyone perforce had to participate, at least some of the time, in farming.

In a few parts of Africa the position was different and land was fertile enough to be kept under permanent cultivation – the plantain groves of Buganda, on the shores of Lake Victoria; the flood plains of the upper Zambezi, the home of the Lozi; and the Ethiopian highlands were such areas. They all saw the quick evolution of centralized state institutions. Yet much of the rest of Africa also saw the rise of kingdoms and empires. Ghana and Mali had many successors in the grasslands of the Sudan. The kingdom of the Kongo was one of many in the coastal tropical forests. Cities have long been established along the East African coast. In the far interior, trade in gold supported wealthy and powerful rulers. Theories abound on how this happened. This whole question lies at the

The Kaduna river, in central Nigeria, has the shifting sandbanks and fluctuating flows that make most African rivers unsatisfactory major commercial arteries – though here pots are being loaded for transport to markets far downstream.

heart of this book. Besides historical studies, the disciplines of archaeology and linguistics can contribute to its elucidation. But before looking at their methods and data, one must consider other theories.

Race. Many foreign writers have, for a long time, looked at African history in racial terms, seeking no explanations beyond the inherent genetic characters of its various peoples. Africa lends itself to this treatment because it has a human diversity like no other continent. There are three races – Negroid, Caucasoid and Bushmanoid. In colonial days many theories on how states developed in Africa were constructed in racial terms. They saw the Negroid peoples as congenitally incapable of the vision, leadership and organization that lie at the foundation of governments.

Using race and language to define ethnic groups or tribes presupposed that both elements have their own inherent and immutable characters. Discussions of race have become fruitless, for varied human characteristics are seen in terms of rigid stereotypes. Each race is then defined by a small number of discrete features, each of which is considered clear, distinct and unchanging. Consequently, a mixture of these features is taken to denote a racial mixture.

In physical anthropology this has resulted in the fragments of a single skeleton or even skull being assigned to a particular race. Serology has recently been used in the same way – in particular, the study of sickle blood cells has been taken to denote certain immutable racial characteristics. Such concepts of race cannot be supported. All human populations vary a great deal. They are also all in a continuous state of change, as they adapt to new environments, new food or different economies. It is thus not possible to define human physical types in rigid terms, let alone assign single bones to a particular race. The weaknesses of this approach are apparent even when discussion is limited to interpreting physical features.

The philosophy that forms the basis of such concepts of race takes its adherents further. If race has an absolute value, particular races can be correlated with particular languages, cultures and even forms of government. In its extreme form, as we shall see in Chapter 2, people with Caucasoid features – tall and lithe with aquiline features – are equated with Hamitic languages. This correlation is extended to include nomadic pastoralism, state formation and even divine kingship. This sort of approach has bedeviled African studies for centuries. It is not simply empirically wrong – and there are now many concrete examples to show this – but logically suspect. The whole concept that lies at its base is philosophically untenable.

Language studies. If ill-founded racial theories have obscured rather than furthered studies of the African past, the work of linguists offers a great deal of help to prehistorians. Language studies are valuable not so much

in understanding the causes or processes of social change as in tracing communities as they obtain a distinct cultural identity and then grow, disperse and interact with neighboring groups. To the archaeologist one of the most striking aspects of linguistics is the enormous abundance of readily accessible material available for study. Not only are the very words or vocabulary of every language a potential field of study, but grammar, tone, gender changes, sound shifts and so on all contain useful information. Africa is particularly suited to such work for it contains a greater number and diversity of languages than any other continent.

Languages change, develop and interact with each other in very similar ways to cultures. When a human population is isolated, the language that it speaks will in time become distinct from those of its neighbors. Successive stages in the process of differentiation can be reconstructed. Such a sequence can, of course, usually only provide a very general indication of date. The rate of differentiation in the development of vocabulary depends on many other factors besides its time. Literacy is the most obvious example.

One of the first linguists to see the relevance of his work to African prehistory was the British scholar Malcolm Guthrie. In his classification of Bantu languages he had recognized a set of words common to most of them. He deduced that these must have been part of an original language. He then plotted the proportion of such words that remained in the vocabularies of a widely dispersed set of Bantu languages. He found a consistent pattern in his results: most original words were found in the languages of the Bantu peoples living in the savanna of southern Zaire. Guthrie considered Bantu must have originated here. The proportion of words declined in the areas due east and west of the core, towards the Indian and Atlantic Oceans. Fewer still remained in the languages of the northern and southern peripheries. Guthrie equated this pattern with the historical pattern of the expansion of Bantu-speaking peoples.

Guthrie's reasoning is now doubted on logical grounds. Areas where there is a high retention of archaic forms do not equate with the point of origin of languages. In practice, conservatism and uniformity are characteristics of late and peripheral language forms. It can be shown mathematically that the languages of immediate neighbors will always be more closely related to each other than they are to more distant languages. Guthrie's radiating pattern is therefore inevitable. It does not have any historical connotations. Nevertheless, Guthrie's studies showed archaeologists the potential of linguistic work in a reconstruction of the past.

The American historian Christopher Ehret has taken a different approach to linguistic reconstruction of the past. When people speaking different languages come into contact with each other, they borrow words. Vocabularies, in particular of loan words, reflect the extent and nature of these contacts. The core of the vocabulary of each language – for instance, the words that describe some of the most fundamental ideas, such as family relationships, numbers, or parts of the body – are much less susceptible to change than others. From a consideration of the sort of words borrowed, linguists can suggest whether groups have been neighbors for a long period, whether a group has dominated its neighbors, whether a group was in the process of absorption or extinction, or whether a group was doing no more than using the technicians or technical knowledge of another.

The languages of Africa are grouped in four families. The Khoisan family is of little concern to Iron Age studies. For the last thousand years it has been spoken only by small groups of hunters living around the edges of the southern African deserts and by pastoralists living near the southern tip of Africa.

The Niger–Congo family includes the western Sudanic and Bantu languages. These meet close to the Benue river in eastern Nigeria. It is probable that Bantu originated here. Bantu speakers now populate the whole of eastern and southern Africa. Between 350 and 400 distinct Bantu languages have been identified. There can be little doubt that the introduction of metalworking, agriculture and village life in eastern Africa equates in some way with the spread of the Bantu-speaking people.

The distribution of the third language family, Nilo-Saharan, is now fragmented. Languages in this family are dispersed through the Sahara desert, the Sudan and parts of eastern Africa – areas that coincide with the sites of the first settled villages in Africa, where fisher folk exploited the swamps and lakes of lands that were once fertile and well watered but are now largely desert. One language group in this family, Central Sudanic, was spoken by the people who introduced farming and herding to the Bantu-speaking peoples.

The fourth family, Afro-Asiatic, includes five Cushitic languages, spoken now in Ethiopia, Somalia and northern Kenya. These languages were once labeled "Hamitic." Racial theorists saw the Hamites as the people who introduced government and kingship to Africa. Though these theories are now discredited, there are substantial grounds for supposing that the Cushitic speakers, who now live in small groups in the Rift Valley of East Africa, were once more numerous and widespread. Between two and three thousand years ago they probably introduced pastoralism to the East African highlands.

In correlating language with other cultural evidence, one must recognize that the relationship between the two is a complex and changing one. Elements of culture can spread to different areas in different ways, in response to stimuli different from those that affect the spread of language. People can adopt a new language without changing their culture, or change their economy and lifestyle without changing their speech. Examples abound in contemporary Africa as well as in history.

Archaeology. The essence of historical linguistics has been to identify distinct groups and trace their growth. They are seen in terms of their geographical distribution and their interaction with other groups. Archaeological studies in Africa have tended to follow a parallel course. (They have the advantage of also being able to date many of the developments.) As languages are divided into dialects, groups and families, so archaeological entities have been defined in terms of assemblages, industries and cultures. Various elements can be traced through phases or periods of time as traditions. These entities are all defined by the forms of certain artifacts – tools, weapons, pottery or buildings. (It is being recognized increasingly that many of these definitions are based on sparse and biased samples and on a few, often arbitrarily selected, traits. These may lack any historical significance or reality.)

In this way firm and detailed archaeological frameworks have been established in many parts of Africa. They outline the changes that have taken place over the last two thousand years in design and technology. Such schemes have become increasingly detailed and refined. Their branches proliferate. New finds can be allocated a place in such designs with ease and precision. The entities can be given a greater appearance of reality when they are correlated with ethnic or language groups.

Still, one must always ask what meaning these units of language and prehistoric cultures may have. What relevance do they have to a study of historical development? The elaboration of typologies – either linguistic or archaeological – contributes little to an understanding of how or why communities have changed. They give little indication of their social structure, their organization, their institutions or their economic base. Neglect of so many of the key elements that make up any society means that it is difficult to locate any impetus towards change or instability within such a society. This means that most prehistorians in Africa invariably seek the causes of change outside the "cultures" that they are studying. For more remote times the causes have been seen in changes of climate or environment. Demographic pressures, generated in nebulous ways – by "success" – that are not susceptible to social regulation, are frequently proposed. For more recent societies it is often suggested that entire populations migrated and that wars, conquests and enslavement brought about rapid and total cultural change. New ideas of government and kingship diffused from the ancient centers of civilization or were carried more rapidly by groups of refugee aristocrats, warriors or statesmen, in numbers too small to leave their mark in the archaeological record. Such concepts merit closer examination. There are certainly well-substantiated historical precedents to support many such interpretations.

The Early Iron Age, in which farming, metalworking and village life were introduced to large parts of eastern Africa, marked a profound, sudden and complete break with the Late Stone Age. It can only be seen in terms of a

fundamental change in the bulk of the population over a wide area. However, this process took centuries to spread through the continent. In no way does it imply that menacing hordes of well-armed warriors marched steadily south through Africa. The later Iron Age may well represent a similar change. Certainly it is difficult at present to see much social, economic or cultural continuity between any of its variants and the Early Iron Age.

In historical times the development of state systems of government in Africa has often resulted from military conquests. Armies have invaded a territory and remained to exact tribute and service from the conquered. Frequently they have established themselves as a permanent ruling aristocracy. Thus ethnic and cultural differences between groups have been perpetuated and incorporated in the organization of society. Often the economies of the two groups have continued to differ and served to reinforce the class structure. In southern Africa many Zulu armies moved north from Natal to escape Chaka's oppression in the early 19th century. The Ndebele settled in Rhodesia, the Nguni in Malawi and Zambia, and the Kololo in southern Zambia. In each territory they introduced new forms of government to the indigenous peoples.

Many states in Africa arose from the interaction between pastoralists – usually the predominant and more aggressive group – and agriculturalists. Fulani cattle herders in the Sudan conquered the sedentary Hausa agriculturalists. Nilotic herdsmen from the eastern Sudan thrust their way into the heart of the Bantu farmlands

Opposite: the full range of pottery wares excavated from an urban dwelling in ancient Ife. It includes cooking, serving and storage vessels and red-painted pots reserved for shrine offerings and ceremonies.

Below: traditional potting in Africa is a domestic task. Vessels are slowly formed by hand, never turned on a wheel.

around the Great Lakes of East Africa in the 15th century. The last of several waves of such invasions was that of the Luo and Masai two centuries later. People in lands bordering those that had been conquered often adopted centralized forms of government similar to those of the people threatening them.

Kingship. For those who see the driving forces of social development in terms of the diffusion of foreign forms of organization, the most important and pervasive institution introduced to Africa was "divine" or "Sudanic" kingship. It is characterized by the unique powers of a single, autocratic ruler, who combined religious and governmental functions. Some see its origins in the pharaohs of Egypt. From here the ideas spread to Nubia and the kingdom of Meroë. Thence it went to Aksum in Ethiopia, to West Africa, and eventually across most of black Africa.

Its various forms were thought to have a great deal in common. Land rights and landownership were vested in the king. He had absolute power over their allocation. Often all cattle were his also. The king reflected and embodied the welfare of the nation. He planted the season's first seed and gathered the first harvest. Should he weaken, the nation suffered. Therefore a disabled king was invited to kill himself to make way for a healthy successor. The king lived in seclusion among a galaxy of courtiers, with a proliferation of titles and functions. His queens – his mother, sisters and consorts – had particular prestige and often power. The office of the monarch was symbolized by many items of regalia. These were often revered more than the king's person.

Forms of kingship that combined many of these attributes can certainly be found through most of sub-Saharan Africa. But are they so similar that they must be explained in terms of a common origin? Sudanic kingship is an abstraction, constructed by combining traits from many different areas and periods. It is an umbrella term. It exists more as an ideal in the minds of anthropologists and historians than in any single African state or social system. It is difficult to argue against a concept formulated in this way. From the very method used in its construction it can be found almost anywhere. It has an inevitable and inherent universality.

Detailed studies have shown that many African kingdoms developed and acquired traits of Sudanic kingship at different periods, often centuries after their dynasties were founded. Nowhere was kingship a single static entity, fully formed from its start. Thus it is improbable that any system of kingship had a single source. In the western Sudan the obvious echoes of ancient Egypt are outweighed by traits derived from the earliest Negroid farmers. Among such farmers, the offices of chief and priest were often combined in a single person. Land cults and rain-making, linking fertility with the ruler's welfare, lay at the root of the belief system. A continuity

Symbols of royalty in Africa are many and various. This antique brass mask from Benin is part of the regalia of the Atah of Idah on the Niger river.

between leadership within village societies, based on family groups, and the monarchical principles of African states is very apparent. There are few signs of any disruptive cultural or political breaks in the development of the more complex forms of social integration.

If the elaborations of Sudanic kingship lend a false and alien sense of unity to the more complex forms of African society, one must still recognize that concepts of religious power are deeply embedded in African forms of government. In village-based societies in Africa, the world view is predominantly religious. Authority is defined in spiritual terms; it is backed by the same forces. Conflicts within a society are settled by an appeal to spirits, who will then take possession of a medium. He is then empowered to investigate and make judgment on the disputes. From temporary spirit possession to more permanent possession, that is divine kingship, is an easily conceived step.

Thus ritual kingship can be seen as a "mental blueprint" permeating African society, a "common fund of political ideas," a "common style," a "common way of thinking." Kingship was created from kinship systems which continue to form the basis of the political structures within

kingdoms. African communities generally evidence a concern for indirect approaches to social relations. They also show a passion for legality and order. All these traits lie at the heart of traditional African society.

If the origins of ritual kingship lie very deep and go back millennia in African history, state government may be much more recent. The state had a monopoly of force. Its institutions controlled, administered and defended the production of the wealth of the community. Many state institutions required religious support to ratify their power. There is no dichotomy between state and religion, no separation of priest and king, in African society. Where the two arms are distinct, religious institutions served the king in many practical ways. The priests of Mwari provided a countrywide network of information and intelligence to the Rozvi kingdom of Rhodesia in the late 19th century. Mwari priests disseminated the king's aims and orders to the community. Today, in the same area, the spirit mediums of the Shona act in a similar way, providing moral authority within traditional societies for the guerrilla armies.

Economic factors. We have seen how the soil and climate, the simple methods of farming, sparse populations and limitless land, and the difficulties of transport, storage and communication affected the possibilities of social and economic developments in Africa. We have seen some of the responses: how particular systems of centralized government have arisen in historical times through wars, conquests and migrations. We have also

Above: the treasure of the emperors of Ethiopia, kept in their coronation cathedral in Aksum, includes votive crowns, umbrellas, drums and traditional, intricately chased, brass crosses.

Opposite: the Oba of Benin, in ceremonial dress of coral beads, officiates at his father's altar. His elbow-rest, in the shape of a ritual box, resembles the ancient stools of Ife.

Below: certain Asante chiefs have the privilege of "translators" in their entourages. They are recognized by their staffs depicting Asante proverbs and covered in gold foil.

seen how many communities throughout the continent have developed their own systems of kingship. In the end, can one make any generalizations about the processes of history and prehistory in Africa?

The institutions of the state depend on the accumulation of an economic surplus for their support. In the African situation, how can this be achieved?

When new land is readily accessible for settlement, the impositions of a king must rest lightly on his subjects if he is not to destroy his kingdom. Dissatisfied subjects can often move away and create new polities or transfer their allegiance to a different ruler. Onerous kingdoms easily fragment. Yet if the tribute of a king's subjects can produce little in the way of a surplus for the state, this still has to be obtained. Many states were forced to look for it outside their own systems of production.

Where land is unlimited and of no commercial value and where the yield of the farmers cannot support the instruments of government, power lies with those who can obtain men. Raiding neighboring territories and taking captives, who were brought home to work as slaves, provided manpower, the instrument of increased production. Raids inevitably grew to become campaigns of conquest. Conquered states could provide continuous tribute in the form of slaves. Once this process was under way, those who were threatened would often readily accept the status of vassals and tributaries rather than face war and the prospect of complete destruction.

However, although the export of slaves to the Americas, through the Atlantic slave trade, was a running sore in West Africa for centuries, it was a late, foreign creation. Slavery seems to have played little part in the development of African states. It was never of major economic significance. Slaves were used as porters in the caravan trade and worked as miners digging for gold for Akan kings from the 16th century. But they only gave the king a marginal advantage over the peasants who did the same work on their own account. Slaves were also used to provide the labor to develop a royal plantation economy in Dahomey in the 19th century. However, this was an alien method of production which was only introduced when the foreign slave trade ceased.

Another potential source of a surplus was trade with an external source. Communities had to look outside themselves and export their valuable raw materials to foreign traders who were in contact with markets beyond the reach of their own traders. To be successful in this, communities had to accumulate sufficient goods in one place to make it worthwhile for foreign traders to visit them. The sources of exportable raw materials – such as copper, gold or ivory – were diffuse. Central control of their production was therefore difficult. Control of markets, and access to them and the traders who entered the country, were a great deal easier. When an authority could guarantee a regular and ample supply of goods, safe travel, fair exchange and a stable economic system, it was assured of foreign commerce. Thus centralized authority grew from a monopoly of foreign trade. The centralized control of distribution, and hence the value of imports, could be determined by the recipients. Foreign textiles, beads and metalwork were converted into prestige goods – the essential elements that determined and displayed a person's status: a measure of rank and wealth. They were used to seal contracts and were exchanged as bridewealth. The system provided positive incentives for loyalty. The availability of prestige goods for distribution attracted followers to a king and enabled him to retain their loyalty. It concentrated increasing wealth and power in the state.

It is possible to see most African economies as divided into two sectors. The bulk of the population, widely dispersed and living in villages, remained tied to traditional farming. It produced only enough food to support itself. Labor was organized in family units. Loyalties remained at the village level. Exchanges in the village may have taken place between blacksmith and farmer, hunter and herder, sometimes on a scale that allowed some degree of incipient specialization. But such exchanges generated no commercial momentum. They did not stimulate production and they made no significant difference to the basic economy. Goods were made to be used in the small communities that produced them. They had no exchange value. They could not be compared in monetary terms. Their circulation was often entirely restricted to certain sectors of the community, such as the village elders. These egalitarian communities had no incentive to change. Their way of life has remained much the same in Africa up to the present day.

The commercial sector of the economy was a product of foreign contacts and of long-distance trade. It was the monopoly of a small group, who by their exclusive access, not to resources but to the outlets by which these could be converted into a useful surplus, became the ruling class. Their control of labor, land or production was minimal: enough to protect the flow of trade and no more. They

Opposite: an Asante king, the Omahene of Akrokerri, is carried to a festival on a palanquin, surrounded by state swords and umbrellas, all traditional items of Asante regalia.

Below left: beaded crowns are a most jealously guarded right of the 16 Yoruba kings descended from the gods. The crowns of Ikirun are displayed once a year.

Below: stools are often particularly sacred symbols of kingship and national identity. In ancient Ife some stools were ground from blocks of quartz, an amazing achievement.

received little in the way of tribute, either in labor or in kind, from the subsistence sector. Nor could they afford to demand heavy duties from the foreign traders. The surplus generated by foreign trade was not employed to increase production in the subsistence sector, but instead it was converted into prestige goods. These perpetuated privilege. They were consumed, hoarded or destroyed ceremonially. They did not stimulate or change the subsistence economy.

Currency, giving a common set of exchange values, and the laws of supply and demand, allowing for production to change in response to consumer demands, never operated. The state determined where exchanges could take place and who could participate in them. It decided what commodities could be traded and on what terms. Crucially, it determined the equivalent values at which goods could be exchanged. This was an administered economy and not a market economy.

Despite these controls, the commercial sector of traditional states generated its own political momentum. It impelled the state towards territorial expansion, encouraging the capture and control of centers of pro-duction, new markets or outlets. It sought greater control of trade to eliminate middlemen. Conversely, it was frequently in traders' interests to subvert the monopoly of the central authority. They would offer people on the periphery of the state better trade terms in order to encourage their secession. They would seek direct commercial relationships with the producers themselves. Foreign participation in the trade frequently introduced an inherent destabilizing influence into the heart of the economy.

The duality of most African economies is generally reflected in the dual nature of African societies. The relationships and interactions between the two sectors and the tensions that these generated were dynamic forces, impelling the societies towards change.

This model of a simple dichotomy in society and economy is in many cases an oversimplification. Often local entrepreneurs and middlemen arose to exploit particular resources. They formed additional elements in society. One contemporary example can be found on the Batoka plateau of Zambia. In the agricultural slack season, groups of Tonga men undertook trading trips over

considerable distances. They not only produced salt and metalwork themselves, but acted as middlemen, trading between other groups. They distributed metalwork from the north and fish from the Zambezi river. However, the wealth they gained was rapidly dissipated. They remained farmers. Their trading activities brought adventure and prestige, better living and some insurance against adversity. But all these benefits could have been found in hunting close to home.

Many other groups lived in a similar way. Systems of regional trade were frequently developed by local entrepreneurs. They could provide the local contacts, local knowledge and expertise, and assurances of security to foreigners. These were precisely the factors that served to attract traders from much further afield into an area. In the late 19th century the Nyamwezi provided the porters, food and local knowledge for Swahili slaving caravans on their way from the East African coast to the Great Lakes. The Chikunda did much the same for Portuguese traders in the Zambezi valley, perhaps following the example of the 14th-century metalworkers of Ingombe Ilede in the same area. In West Africa the Mande peoples, under a variety of names, played a key role as entrepreneurs for the states of Mali, Songhay and Asante. Such professional traders formed a distinct class. They resided in special quarters in many interior capitals and influenced their policy.

Enough has been said to show that if the constraints on social and economic development were similar in many places, the way people adapted to them differed a great deal. It is most improbable that there was a simple and uniform solution. The model sketched here is derived mainly from historical studies, where detail and precision are much more readily available. The reconstruction of the social and economic structures of prehistoric Iron Age Africa, which formed the foundation for the historical states and kingdoms, has scarcely begun.

Side-blown horns can be ancient, rare and precious symbols of a community's identity. *Above:* the bronze *siwa* of Lamu and ivory *siwa* of Pate, islands off northern Kenya, date back to the 17th century. *Below right:* the *siwa* of Mbweni, now an insignificant fishing village of Tanzania. *Below:* horns in use in an Asante court.

2. Concepts of Africa

Africa has seen few of the dramatic revelations that illumine the story of archaeology in other continents. No unknown civilizations have come to light. No explorer has stumbled upon the ruins of cities, lost in tropical jungles. Few excavators have the good fortune to uncover the riches of unknown peoples. The reasons are readily apparent. Until just over two thousand years ago there had never been any permanent settlements south of the Sahara desert. Kingdoms rose in Africa only within the last thousand years or so. This means that none of the symbols of an African state – monumental buildings, regalia, sculptures of kings, gods or founding fathers – are particularly old. They have not had time to be abandoned, vanish or become buried. A great many are still in the palaces of traditional rulers. This short time span also means that cultural continuity between contemporary African societies and the earliest kingdoms is still real and alive. The past is remembered in dynastic genealogies, recounted in the courts of kings. The heroic exploits of ancestors are retold in myth and reenacted in ritual, dance and festivals. Historical events, wars, conquests and migrations, are embedded in the people's memory. They are learned and recounted by specialist historians.

This is not to say that African societies have not developed and changed a great deal over the centuries. In the last five hundred years, all over the continent, indigenous institutions have been subjected to particular strain from external economic exploitation and slave trading. The damage that these have caused has been deep and extensive. In the 19th century, when penetration of the interior by European missionaries, traders and explorers started to pave the way for direct colonization, the strains were particularly apparent. So much so that many of the foreign visitors found the local people indolent, degraded and untrustworthy. Their society looked primitive and stagnant. There was no reason to suppose that things had not always been as horrible. In these circumstances, the standard bearers of European civilization naturally believed that their influence could only be beneficial. They certainly did not comprehend that Africa's backwardness could have been at least in part the result of the actions of their predecessors. If Africa's primitiveness was inherent, Africans were by nature destined to be the passive recipients of alien cultures and to fulfill the roles of servants and slaves. The springs of human creativity and art, culture and civilization, lay elsewhere.

When African achievements in art and architecture were "discovered" they were naturally interpreted as the work of civilized foreigners from Asia or Europe. Millennia before, prehistoric colonists must have in-troduced their alien cultures to Africa. This attitude is reflected in the writing of the most eminent philosophers and historians of Europe. Georg Wilhelm Hegel, in his *Philosophy of History*, published in 1854, observed that: "Africa is not an historical continent; it shows neither change nor development, and whatever may have happened there belongs to the world of Asia and of Europe . . . nothing remotely human is to be found in the [Negro] character . . . Their condition is capable of neither development nor education. As we see them today so they have always been."

As late as 1961, the British historian Hugh Trevor-Roper wrote: "At present there is no African history: there is only the history of the Europeans in Africa, the rest is darkness . . . and darkness is not a subject of history. Please do not misunderstand me. I do not deny that men existed even in dark countries and dark centuries, nor that they had political life and culture, interesting to sociologists and anthropologists: but history, I believe, is essentially a form of movement and purposive movement too. It is not a mere phantasmagoria of changing shapes and costumes, of battles and conquests, dynasties and usurpations, social forms and social disintegration. If all history is equal, as some now believe, there is no reason why we should study one section of it rather than another; for certainly we cannot study it all. Then indeed we may neglect our own history and amuse ourselves with the unrewarding gyrations of barbarous tribes in picturesque but irrelevant corners of the globe: tribes whose chief function in history, in my opinion, is to show to the present an image of the past from which, by history, it has escaped."

Attitudes like these have prejudiced many investigators. Such preconceptions have distorted their findings. Thus, if the Oni of Ife, king of the town that is the spiritual center of the Yoruba people of Nigeria, could name the subjects represented in the ancient sculptures, carved and molded with supreme sensitivity and unearthed in his capital, placed in his people's shrines, and guarded by his priests, this was not taken to indicate that Yoruba craftsmen may have made them or kings commissioned them. If local people could recount the history of Great Zimbabwe and describe the religious ceremonies once held there, this did not mean they were responsible for the buildings. Such things only indicated that foreign artists had, down the ages, been absorbed by the local populace. Their blood, race and culture had been diluted, weakened, coarsened and nearly extinguished by their Negroid subjects. Besides the monuments, the only trace of their passage was to be found in the thin lips, sallow skin or pointed noses of particularly eloquent informants. The gap between historical reality and foreign interpretations of it is so wide in Africa that any study of the development of prehistorical research must take account of such attitudes. It must seek to discern the pressures and motives that molded them.

Previous page: a griot *or bard. The court bards of the Manding kings were custodians of oral traditions. Each could recite the history of the dynasty and kingdom.*

The Arab geographers. This negation of African achievement is a phenomenon of the colonial period and the years that led up to it. It was not reflected in the first contact between foreign travelers and African kingdoms. The first indication of the cultural and economic riches of Africa came from Arab scholars. After Islam had been established along the southern shores of the Mediterranean, caravans crossed the Sahara and linked the West African Sudan to the commerce of the Islamic world. Great trading cities grew up in the Sudan. Their wealth was a living reality to the Islamic world. With the caravans went adventurers, scholars and merchants. They returned with tall stories, with detailed descriptions of towns and people, and with assessments of the possibility of trade. Their reports formed the substance on which the Arab geographers worked.

At the end of the 8th century, al Fazari, geographer at the court of the caliph of Baghdad, mentioned the ancient kingdom of Ghana in the western Sudan for the first time. A century later, al Yakubi recorded that gold mines and many tributary states were the basis of the king of Ghana's greatness. In 1067 al Bakri, a Spanish-Arab living in Cordoba, gave the fullest picture of Ghana. He described how the capital of Ghana was divided into two. The commercial area catered for the foreign merchants and had a dozen or more mosques. Some distance away, on the other side of the town, lived the king, in a palace built in traditional style. The elaboration and wealth of his court

In the Catalan Atlas, Mansa Musa receives a Saharan merchant. Between them are depicted *Tagaza*, *Ginyia* (Guinea), *Melli* (Mali), *Sudan* and *Tembuch* (Timbuktu).

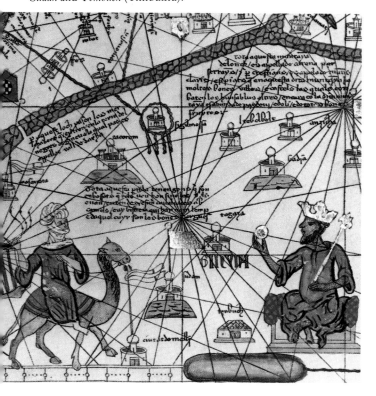

were immense. In audience he was surrounded by governors and viziers and flanked by pages bearing gold-mounted swords. Gold ornaments were everywhere. Even the trappings of the horses and collars of the dogs were of gold and silver. The kings of Ghana took such splendor beyond the grave. At death, the king's corpse was laid in a chamber under a domed tumulus of earth, surrounded by jewels, food, drink and servants. Ghana was powerful enough to put 200,000 men, including 40,000 bowmen, into the field. Its wealth came from taxes on the copper and salt passing through the capital to the southern forests and on the gold from the south that passed north.

The wealth of black Africa was displayed in full view of the Arab world when Mansa Musa, the king of Mali, stayed in Cairo during his pilgrimage to Mecca in 1324. Twelve years after he had passed, al Omari found the event still vivid in his benefactor's memory: "This man spread upon Cairo the flood of his generosity: there was no person, officer of the court, or holder of any office of the sultanate who did not receive a sum of gold from him. The people of Cairo earned incalculable sums from him, whether by buying and selling or by gifts. So much gold was current in Cairo that it ruined the value of money." At home the court of the Mansa was as splendid, as al Omari recorded: "The sultan of this kingdom presides in his palace on a great balcony ... flanked by elephant tusks ... his arms stand near him, being all of gold ... Behind him there stand about a score of Turkish or other pages which are bought for him in Cairo ... One of them ... holds a silk umbrella surmounted by a dome and a bird of gold."

A generation later, Ibn Battuta visited Mali. He was a Muslim scholar, lawyer and theologian of rigid orthodoxy. He had devoted his life to travel. Born in Tangier, he visited places as distant as the Upper Nile, the Crimea, India, Samarkand, China and Sumatra. In his eyes, the pomp of the Mali court was as great as any he had seen. The king's subjects lived in security. Injustice was particularly rare: "The Negroes are of all peoples those who most abhor injustice." Travelers enjoyed complete safety: "The traveler has no more reason than the man who stays at home to fear brigands, thieves or ravishers." The people were pious: "On Fridays, anyone who is late at the mosque will find nowhere to pray, the crowd is so great ... They zealously learn the Koran by heart. Those children who are neglectful in this are put in chains until they have memorized the Koran." Only some pagan customs jarred: "Women go naked into the sultan's presence, too, without even a veil ... they have buffoons who appear before the sultan ... a good number of Negroes eat the flesh of dogs and donkeys."

Across the continent, the trading cities of the East African coast attracted the same attention in the Islamic world. The seaborne commerce of these cities with Asia had a history even longer than that of the caravan trade of the Sudan. The earliest record of the part East Africa played in the commercial network of the Indian Ocean is contained in the *Periplus of the Erythraean Sea*, written in the 2nd century AD. At this time the furthest trading post of the ports of the Red Sea and Arabia was Rhapta, "the last mainland market-town." About the same time Claudius Ptolemy described it as "the metropolis of Barbaria, set back a little from the sea ... around which there live man-eating savages." It has not yet been located but probably lay on the coast of Tanzania.

By the 10th century, when al Masudi took passage from Oman to the East African islands, the Zanj, the inhabitants of what is now Tanzania, were significant traders: "The land of Zanj produces wild leopard skins. The people wear them as clothes, or export them to Muslim countries. They are the largest leopard skins and the most beautiful for making saddles ... They also export tortoise shell [and] ivory ... There are many wild elephants ... The Zanj rush upon them armed with very long spears, and kill them for their ivory. It is from this country that come tusks weighing 50 pounds and more. They usually go to Oman, and from there are sent to China and India. This is the chief trade route, and if it were not so, ivory would be common in Muslim lands."

While al Omari was writing in 1336 of Mansa Musa's pilgrimage and the economic upheavals it caused, Ibn Battuta was visiting the now well-established commercial city-states of Africa. He found Mogadishu "a very large town" with a closely regulated system of trade, conducted through local agents and controlled by the sultan. "When a ship arrives, it is the custom for it to be boarded by the sultan's *sanbuq* [a small boat], to inquire whence it came, who are the owners and who its captain is. They also inquire the nature of the cargo and what merchants or

The harbor of Hais on the Somali coast of the Red Sea, probably one of the ports mentioned in the *Periplus*. Myrrh and frankincense were exported from its hinterland.

Africa, from a map made by Juan de la Cosa in 1500. New York Public Library.

other persons are on board. All this is told to the sultan who invites as his guest anyone worthy of such honor ... Not one of the merchants disembarks except to go to the house of his host ... save frequent visitors to the country. In such a case they go where they like. When a merchant has settled in his host's house, the latter sells for him what he has brought and makes his purchases for him. Buying anything from a merchant below its market price or selling him anything except in his host's presence is disapproved of by the people of Mogadishu. They find it of advantage to keep to this rule."

From Mogadishu and Mombasa, Ibn Battuta sailed on to Kilwa, "the principal town on the coast, the greater part of whose inhabitants are Zanj of very black complexion." He found Kilwa "one of the most beautiful and well-constructed towns in the world. The whole of it is elegantly built. The roofs are built with mangrove poles. There is very much rain. The people are engaged in a holy war, for their country lies beside that of pagan Zanj. The chief qualities are devotion and piety: they follow the Shafi'i rite."

Europe encounters Africa. Accounts of Africa filtered through to western Europe. In 1154 al Idrisi compiled reports of Africa by his Muslim compatriots for Roger, King of Sicily, in whose court he had resided for many years. Jewish merchants who had traveled with the Saharan caravans, gave the Majorcan cartographer, Abraham Cresques, enough information for him to reproduce their routes with considerable detail and accuracy in his Catalan Atlas of 1375. Hassan Ibn Mohammed, a Spanish Muslim captured by Christian pirates, was received by Pope Leo X in 1512 and described his travels to the Niger towns of Timbuktu and Gao. The pope in return christened him Leo Africanus. His descriptions were published by Giovanni Ramusio for the merchants of Venice. In Britain Samuel Purchas reproduced them in his anthology of travel, *Purchas, his Pilgrims*.

Although Europe knew of the commerce and riches of the kingdoms of black Africa, access to these markets was denied by the Islamic powers of North Africa. Islamic hostility also blocked Christian trade with India and the east. Portugal initiated a systematic campaign to outflank Islam by the sea. Her navigators sought to open a sea route to Africa and the Indian Ocean. By 1442 Portuguese ships were raiding the camps of the desert Tuareg along the coast of Mauritania. They were also taking slaves from the villages of Senegal. The first gold dust from Africa was brought back to Lisbon. Within a decade Portugal was minting coins from African gold – the first gold coinage she had been able to afford for 70 years.

In the 1470s ships of the Portuguese crown entered the Gulf of Guinea. Forts were built along this coast and the first tenuous contacts were made with the forest kingdoms of West Africa. Access to the gold mines, whose products had fueled the caravan trade of the Sahara for many centuries, was within grasp. The entire trade of the West African Sudan faltered. Gold started to pass south to the new outlets on the Atlantic coast.

In 1486 a Portuguese envoy, João Affonso d'Aveiro, entered the city of Benin, capital of the most powerful forest kingdom. Here he heard of an even more powerful state further inland. Its king, the Ogane, was a religious leader who sent to each new king of Benin messengers bearing royal insignia: a staff, a crown that looked like a Spanish helmet, and a Maltese cross. Only through these ceremonies was the royal succession of Benin legitimized. It seemed to the Portuguese that they were at last within reach of the ally they had most sought.

Since 1165, when he had dispatched a letter to the emperor of Byzantium, the Christian kings of Europe had speculated on Prester John, the great Christian king and priest who ruled in Africa beyond the borders of Islam: "I, John the Presbyter, Lord of Lords, am superior in virtue, riches and power to all who walk under heaven. Seventy-two kings pay tribute to us. Our might prevails in the three Indies, and our lands extend all the way to the furthest Indies ... our country is a home and dwelling place of elephants ... lions ... tigers, hyenas and wild men. Thirty thousand people eat at our table each day, apart from casual guests, and all receive gifts from our stores ... this table is of the richest emerald and is supported by four pillars of amethyst ... at our court there are many servants who hold high spiritual offices and honors. Our steward is a primate and king: our cupbearer a king and archbishop ..."

Native Christian priests from Ethiopia, who traveled as far as the court of Portugal as envoys of their emperor, seemed to confirm Prester John's existence. It now seemed that the Ogane, the secret ruler whom Benin held in such

reverence and whose emblem was a cross, must be Prester John himself. After d'Aveiro's report reached Lisbon, a new attempt was made to reach Prester John by sending an agent through the Muslim lands. Pero de Covilhao, disguised as an Arab merchant, left Lisbon in 1487 and traveled to Aden and south India. From there he took passage on a trading dhow to Sofala, scouting the possibilities of rounding Africa from the south. In 1493 he reached the court of the emperor of Ethiopia, where he took up residence for more than 27 years. The troubled alliance between Prester John, emperor of Ethiopia, and the Portuguese was never to give them the power in the African interior that they sought.

Meanwhile, Portuguese ships steadily probed their way further down the coast of West Africa. In 1482 Diogo Cao had anchored in the waters of the Congo river. In 1490 the king of the Kongo was baptized and started to model his kingdom on that of Portugal. In 1498 Vasco da Gama finally rounded the southern tip of Africa and entered the Indian Ocean. A new world was opened.

In their effort to capture the Indian Ocean trade from the Swahili city-states, the Portuguese built and garrisoned forts at Kilwa and Sofala. From Sofala, gold was exported from kingdoms far inland to Kilwa and other cities of the northern coast. The Portuguese were soon aware of the potential wealth of the interior. "The land is rich in gold; if the people were covetous, a great quantity could be obtained; but they are so lazy in seeking it, or rather covet it so little, that one of these Negroes must be very hungry before he will dig for it." But there was more. Viçente Pegado, captain of Sofala in 1531, was told of a great ruin that stood among the gold mines of the inland plains: "A square fortress, of masonry within and without, built of stones of marvelous size, and there

The castle of St George of the Mine – now Elmina – was the main trading port of the Portuguese in the Gulf of Guinea from 1482 until its capture by the Dutch in 1637.

like strong bulwarks ... the Kaffirs consider to be the means by which Monomotapa obtain dominion over all Kaffraria." (The Munhu Mutapa ruled the inland kingdom with which the Portuguese traded in gold in an uneasy partnership that lasted for the next two centuries.) But there were also more romantic notions that held out the promise of wealth beyond even that of Prester John: "Some aged Moors assert that they have a tradition from their ancestors that these houses were anciently a factory of the Queen of Sheba, and that from this place a great quantity of gold was brought to her ... Others say that these are the ruins of the factory of Solomon, where he had his factors who procured a great quantity of gold from these lands ... they say further that the gold of Ophir which was brought to Solomon was from the place called Fura [a mountain near the Monomotapa's capital]."

A start in prehistory. There is little doubt that the ruin that the Portuguese knew was Great Zimbabwe. It had been the capital of a Shona state for 300 years and had only lost its power a few decades before the Portuguese heard of it. Indeed their partner, the Munhu Mutapa, ruled a state that had succeeded to part of the territories of Great Zimbabwe. But this has only been established by the archaeological work within the present century. In all their dealings with the interior, the Portuguese saw few further ruins and discovered nothing more. Their more romantic speculations remained uncontested for over three centuries.

In 1862 the Revd. A. Merensky, who for many years had worked as a missionary in the northern Transvaal, set

Above: Prester John surveys his kingdom from his mountain fastness of Ethiopia. A detail from a 16th-century Portuguese map.
Right: Great Zimbabwe, from a photograph taken on the march north by Rhodes's occupying force. "We are about to make this rich country again disgorge the gold which has so long lain hidden around these prehistoric remains."

appears to be no mortar joining them ... This edifice is almost surrounded by hills, upon which are others resembling it in the fashioning of the stone and the absence of mortar, and one of them is a tower more than 12 fathoms high. The natives of the country call all these edifices Symbaoe, which according to their language signifies court ... When, and by whom these edifices were raised ... there is no record, but they say they are the work of the devil, for in comparison with their power and knowledge it does not seem possible to them that they should be the work of man."

Was this yet further evidence of Prester John? "These edifices are very similar to some which are found in the land of Prester John ... It would seem that the prince who was lord of that state also owned these mines, and therefore ordered these edifices to be raised." There were other more prosaic explanations. "The great stone edifices which are called Symbaoe by the Kaffirs and which are

out to visit Great Zimbabwe. He had not only read the Portuguese chroniclers' accounts of the mysterious ruins of King Solomon, but had collected descriptions of an enormous ruin north of the Limpopo river, from Africans who had visited it. Misfortunes forced him to turn back. His information was, however, published in Capt. Hugh Walmsley's *The Ruined Cities of Zululand*, a romantic travelogue, cast as fiction, in which Merensky appears, thinly disguised as the intrepid companion of a British army officer. Together they traveled up the Sabi river, the "Golden River, down whose stream the boats of bygone days floated gold, cedar-wood and precious stones ... from ... the gold fields of Solomon ... where ... the ruined cities of the mighty old Egyptians, the ancient gold diggers, crumble into dust."

This journey became a reality when Merensky helped Karl Mauch, a German explorer and geologist, to travel north towards "the most valuable and important, the hitherto most mysterious part of Africa, the old Monomotapa or Ophir." In 1871 Mauch reached the village of Mapansure, a Shona chief living north of the Limpopo river. He was given "most exciting news": "White men once lived in this country." There were "quite large ruins which could never have been built by blacks." He was taken to these a few days later. "After two and a half hours' walking, a bare, large and rounded granite hill was reached, from the summit of which a preliminary view of the mountain could be had ... The western slope of the rocky mountain is ... covered with ... stone fragments ... these probably had been walls of a fortification ... I ambled around a little between extensive ruinous walls and saw a short distance away an apparently round edifice ... Presently I stood before it and beheld a wall of a height of about 20 feet, of ... granite bricks. I did not have to look for an entrance for long, for very close by there was a place where a kind of footpath, which apparently is used quite frequently, led over rubble into the interior. Following this path I stumbled over masses of rubble and parts of walls. Dense thickets and big trees prevented me from obtaining an overall view from any point."

For nearly nine months Mauch lived near Great Zimbabwe. On the two further visits that he was allowed to make to the ruins, he mapped the largest ruin and retrieved objects of metal and carved stone from among the ruined walls. "With patience, prudence, cunning and some lying" he also managed to meet a man whose family had had charge of the religious ceremonies that had been held within the ruins for generations. "I made him know that by the reticence and silence which he showed towards me he was not doing anything good, as I would straight away go to my Captain, who would rebuild Zimbabye again and would, instead of electing him as high priest, install somebody else. This had the desired effect. True to his promise he arrived and showed himself very willing to answer the many questions that I put to him."

Mauch interpreted all that he heard in the light of Merensky's belief in the Biblical associations of the ruin.

The diary (*below*) of Karl Mauch (*below left*) describes his visit to Great Zimbabwe on 11 September 1871. Of the gong, he writes: "Its use was a complete riddle to me, but it proves most clearly that a civilized nation must once have lived here."

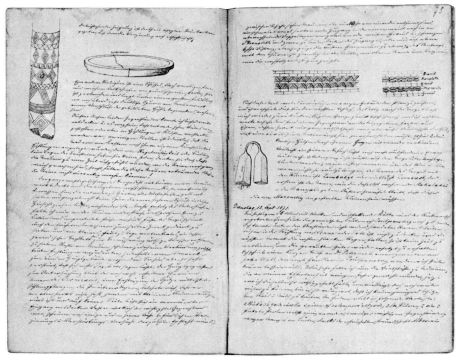

The smell of a sliver of a wood beam from the ruin was conclusive. "A comparison of it with the wood of my pencil shows great similarity and therefore I suppose . . . it must be cedar wood . . . it cannot come from anywhere else but from the Libanon . . . A very telling witness to the fact that these ruins are an imitation of Salomo's buildings." Great Zimbabwe was Sheba and the largest ruin was a copy of the Queen of Sheba's palace. The religious ceremonies were clear imitations of the festivals of the Jews of the Old Testament. Mauch's informant must be "a descendant of the high-priestly officer, that Salomo sent out with the Queen of Sheba who, with her whole entourage, had converted to Judaism." Mauch's tenacity in reaching Great Zimbabwe, his patience and endurance and his skill in recording the plans and descriptions of the ruins in the end had taught him nothing.

The Portuguese chronicles that had inspired Merensky, Walmsley and Mauch led on to Rider Haggard and his novels of Africa, *She* and *King Solomon's Mines*. The same ideas acquired political overtones when they were taken up by the financiers and advocates of colonial expansion in Africa. Cecil John Rhodes bought Mauch's relics from Great Zimbabwe and got others from later hunters and prospectors who had traveled to the ruins. He believed: "You will find that Zimbabye is an old Phoenician residence and everything points to Sofala being the place from which Hiram fetched his gold the word 'peacocks' in the bible may be read as parrots and amongst the stone ornaments from Zimbabye are green parrots, the common kind of that district for the rest you have gold and ivory, also the fact that Zimbabye is built of hewn stone without mortar." Such theories, in the words of the first Administrator of Rhodesia, "helped fire his imagination and shape his policy." Rhodes formed a company under royal charter to colonize the territory of Great Zimbabwe. At least in part, the ruins were seen as a

Above: using laborers like these convinced the first excavators that the Shona were too "backward" ever to have built the ruins.

Left: members of the Rhodesian Ancient Ruins Ltd, with an exclusive right "to explore and work for treasure," pillaged more than 50 ruins between 1897 and 1900.

promise of wealth and a guarantee of the legitimacy of colonial rule. Both had been realized in Biblical times. In the face of such precedents, the rights of the existing barbarous inhabitants paled into insignificance.

Investigations of Great Zimbabwe. Within a year Rhodes invited Theodore Bent to investigate Great Zimbabwe. Bent was an antiquarian who had traveled extensively in the eastern Mediterranean, Asia Minor and the Persian Gulf. He knew something of the ancient civilizations of the east. He started to excavate within the main walled enclosure of Great Zimbabwe. From his local foreman and guide, one senses something of Bent's problems, methods and attitudes, faced with a new area and strong preconceptions about African creativity and skill. "Mr. Bent had various moods about the origin of the Ruins, some days he thought that they were Phoenician and at other times he thought they might be Egyptian as we had not found anything in the nature of an inscription which would have been a guide. One day we found a piece of white glass with some ornamentation in gold and he thought it was Chinese glass. One day he came to me looking rather depressed and said 'I have not much faith in the antiquity of these ruins, I think they are native.' I asked why, he said 'Everything we have so far is native.' I did not agree with him and said so, I did admit that natives had occupied the place after the evacuation by the original builders but I would not agree that African natives had built them. A day or two later he had changed back to Phoenicians and stuck to the idea." Bent could get no help from traditional history even if he had wanted it. "He could not get much reliable information as there was not a Chishona linguist in the country. The interpreters we had at Zimbabye were good Xhosa and Zulu speakers but they could not speak or understand Chishona and they had to depend on shouting and gesticulations to make a native half understand."

When Bent finally came to interpret his work in *The Ruined Cities of Mashonaland*, he could see resemblances in the art and architecture of Great Zimbabwe to the monuments of Assyria, Phoenicia, Cyprus, Malta, Sardinia, Egypt, Sudan and south Arabia. Yet nothing pointed unequivocally towards a particular alien civilization. Bent was forced to conclude: "A prehistoric race built the ruins . . . which eventually became influenced and perhaps absorbed in the . . . organizations of the Semite . . . a northern race coming from Arabia . . . closely akin to the Phoenician and Egyptian . . . and eventually developed into the more civilised races of the ancient worlds."

Bent's work was followed by a series of disastrous excavation campaigns by local colonists. They shoveled great quantities of stratified deposits out of the walled enclosures in an obsessive search for the exotic. In sharp contrast to this, Great Zimbabwe also saw the first scientific excavation ever conducted in black Africa. In 1905 the British Association for the Advancement of Science commissioned David Randall-MacIver to investigate the ruins of Rhodesia. The controversy that his findings caused among the settlers of southern Africa lasted a generation. As a result, in 1929, the British Association invited Gertrude Caton-Thompson to repeat Randall-MacIver's investigations.

Both Randall-MacIver and Caton-Thompson were eminent professional archaeologists at the height of their careers when they were invited to go to Great Zimbabwe. They had both had considerable field experience in the Middle East. Both approached the problems of Great Zimbabwe as outsiders, with little local knowledge and no local archaeological advice or background information to assist them. As a result, both decided to visit and excavate several ruins, throughout the country, before they commenced work at Great Zimbabwe. Most importantly, both used the best archaeological methods that had been developed in their time in Europe, seeking precisely identifiable and datable objects, those that were securely stratified within sealed deposits, associated with the monumental structures. Both also published full reports on their work, with all the apparatus of scholarship – full catalogs of finds, illustrated stratigraphic sections and typologies of local artifacts.

Local settler reaction was immediate and hostile: "I was so historically offended that I felt I never wanted to go near the place again. To me it was as if Stonehenge had been brought to England by William the Conqueror."

The sort of discussion that resulted in Britain is reflected in the pages of the *Geographical Journal* that first reported Randall-MacIver's findings. Sir Arthur Evans, excavator of the Minoan civilization, "was long ago negatively convinced that the supposed evidence of early contact with Arabia or Phoenicia had no real basis. In fact, it seemed to me that there was nothing in the architecture or the remains discovered in common with either early Arabian or Phoenician models as far as they were known . . . the great presumption . . . was that the existing ruins were simply enlarged examples of native kraals." Hercules Read, Curator of the British Museum, had, at Rhodes's request, examined his relics from Great Zimbabwe. "Nothing that was brought to me differed from what might have been made either by the existing or recently existing natives, except in cases where they were importations of a well-known date. That is to say, there was Arab pottery and Chinese porcelain . . . of about the 13th century." David Hogarth, then the leading Arabist in Britain, pointed out that "The whole Semitic theory . . . rests also on a great deal of vague generalization . . . I was not convinced by Mr. Bent's evidence. I was always very much impressed by two facts: one that no real evidence of high civilization was offered, either by the architecture, or

Gertrude Caton-Thompson behind her excavation on the slope below the Hill Ruin, which yielded imported beads and other finds from a rubbish dump buried 17 feet beneath later debris.

still more by the smaller finds, particularly those much-vaunted steatite phalli and birds."

Recognized authorities on African life expressed contradictory opinions. Frederick Courtenay Selous knew the country and people so well that he had been chosen to guide Rhodes's occupying column into Mashonaland. He could not see "any evidence that a highly cultured civilized people ever lived in that country, who were destroyed by the sudden incursion of a barbarous race . . . Given a powerful chief in Mashonaland a hundred years ago, at a time when the natives were still accustomed to building walls of well-fitted granite stones, and I see no reasons why such a chief could not have had such a building as the Great Zimbabwe put up." Sir Harry Johnston, Administrator of Nyasaland, had "never been exactly to the part of Africa where these ruins are situated." Nevertheless, he "remained relatively unshaken that there was at a period at least as early as the birth of Christ – I believe earlier – an incursion into this country of a Semitic race of teachers."

The significant thing is that all these represented subjective opinions, however cautious and experienced. Randall-MacIver had obtained the objective evidence. It was clear, precise and irrefutable. His excavation yielded imported goods of known date and type, sealed beneath clay floors, in association with the stone walls. There was no significant earlier material and there was no other alien material. Great Zimbabwe could be dated: its African nature, its origins and culture were firmly established.

Within a welter of local emotion, Randall-MacIver and Caton-Thompson independently established that the objective and scientific methods of archaeology could be employed to investigate isolated sites in the furthest interior of Africa just as they could be used in uncovering the ruins of the ancient literate civilizations of the Middle East. The chronology and culture of the builders in stone whose contacts with the outside world were tenuous, obscure and indirect and who had no knowledge of writing, could be determined by archaeological methods. Comparisons of style in sculpture or building could not match these methods. Generalizations about the African character were both irrelevant and demonstrably wrong. Certainly, they had no place in the argument. Scientific archaeology had been introduced to Africa at a key site. The political, financial and racial implications of the archaeological interpretations of Great Zimbabwe were both obvious and crucial. Scientific method had triumphed.

Benin. Six years after Mashonaland was occupied, a British punitive expedition entered Benin to exact retribution for the killing of an Acting Consul General. After 400 years of trade with Europe, the kingdom's independence was at an end. In the early 17th century Dutch merchants had described Benin as a town with streets "seven or eight times broader than the Warmoes street in Amsterdam," running straight as far as the eye could see. The king's palace alone "occupied as much space as the town of Haarlem and is enclosed within walls . . . with fine galleries, most of which are as big as those on the Exchange at Amsterdam. They are supported by wooden pillars encased with bronze, where their victories are depicted, and are carefully kept very clean." Now the British found "only a straggling collection of houses, built in clusters here and there, in little or no order. The number of ruins testified to the fact that it was once very much larger." The palace was still the most imposing building in the town: "Entered through a doorway, the big door of which is lined with sheets of brass with stamped figures of men and leopards' heads . . . On the other side of the compound . . . the wall is partly roofed in, and along this is

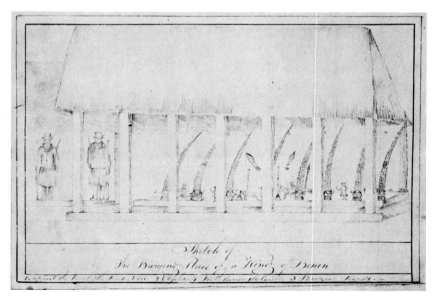

The earliest drawing of a Benin shrine or tomb, by Giovanni Belzoni, the former circus strongman, who amassed an enormous collection of Egyptian antiquities before going to Benin and his death in 1823.

a row of brass heads, and on top of every head is a long, heavy weather-worn finely carved ivory tusk ... Between the brass heads were brass castings of men on horseback, in armour, in chain mail ... All the articles were thickly encrusted with blood, and a fearful smell pervaded the place ... Through this compound ... is the king's meeting house ... The first thing that strikes you here is the metal roof on which, just facing you, is an immense brass snake crawling down with its big head close to the gutter ... All the rafters are of wood carved with rough figures; some of the rafters have been covered with brass sheeting on which figures have been punched. The roof is supported by over one hundred pillars of bronze sheets riveted together, giving a very good effect."

Carvings and sculptures of every size and form were looted by the expedition before fire razed the town to the ground. H. Ling Roth, brother of the surgeon of the punitive expedition, in the most detailed and comprehensive study of Benin and its art, written in 1903, showed that many of the bronzes depicted Portuguese soldiers in 16th-century dress, delineated in such precise detail that it was impossible to claim that they were not contemporary representations. Nor was there any question that they were imports. "There was no such high-class art in the Iberian peninsula at the end of the 15th century; and we know there was not much of this art in the rest of Europe." Consequently, although "their pottery was exceptionally crude and their superstitions were of the lowest, it seems as though the only conclusion we can arrive at is that we have [in the bronzes] a form of real native art." Benin went to its downfall in a river of human blood, sacrificed with appalling cruelties, squalor and profligacy. Yet it had to be recognized that it had produced works of aesthetic and technical proficiency and merit unmatched in Europe. At the time this conclusion was particularly forceful because the sculptures had a realism to which high Victorian taste could readily respond.

Above: a Benin statuette of a Portuguese soldier in 16th-century armor.

Opposite: members of the punitive expedition of 1897 surrounded by plaques looted from the palace of Benin.

Below: a desecrated altar in Benin. The carved staffs symbolize authority, transmitted to the Oba from his predecessors. The wands were evidence of his personal commands.

The origins of this creative flowering were not pursued. No prehistorians were attracted to a study of the West African past until 1910, when Leo Frobenius landed in southern Nigeria to study the Yoruba. They were Benin's western neighbors and, it had always been assumed, the source of much of their culture. Where foreign archaeologists had spent, at most, a season at major sites like Great Zimbabwe, Frobenius was to devote his life to a systematic investigation of the prehistory of all Africa. His stimulus had come from a Berlin newspaper, which had described Africa in Hegelian terms: "No historical enigma ... calls for solution, because ... civilization proper in this continent begins ... with the Mohammedan invasion ... Before the introduction of a genuine faith and a higher standard of culture by the Arabs, the natives had neither political organization nor ... any religion, nor any industrial development ... If the soil of Africa is turned up today by the colonist's plowshare, no ancient weapon will lie in the furrow; ... excavation will reveal no ancient tomb, and if the ax effects a clearance in the primaeval forests it will nowhere ring upon the foundations of an old-world palace ... 'Black Africa' is a continent which has neither mystery nor history." Frobenius realized the absurdity of this outlook. It seemed, for instance, immediately obvious that Africa's wide diversity of cultures could only be the product of different historical developments. This he set out to demonstrate.

Frobenius also saw an immediate practical significance in his work. Colonial administrators were seeking to mobilize Africa's labor power and harness it to Europe's requirements. Africans were uncooperative and appeared impervious to the European virtues of industry and ambition. To Frobenius it seemed the causes and origins of such perversions could only be found if one examined how healthy African societies function. This demanded a historical perspective. Africa had changed through time. All that now seemed squalid and degraded should not be allowed to obscure the culture of the past. "The African lacks the faculty of preserving the treasures of civilization intact and of keeping his inheritance undefiled. All he does is to overlay the ancient records with such a mass of odd or humorous, artless or extravagant, but nearly always tasteless flourishes, that the eye needs a prolonged and most careful training before it can recognize the original text ... Learning to see is the most difficult of things in the laborious study of African history."

"Like a thunderclap – Frobenius!" Frobenius realized that the African past should not be studied only through written documents or great monuments, though he knew that these existed. He had, for instance, already excavated the tombs of early kings beside the Niger river. Instead, there were two basic methods of research. The first was to collect and interpret the myths and traditions of local people: "the godlike strength of memory in those who lived before the advent of the written word." The second

method was archaeological excavation: "We threw ourselves upon the ground ... and pressed our ear upon the hard-bound earth, to hear perchance the footfalls of men long passed away ... We dug; we went into the depths; we let the light of day shine in upon palaces of ancient days and disused mines and workshops in decay. We strove to get upon the track of every single human impulse."

A Yoruba sailor in Hamburg's dockland had first told Frobenius of his home, Ife, the holy city of the Yoruba, the center and origin of man and his world. Its ruler, the Oni, was first in honor among all Yoruba kings. He had to approve and validate their coronations. He was probably the Ogane, of whom the people of Benin had told the Portuguese, who had believed that he must be Prester John. Frobenius was also told that the "heads of ancestors turned to stone" were to be found buried in Ife. He found a run-down town. Large parts of it were derelict and much of the palace in ruins. Sixteen years before, civil war had broken out in Ife and for a long time the city had been abandoned. These disorders – and there had been others not long before – had badly damaged the city's confidence and sense of continuity.

Below: Leo Frobenius. *Opposite:* his assistant, drawn on the spot by the expedition's artist, examines finds, standing in the extraordinary excavations deep beneath the Olokun Grove.

Frobenius immediately set out to visit the shrines of the Yoruba gods. His first impression was disappointing. Many were simply groves in the tropical forest. They had no buildings and their cult objects were unimpressive – crude carved stones at most. Still, they seemed the best place to start looking for antiquities. Within days, while watching the rites at one shrine, Frobenius "happened upon one or two bits of reddish-brown terracotta embedded in the earth ... They were pieces of a broken human face and when I saw these fragments, I grasped the full meaning of what I had been told ... Here were the remains of a very ancient and fine type of art, infinitely nobler than the comparatively coarse stone images ... These meager relics were eloquent of a symmetry, a vitality, a delicacy of form directly reminiscent of ancient Greece."

With this encouragement, Frobenius's assistant started to sink shafts and tunnels in the grove of Olokun, Yoruba goddess of wealth and the sea. Eighteen feet below the ground, his extraordinary "burrowings" were still producing pottery and "exquisitely life-like terracotta heads, with clear-cut features and purity of style." To cap it all, after much hesitation and reluctance, the priest of the Olokun Grove showed Frobenius "a head of marvelous beauty, wonderfully cast in antique bronze, true to the life, encrusted with the patina of glorious dark green. This was,

in very deed, the Olokun, Atlantic Africa's Poseidon." Frobenius was deeply moved. "I looked around and saw the blacks, the circle of the sons of the 'venerable priest,' his Holiness the Oni's friends, and his intelligent officials. I was moved to silent melancholy at the thought that this assembly of degenerate and feeble-minded posterity should be the legitimate guardians of so much classic loveliness."

Frobenius looked at the culture, myths and antiquities of Ife for clues to its origin. The calm repose and realism of the sculptures were reminiscent of Classical Greece. The pantheon of Yoruba gods, their attributes, their vivid lives and complex responsibilities echoed Mount Olympus. The architecture of the houses and palaces, where rooms opened off enclosed courtyards, open to the sky, resembled the impluvia of early Mediterranean, particularly Etruscan, buildings. The Yoruba concept of the universe, their educational system, the organization of their society and their statecraft supported a Greek connection. There appeared to be no local precedent for this high culture.

In his approach to historical problems in Africa and the means of their solution Frobenius was overawed by the richness of his material. He recognized the value of archaeological techniques, but his excavations became simply another means of acquiring art objects. They owed

nothing to scientific methods. Though the number of objects he gathered was phenomenal, his assessments of them had exactly the same subjectivity and the same emotional core as those of Cecil Rhodes or Theodore Bent. The scholarship, discipline and precision of Randall-MacIver found no echo in Frobenius. In the end, Frobenius was satisfied that Ife and Yoruba culture must be the last relics of Atlantis, the island of Poseidon, lost in the oceans beyond the Pillars of Hercules.

Frobenius's contribution to African prehistory fortunately did not end here. The stimulus of Ife enabled him to make a more telling contribution in another sphere. After leaving Ife, he traveled north to the Hausa states of the western Sudan. Here Britain was establishing a policy of indirect rule. British authority was transmitted through the Hamitic-speaking Hausa sultans and emirs to their Negroid subjects. This policy reflected the conviction that the Hamitic peoples had an inherent competence as builders and administrators of state organizations. Frobenius saw it differently. To him the Hamites were former slave owners and the instigators of the slave trade that had deprived Africa of productive manpower. Frobenius believed that Hamites, with this cultural background, could contribute little to Africa's main value: as a source of labor for the European economy. In these circumstances, he believed that Hamites should not be given the powers proposed by British administrators.

Beyond his logical objections, Frobenius's emotional sympathies lay with Negroid agriculturalists of the West African forests – the "Ethiopian" peoples. Frobenius associated Ethiopians with a mysticism and a non-rational spontaneity. They showed a sense of communion with nature, inductive forms of reasoning and a concern for myth. For Frobenius these characteristics echoed the innate personality of the Germanic peoples from which he himself sprang. The Ethiopian personality was undoubtedly due to the long influence of Atlantic civilization on the cultures of West Africa, exemplified by the arts of Ife.

Many see the essence of Frobenius's work in West Africa as this revelation of the African personality. Leopold Senghor, now president of Senegal, developed his beliefs in a distinctive African personality into the concept of "negritude" and embodied this in powerful poetry and drama. This philosophy has given many newly independent African nations a sense of identity, pride and purpose. Senghor fully acknowledges his debt to Frobenius. "Suddenly, like a thunderclap – Frobenius! All the history and prehistory of Africa were illuminated to their very depths. And we still carry the mark of the master in our minds and spirits, like a form of tattooing carried out in the initiation ceremonies in the sacred grove." The Ife revealed by Frobenius embodies more than any other place the spirit of negritude. In 1971 President Senghor paid homage in Ife. "Here, in olden times, flourished the Negro soul and imagination, creating myths, composing prayers,

developing art." The primeval man of Ife "had no need to make books or build museums. His function was to express life through prayer and art, by symbolism. Thus he helped other men, all men, to lead a better life. The man of Ife, who was greeted by the West through the voice of Leo Frobenius the German, was endowed with poetic powers. His mission was to help shape the world . . . In the sculptures of Ife are depicted all the art, history and philosophy of Africa. And from them Western Europe discovered the forgotten notions of art in prayer, gravity in joy, dignity in suffering, restraint in the broad sweep of a gesture."

The discipline and science of MacIver, the British archaeologist who restored some sense of historical reality to Great Zimbabwe, stands at an opposite pole to the poetic mysticism of Frobenius and Senghor. Both have played a part in establishing the authenticity and contemporary significance of African prehistory. They both fashioned new concepts of Africa.

An Ife bronze, said to be of the deity Olokun. Frobenius acquired a very similar head at the Olokun Grove, now lost. The head said to have been left in Ife by Frobenius was shown in 1949 to be a recent European casting.

Meroë and Aksum

Meroë lies on the Nile above its confluence with the Atbara, flowing from the Ethiopian highlands. It represents dynastic Egypt's furthest penetration south and its closest contact with black Africa. The interaction of the two provides much of Meroë's interest and significance. Nubian kings who had conquered Egypt briefly were driven back out by the Assyrian invasion of 671 BC and founded a new kingdom in their homelands. Its capital was established at Meroë soon after 600 BC. Egyptian influences dominated for about 300 years, but gradually southern connections grew. Egyptian hieroglyphs gave way to a Meroïtic script in the 2nd century which has yet to be deciphered. It may represent a Sudanic language or have Kanuri elements (spoken today near Lake Chad). Meroë's influence on black Africa is still unclear. Old ideas of the diffusion of Sudanic institutions of kingship have been discarded. How and when ironworking spread is disputed. Meroë was in decline by the 1st century AD when Nero's spies reported it not worth conquering. In Ethiopia a rival power grew: Aksum. Meroë was finally abandoned in the face of Aksumite and other invasions in the 7th century AD.

Below: the "Lion Temple" of Naqa is thoroughly Egyptian in style. The entrance pylons show the king and queen smiting their enemies. They comply strictly with Egyptian artistic conventions but the queen is distinctly plump and thus conforms to black African ideals of beauty.

The lion god, Apedemek, to whom the Naqa temple was dedicated, has no place in Egyptian iconography. He is distinctively Meroïtic and the kingdom's most important deity. On the side of the entrance pylon at Naqa (*left*), Apedemek is depicted with a snake's body, rising from a flower. On the rear wall (*above*), as a three-headed and four-armed creature, he receives the adoration of the royal family. Their elaborate jewelry and clothes are perhaps more African than Egyptian.

Below: the elephant played as prominent a role as the lion in Meroïtic iconography and ritual. Here a frieze of elephants appears on the sandstone walls of a temple at Musawwarat es Sufra, 10 miles northeast of Naqa. Ramps and enclosures around temples at Musawwarat look as if they could have been used in training the beasts. Certainly, the elephants of Butana provided Meroë's main export – ivory.

Above: Naqa lies upstream of Meroë, and a day's march east of the Nile. It was probably a staging post on routes to the Red Sea. The two best-preserved temples were built by King Natakamani, the last great builder of the Kushite dynasty, at the start of the Christian era. The Lion Temple is thoroughly Egyptian, the temple in the foreground Classical and Hellenistic. Only the winged disk and frieze of cobras above the central window clearly show Egyptian influences.

Opposite: excavations at Meroë.

Below: Meroë from the air. The royal city lies on the Nile and the river provided irrigation and alluvium. Meroë's main trade did not pass down the Nile but eastwards to the Red Sea, the Arabian kingdoms, and India, connecting with the wide-ranging Hellenistic network.

Below: a heap of slag, waste product of an extensive ironworking industry. It is too early to determine if Meroë was the source of smelting knowledge for Bantu-speaking Africa. *Right:* a recently excavated furnace.

By the 5th century BC, migrants from southern Arabia, including Saba, had established a literate, urban civilization among the farmers of the Ethiopian highlands. From the intermingling of these two peoples and cultures grew the kingdom of Aksum. It entered history as "the most important ivory market in northeast Africa" in the *Periplus*. Supplies came from as far away as "beyond the Nile" and Butana. Aksum, like Meroë, formed part of the Hellenistic trade network through its port of Adulis on the Red Sea. In the 4th century King Ezana, like the Emperor Constantine, became a Christian. Like Constantine too, he was a military expeditionary leader: Meroë was pillaged by Ezana. In the 6th century AD Aksum fell into decline. Its Arabian colonies fell to Persian armies and in the 7th century Islamic Arabia stifled the Red Sea traffic.

The most dramatic surviving monuments in Aksum are a group of locally quarried granite stelae. As many as 119 survive, the largest still standing 71 feet high (*above*). These were always believed to mark royal graves, but it was excavations by the British Institute in Eastern Africa in 1973 and 1974 that revealed a remarkable series of tombs beneath the stelae. Behind the tallest stelae, shown here, lies a network of rough-hewn shafts, passages and chambers: catacombs 25 feet below the ground. They were entered for the first time in centuries in 1974. Bones and grave goods were visible in the thin layers of mud on the floor but they were resealed before excavation.

Right: the largest stela in the main Aksum field, over 100 feet long and the largest single stone ever quarried or erected in the ancient world, has fallen. The stelae are architectural fantasies, many-storied mansions of the spirit reaching skywards. But the carving represents Aksumite building techniques in realistic detail. Rubble masonry walls were reinforced with a timber framework. Longitudinal beams, slightly inset, broke the wall surfaces. They were joined by cross-timbers, slotted over the longitudinal members and projecting from the walls as round-ended "monkey heads."

Left: the stelae ended in crescentic caps that held bronze plaques. Only the rivet holes remain. Probably they bore representations of the crescent and disk of Ilmuquh, the Sabaean moon god. The rivet holes and carved details of the timberwork of the uppermost windows are visible in this fallen top.

Below: excavation in 1973 of granite steps leading down to a tomb in the main stela field. A symbolic house, complete with a door carved in realistic detail on a great slab of granite, was erected over the tomb – hence it is called the Tomb of the False Door.

Right: the entrance to the antechamber of the so-called Tomb of the Brick Arches. Similar doorways, 18 feet high, led to two burial chambers. The start of exacavation – soon discontinued and not so far resumed – revealed the first of a mass of grave goods – fragments of gold, silver and bronze, goblets and flasks of glass, iron weapons and a mass of potsherds – disturbed and pillaged by grave robbers. This shape of arch – later a characteristic of Islamic architecture – is first found in Christian Syria in the 4th century AD – presumably the source of the motif in Aksum soon afterwards.

Outside Aksum lies another field of stelae, the Gudit field – named for Judith, the formidable native pagan queen who destroyed Aksum and Semitic influence in ˙ ˌe 10th century AD. Despite the name, there is no evidence to connect her with the stelae.

Left: one tomb was excavated in the Gudit field outside Aksum, an earthen chamber at the base of a 12-foot shaft. Here a number of grave goods were recovered, including 80 pottery vessels of a red ware. Glass goblets and flasks, probably made in Egypt, have been attributed to the 3rd or early 4th century AD.

3. Villages and Farmers

The kingdoms of Africa are rooted in village life. Kings, courtiers and administrators fulfill many of the functions of village elders. They carry out their duties in the same ways. State institutions develop from those that regulate village life. A self-sufficient village economy continues to feed and support the bulk of any kingdom's subjects. Towns and capitals are structurally and functionally not very different from large villages. Continuity in population, culture and history is immediately apparent.

Village life, based on cultivated crops which ensure a regular supply of food, is often contrasted with the arduous life of hunting bands. They depend on wild plants and animals in their constant and uncertain quest for food. On the other hand, life for the villager is leisured, with time for arts and crafts. It provides opportunities to accumulate possessions while existence for the hunter is miserable, impoverished and brutish. To those who believe in these two images, the differences in life-style are so wide-ranging and clear-cut that the spread of farming must be readily recognizable in the archaeological record. This dichotomy is a false one. No single technology offered the best means of progress. Different habitats

Previous page: finger millet – *Eleusine* – collected for threshing and winnowing. There is now evidence for *Eleusine* near Aksum in the third millennium BC – making it the oldest African domesticate.

In the period of increased rainfall between 7000 and 2000 BC, the Saharan mountain ranges, like Tassili N'Ajjer, contained thriving settlements of fishermen, hunters and, later, herdsmen.

produced different stimuli. These generated different responses. There was no sudden transformation from hunting to farming. The search for the origins of agriculture in a single place and time is doomed. It is much more fruitful to try to understand the processes of change, by which man in different regions and in different ways responded to new social, technological and environmental pressures and opportunities.

The last hunters and gatherers. The sort of environment that offered the greatest stimulus for development was one in which many different resources occurred within a short distance of a settlement. In this way the Nile valley was rich in opportunity. The river contained fish. Crocodiles and hippopotamuses on the banks could be killed for meat. Riverine swamps and marshes yielded many edible water plants and tubers. They also sheltered wild fowl. The dense riverside bush was the home of large antelope and predators. Cereals grew wild on the fertile flood plain. The open desert and steppe of the valley edges was the home of small game, like gazelle. The richness and variety of these resources meant that, throughout the year, different species of animal could be hunted and plants collected without any need to move camp.

In Egypt many communities of hunters and fishers, who lived between 15,000 and 9000 BC, have been investigated. A direct result of sedentary life and the intensive exploitation of a geographically restricted and very rich environment was an increase in population. The resulting pressures produced an increasing sense of group identity and unity and a sense of territory. Extensive cemeteries of culturally distinct groups, many of whom had been killed in war, are archaeological evidence that illustrates the density, permanency and rivalry of the new "tribes." The early settlements of the Nile valley clearly demonstrate that village life in Africa was not the prerogative of farmers.

Foragers are inevitably extremely conscious and aware of the potential of their natural environment. They seek out and test every available plant to find a use for it. Seeds of wild grasses were an obvious potential food source. Today, even in surroundings as apparently hostile as the mountains of the Sahara desert, the food value of such plants is still enormous. One study of Tuareg communities in the Ahaggar mountains of Algeria shows that, ot the 446 varieties of wild plant that grow in the mountains, 80 produce edible food. Twelve of these are regularly collected. Four are very important food sources. In a good season here a household can, in a very short time, collect enough wild grain for a year's food supply. When food is short, or in any year when crops fail, the wild grasses are a farmer's "famine foods." At other times they at least make a change and are often used as a relish with cereal staples.

In the Ahaggar the ground around abandoned Tuareg camps is often covered in rich stands of self-seeded cereals, which can be cropped two or three times a year. This source of food and its connection with human occupation

In the Ethiopian highlands, a native grass, teff, was domesticated before wheat and barley were introduced. In the first millennium BC it spread to Arabia but it could not compete with more productive cereals.

would not have been overlooked by peoples who were acute observers and as sensitive to nature as hunting communities. Wild grasses were therefore a widespread, rich and easy source of food, long before domestication led to their systematic cultivation and improvement.

The open savanna and steppe country of the Sudan and Sahel regions, which cut right across Africa south of the Sahara desert, was the original home of the main indigenous grain crops of Africa. Several different species of millets and sorghum, each adapted to particular rainfall and soil conditions, are the staple crops of Africa. All are summer crops, with a short growing season. This sets them apart from cereals such as wheat and barley, the crops that were domesticated in southwest Asia, to initiate the "Neolithic revolution" of the Levant and Europe. These need rain in winter. The Mediterranean shores of North Africa, the valley of the Lower Nile and the highlands of Ethiopia are the only places in Africa where they can grow.

This raises some of the key problems in a discussion of farming. Is one concerned with diffusion from an external source, whether of people, things or ideas? Is the rise of agriculture in Africa due to the migration of successful and therefore prolific farmers and their crops from outside Africa, overcoming or assimilating weakened and improvident hunters? Does it represent the spread of ideas or of technology? Were concepts of selecting, planting, tending and controlling plants for food developed in one area for a particular group of plants and environments, and then adapted by different people to new situations? Or were the things themselves – domesticated seeds, plants and animals – carried to new areas?

Farming systems. Before exploring this further, one must recognize more of the implications of growing crops in the savanna. Cereals need fields open to the sun and rain. This means that land must be cleared of trees and bush. Growing crops must be kept clear of weeds (though groundnuts and cucurbits can, with profit, be grown between cereal plants, to provide ground cover and prevent evaporation and erosion). Cereal farmers tend to rely largely on a single crop. Fields tend to be large and can only be used for limited periods. Grain crops make high demands on the soil. Fertility is therefore rapidly exhausted. New fields must be cleared and planted every few years, to give old lands time to rejuvenate themselves. The archaeological evidence for cereal growing is usually readily recognizable. The hoes for tending fields, the sickles for harvesting, the stone querns and rubbing stones for preparing the grain, the pottery cooking vessels and the remains of storage bins and pits are frequently preserved. Impressions of seed grains in ceramics or plasterwork provide direct evidence of specific cereals. The snag is to know if such grains are from wild or domesticated varieties. This crucial distinction has frequently been blurred, particularly when the dichotomy between hunting and farming seemed absolute. Precise identifications are essential.

In the tropical forests of Africa farming methods are very different. Here grain crops were an insignificant source of food. Clearings in the forest were used to grow a considerable range of plants in a confined area. For instance, tubers like yams and cocoyams, trees like plantains and oil palms, and kola nuts are normally grown together. Each has a different root system, growth pattern and ripening time. Each fills a specific ecological niche and exploits a different range of the light, warmth, moisture and nutrients available. This system assures satisfactory yields of at least a few crops, whatever the circumstances. Not every crop will fail in any one year. The crops also complement each other in the nutrients they provide in the diet – carbohydrates, proteins and vitamins. Plots tend to be around houses and benefit from the fertilization of manure and rubbish. They frequently remain permanently under cultivation.

Because this system reproduces natural forest conditions, it is difficult to discern evidence of it archaeologically. The crops themselves need little attention. Storage containers are not essential, as they are elsewhere. The equipment used to cultivate, harvest and prepare the crops is minimal and does not survive long. Wooden digging sticks, mortars and pounders soon decay. The crops

Below and right: the hoe is the traditional implement of African farmers. It can be used by every member of a family but it does not reinvigorate the soil like a plow. It is ineffective against grass roots and inclines farmers towards lighter and less fertile soils. After Livingstone.

Above: in the tropical forests, a variety of crops, particularly root crops, can be grown in small, permanently cultivated clearings.

themselves are not propagated by seed and many produce little or no pollen. Their remains are never carbonized or preserved.

The whole process of tropical vegeculture is a manipulation of the existing environment rather than the creation of a new one. It is easy to envisage that present systems of tropical vegeculture are the result of millennia of gradual adaptation. The first foragers in the forests probably gathered wild tubers and discarded parts of them around their camps. This would increase propagation: they would soon have recognized that this resulted in the gradual enrichment of the food plants in a particular area and that this process could be used to advantage, encouraged and eventually be deliberately controlled. Forest cultivation is thus a process that arose gradually and naturally. Initially it can scarcely be distinguished or separated from casual collecting or more intensive natural exploitation. The prehistory of tropical farming will never be easy to discern. Systematic research in this field has scarcely begun.

The places where savanna and forest meet offer particular challenges and rewards for cultivators. Many important crops are natives of the forest fringes. Yams are tubers designed to store moisture. Therefore, they are inherently plants adapted to regions like the forest edges, with high but markedly seasonal rainfall. Oil palms need sun and cannot exist under closed canopy forest. Here also the agricultural systems based on cereals and root plants meet and coexist. They provide a corresponding enrichment of agricultural opportunity.

With slash-and-burn agriculture, branches are lopped from the trees, piled together and burned. The ash fertilizes the land. The tree stumps can be left in the ground.

The fertile Sahara. In looking at the origins of agriculture, one is looking for evidence of permanent settlement in areas of diversity and challenge. The mountains of the central Sahara should hold some of the answers. In the desiccated wastes of this desert several great mountain massifs rise. From east to west, the mountain ranges of the Air and Adrar, Ahaggar, Tassili, Tibesti and Ennedi form an almost continuous crescent of land up to 9,000 feet above sea level. They stretch into the desert from the savanna and provide a link between the two environments. On the west the mountains are accessible to the bend of the Niger river. On the east they reach towards the valley of the Upper Nile.

From about 7000 to 2000 BC the climate in this part of the Sahara was significantly cooler and wetter than it is today. The plains were a dry, open steppe, covered with grass and populated with gazelle and antelope. What are now dry wadis were rivers, fringed with dense bush or forest. Sediments and raised beaches show that swamps and lakes lay at the foot of many hills. They held Nile perch, crocodiles and hippopotamuses. Pollen samples indicate that the foothills were covered in a Mediterranean flora of pine, cypress and juniper. The mixed oak woods of the upper slopes supported indigenous wild cattle and Barbary sheep. Heathlands covered the highest plateau. This rich ecological situation was very like the Nile valley. There were rapid changes of habitat, supporting different game and edible plants. They were accessible from the same camps. The zones were also restricted, demanding social cohesion and stimulating new methods of exploitation. When climatic fluctuations occurred, the rapid changes in altitude, the great area covered and the link with the southern vegetational zones insured that the flora and fauna could move to more suitable areas. They were not faced with extinction.

In many parts of the central Sahara camp sites have been excavated. Most often they were on the lower slopes of hills, sheltered by boulders or overhangs from the sun and wind. Often they overlooked the lakes and open country

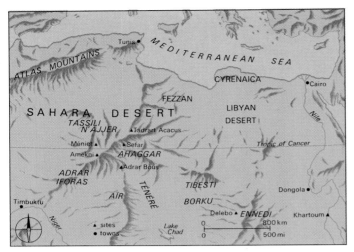

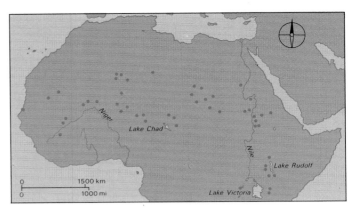

Above: the distribution of bone harpoons and "dotted wavy line" pottery. After Sutton.
Left: early settlements in the Sahara.

of the plains. Few have revealed structures, dwellings or even spreads of tools forming single, undisturbed horizons. All of them contain potsherds. Pottery, a heavy and fragile form of container, is generally a good indicator of settled life, even if it does not necessarily correlate absolutely with farming. The decoration of almost all the Saharan pottery was extremely distinctive. Rows of stab marks and lines cover much of the surface. They were made with the spines of a catfish – a large, edible fish whose spines can cause unpleasant sores and are therefore broken off by fishermen as soon as they are caught. This pottery is known to archaeologists as "dotted wavy line" ware. With the ceramics were microliths and bifacially flaked stone arrowheads. Beads were chipped from ostrich shell. Grindstones show that grass seeds were collected and eaten. The most distinctive weapons were harpoons, cut from bone, with one or two rows of barbs.

"Dotted wavy line" pottery and harpoons have been found over very wide areas. Two important Saharan sites are Amekni, near Tamanrasset, in southern Algeria, towards the southwest end of the Saharan mountain chain, and Meniet, about 150 miles further into the desert. Both contained pollens and grains of grasses that the excavators felt, from their size, could indicate domestication. But there were only one or two specimens and the criterion of grain size is not reliable. "Dotted wavy line" pottery has also been found in many camps beside the Nile near Khartoum and near Lake Turkana (formerly Lake Rudolf) in the desert plains of northern Kenya. A sherd of pottery, found with an obsidian stone industry at Gamble's Cave in the Rift Valley of Kenya, is also considered to bear the same distinctive form of decoration.

Villages of fishermen. The uniformity of the pottery decoration and the distinctive harpoons have led John Sutton to propose that a single "civilization" once covered much of the Sudan, exploiting the lakes and rivers. The characteristic artifacts reflect specialized methods of fishing – by harpooning – and of cooking the produce – by using ceramic stew pots. Sutton suggests that this technology was so successful that large villages could be established and inhabited for long periods of time. Other methods of food production presented no advantages. There were therefore no incentives to develop farming or herding economies. To some, these societies look stagnant. For the African fisherman, the aquatic resources were more than enough to live on. Change had no attractions.

This model is probably too simple. The characteristic forms of artifacts mask considerable regional cultural diversity. When the ceramics are examined closely, they show clear differences in fabric and manufacturing technique. Similar changes are visible in the stone tools. Other significant distinctions between areas will doubtless become obvious when complete artifact assemblages are compared in detail. At present, these are obscured by the overwhelming weight that is being given to the presence or absence of one or two stylistic traits. What the assemblages of stone tools already show is a clear unbroken sequence and continuity between local Stone Age hunting and gathering communities and the fishermen and potters that succeeded them. There was no total and overall cultural unity. Hunters of many different "cultures" and areas adopted the new pottery and fishing equipment at much the same time.

The appearance of pottery in many different areas in the late seventh millennium represents the rapid spread of a new idea, a new technology. For many centuries after the communities in the central Sahara and on the Upper Nile had developed pottery, people on the Lower Nile, in the Nile delta and along the North African coast were without it. Pottery only appears in Cyrenaica in the mid-fifth millennium and in lower Egypt in the fourth millennium. The desert between the Upper Nile and the Saharan ceramic sites – areas that lie astride the sole link between the central Sahara and the early pottery users of southwest Asia – only adopted pottery in the mid-third millennium. This distribution pattern shows therefore that settled villages in Africa must have invented and developed their own pottery industry without external influence.

The start of cattle herding. At the start of the fourth millennium, over two thousand years after village life was established in the Saharan mountains, there was a shift towards a more pastoral economy. Wild cattle already roamed the mountain woodlands. The indigenous beast, *Bos africanus* or *ibericus*, was short-horned and humpless. It is very probable that it was first domesticated by Saharan communities. Certainly no domesticated animals were imported from Asia or the Mediterranean lands. The earliest domesticated cattle in Egypt had long horns. Short horns only appeared there about the mid-third millennium.

Deposits in Cyrenaican caves show that domesticated sheep and goats were herded there early in the fifth millennium. Sites on the Upper Nile – including Shaheinab, one of the first to be excavated – contain domesticated sheep in contexts that are perhaps as early as those of Cyrenaica. Indeed, sheep herding distinguishes these "Khartoum Neolithic" sites from their immediate predecessors, the "Early Khartoum" or "Khartoum Mesolithic" fishing camps. Another "Khartoum Neolithic" site on the Nile, Kadero, has recently produced a great many cattle bones, far outnumbering those of sheep or goats. It is dated to the late fourth millennium and the cattle appear to have been domesticated. Kadero provides evidence that cattle keeping on the Upper Nile may have started as early as it did in the Sahara.

The people of the southern Sahara could well have been stimulated in their experiments in the domestication of their indigenous cattle by the example of small-stock herding reaching them from Cyrenaica. There may have been strong climatic reasons why such innovation was urgent. Gradual desiccation of the Sahara may have decreased the game herds. As lakes and swamps diminished, hunting and fishing may have become only marginally worthwhile – though both continued in some form for centuries. The social and economic role of cattle, as a means of accumulating wealth and reinforcing group alliances, may have made cattle breeding particularly socially significant.

There are still many unsolved problems in considerations of pastoralism in the Sahara. The Saharan sites are unusual in that there is so far no evidence that there was any close relationship between man and cattle prior to domestication; for instance, no specialized hunting methods were evolved. Wild cattle do not seem to have been a major or exclusive food source. Yet evidence of such a symbiosis is the logical and usual precursor to experiments in domestication. Pastoralism is usually a specialized offshoot of more general forms of husbandry. It is adopted by established farmers in order to meet special ecological circumstances. Elsewhere, pastoralists always remain dependent on agriculture for at least some of their needs. Yet, in the Sahara, pastoralism seems to have been the only form of food production for centuries.

There is some evidence, from human remains and the people depicted in rock paintings, that the Saharan pastoralists were not Negroid, unlike the first pottery users. The change to pastoralism may therefore reflect a change in population. Certainly a change in pattern of settlement is apparent. Camps were now established far into the plains. Adrar Bous, in the Tenere desert, east of the Air massif, is one. The villages here each covered a considerable area. Their populations may have been large, but the dwellings were fragile: little more than windbreaks of grass set in a ring of stones. They look as if they were the seasonal camps of nomads.

Tadrart Acacus, a pastoral camp north of the Tassili mountains, has produced dates of the mid-sixth and very early fifth millennia. Domesticated cattle may not have been present at this time: the evidence and association are uncertain. An early fourth-millennium date from this site has clearer associations with a pastoral group. The skeleton of a short-horn cow excavated from a camp at Adrar Bous

Evidence of early pastoral settlement at Adrar Bous in the Tenere desert included (*below left*) three circular concentrations of stone, possibly the bases for storage bins, and (*below*) the nearly complete skeleton of a short-horn domestic cow (dated to 3810 ± 500 BC) excavated in a midden at Agorass in-Tast.

is dated to 3810 BC. In the Tassili mountains rock shelters and overhangs were enclosed behind stone walls to form pens for cattle and small stock. Many of these enclosures have been dated to the fourth millennium.

The painted friezes on the walls of the Tassili shelters have given a vivid insight into the lives of the first herders. Large mixed herds of cows and oxen, many with dappled hides, were drawn with minute attention to detail. The great, curved, lyre-shaped sweep of the long-horn and the contrasting, short, forward-curving horns of the short-horn occur in the same herds. Most beasts were probably kept for meat and not milk, for the cows are shown without udders. The herds move across the walls, tended by people in a variety of costumes. Many of them resemble the Fulani pastoralists of the Sudan today.

After 2000 BC rain had become so rare and uncertain in the Saharan highlands that husbandry was barely possible. Herdsmen moved into the plains and followed the richer vegetation that fringed the drying rivers and wadis towards the southern savanna. At Karkarichinkat, in the desert north of the Niger river, at its northernmost point before it bends south and flows towards the tropical forests, excavations in 1968 illustrated the last stages of this process. Low spreads of settlement debris, deposited throughout the early second millennium, showed that more cattle were being eaten in the Niger villages than all other animals combined. The rest of the meat came equally from small stock and game. Though the rainfall of these villages was about 8–12 inches per annum, twice what it is today, and though the shallow alluvial valley contains a fertile soil, there was no sign of cultivation.

A painted rock shelter in one of the sandstone gorges of the Sefar massif in the Tassili N'Ajjer mountains.

The first farmers. It is from one of the marginal areas of the Sudan, in a period that follows immediately after Karkarichinkat, that the first clear, direct and incontrovertible evidence of crop growing in Africa has been obtained. In 1960 Patrick Munson investigated a series of sites at Dhar Tichitt in Mauritania. Here some sites were established on the crest of a line of cliffs and others beside the dried lakes and swamps at the foot of the cliffs. Direct evidence of cultivation comes from casts of domesticated millet incorporated in pottery vessels. A succession of sites, divided into eight phases, illustrates the social and economic changes that the new economy entailed.

As the lakes dried, the first two phases, starting about 1750 BC, saw the disappearance of hunters who had used microlithic arrowheads. In the next two phases, from 1500 to 1100 BC, the rainfall improved and fishing started up again. Encampments now contained pottery. Small stock were herded. Wild grasses – including a form of millet – and berries – the "famine foods" of today – were harvested and stored in pits. In the fifth phase large villages of stone houses were built. Sedentary life had been adopted. Cereal cultivation may have lain at the root of this crucial social transformation, though the direct evidence is slight. In the succeeding phase, dated to about 1100 BC, the issue is no longer in doubt: 72 of the 121 grain impressions on pottery of this phase were of *Pennisetum* millet. Half of these clearly belonged to a domesticated variety. Villages were now fortified and sited along the cliff tops. In the succeeding phases, from 750 to 400 BC, the villages split up and people scattered. Concentration on millet cultivation, even at the expense of livestock, did not bring the prosperity needed for the villagers to defend themselves against attack, or the flexibility to respond to a steadily deteriorating climate.

Dhar Tichitt itself is perhaps a late and peripheral site in the history of early Saharan or Sudanic agriculture. It does not necessarily reflect the first steps taken in cereal cultivation. What it does show is the wide-ranging effect that the introduction of agriculture had on Saharan communities. Equally important, it also illustrates the questions that must be asked, the scale of fieldwork that must be done and the sort of evidence that must be recovered if archaeologists are to investigate the social implications and processes involved in the development of agriculture. Munson's work at Dhar Tichitt is the sort of research that is desperately needed in prehistoric studies in Africa.

As the Sahara gradually became desert, people drifted away and created new demographic pressures on the desert fringes: in the savanna, on the edge of the tropical forests of West Africa and near the Nile. There were indirect repercussions even further away, in Ethiopia and East Africa.

Opposite: domesticated long-horned cattle – including milk cows – from the Tamrit shelter in the Tassili.

Right: an undated painting of cattle in Genda Biftu, a shelter on the northeast edge of the Ethiopian plateau.

Below: herds of cattle and a pastoral encampment from a Tassili rock shelter.

Penetration of the forest stimulated new developments. Its agricultural potential was quite different. Commonsense interpretations of the lengthy, almost unintentional and inevitable development of the permanently farmed forest clearings, growing many different crops, have already been discussed. We have also seen how archaeological evidence for this is very difficult to trace and at present is almost entirely lacking. The sort of inferences that can be made from the botany of yams and oil palms suggest that their domestication is linked to a start in cultivation where savanna and forest meet. Heavy, flaked tools of stone – which archaeologists interpret as adzes or hoes – and ground stone ax heads are found in the forest. They have never been dated or associated with other artifacts or occupation deposits. Their context is not clear. They certainly cannot, by themselves, be considered as evidence of farming. Speculation on these lines is based on misinterpretations of the old European theories that equate "Neolithic" polished stone tools with the first farming.

A group of sites in Ghana tells us something about the first farmers of the forest. These sites occur in several

An extensive, low mound of debris that marks a pastoral settlement at Karkarichinkat. The once fertile alluvium has been degraded to desert.

widely separated areas where forest and savanna meet. In the north they are near the forests that fringe the Volta river, where it flows into the savanna. Within the forest zone, there are sites on the less densely wooded sandstone uplands. Near the coast, where the grassland of the Accra plain extends down to the sea, there are further sites. The type-site is Kintampo, although Ntereso was the first excavated site. Both are dated to between about 1600 and 1200 BC. Villages were made up of substantial houses, built of wattle and daub or blocks of lateritic clay. These were the earliest permanent dwellings in tropical Africa. Small short-horn cattle and sheep or goats (also small specimens, reminiscent of the animals of the "Khartoum Neolithic") were kept. Bone harpoons, hollow-based arrowheads and fish hooks have suggested a cultural connection with the Nile to some prehistorians. However, Kintampo pottery is quite unlike the "dotted wavy line" ware of the Nile. Though excavators have tried several methods to recover seeds, Kintampo villages have so far given no direct evidence of domesticated cereal crops. Nevertheless their economy can scarcely have been exclusively pastoral, in the sort of environment they chose to inhabit. The consistent choice of the forest fringes for their villages is an important indicator that the Kintampo farmers cultivated both cereals and yams.

It is easy to visualize the progress of farming from the Sahara, through the desert fringes and river valleys of the northern Sudan, into the tropical forests of West Africa, as a single continuous process. In East Africa complex interrelationships between different environments and vegetation zones demanded more individual responses.

East African cattle herders. At the very start of the first millennium BC pastoral groups settled in the highlands of western Kenya and the adjoining regions of Tanzania. The open grassy plains of these areas were the home of great herds of antelope. Today their remnants attract many foreign tourists to famous game reserves like those on the Serengeti plain or in the Ngorongoro crater. This is a tectonically unstable area of earthquakes and volcanoes. Ngorongoro is a vast extinct crater. The mountains that delimit the highlands – Elgon, Kenya and Kilimanjaro – are all volcanic in origin. The Rift Valley – the great fault in the earth's crust that bisects the highlands – has many small lakes on its floor. In the remote past these were often dammed by lava flows or drained by earthquakes and faulting. The valley floor is noticeably hotter and drier than elsewhere in the highlands.

The highlands contain areas of excellent arable land, but it is their grazing that is preeminent. Settlements of early pastoralists have only recently been discovered in the highlands. The only two villages excavated so far are Narosura, on the edge of the Rift Valley in northern Tanzania, and Prospect Farm, on the valley floor in Kenya. However, excavations at both sites have as yet told little. Both sites have been badly eroded and largely destroyed. The occasional postholes that have been revealed say little of settlement size or density. They do not even indicate the plan or structure of the houses. At Narosura small stock outnumbered cattle in the food

A sandstone shelter at Kintampo became a quarry and factory producing querns. Well over 1,000 blanks were recovered from debris sealing dark lenses of Kintampo material.

Above: the Rift Valley of Kenya, near Lake Naivasha. Steps caused by successive faulting are clearly visible in the scarp.

Right: early pastoral sites in East Africa.

Below: one of a group of 60 cairns at Kapkures in western Kenya; 40 feet across, it contained a hoard of obsidian flakes, pottery and the remains of a young ox that had been eaten. Scale in feet.

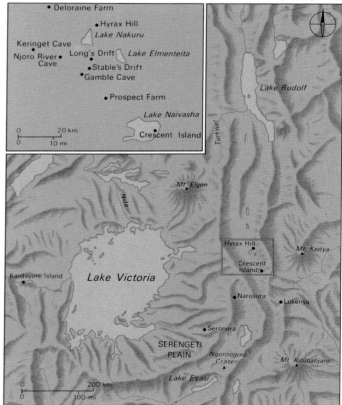

debris but the economy was certainly primarily based on cattle herding. Life may, as today, have been predominantly nomadic.

More abundant, if not more revealing, material comes from burials. In 1938 Louis Leakey exposed the remains of 80 cremated burials in the Njoro River Cave, another Rift Valley site. It seems likely that each body was buried with a small, shallow, thick-walled bowl, pecked or ground from volcanic tuff. Almost as many of these bowls were recovered as there were burials. These curious and distinctive vessels are also found on almost every other site, hence the popular name for the group, the "Stone Bowl Culture." The bowls absorb too much heat to have been used for cooking. Some have traces of carbon or ocher within them. Perhaps they were lamps, palettes for paint or containers for funerary gifts.

Cremation was not the only way by which the dead were disposed of. Many burials were covered with stone cairns. Some had stone-lined shafts at their center. Some were up to 50 feet across. They cluster in groups of up to a hundred cairns. Many contained stone bowls and long knife blades flaked from obsidian, placed beside the corpse as funerary goods. Although the first pastoralists had lost their distinct cultural identity by about 100 BC, burials under cairns took place in East Africa for many centuries – indeed millennia. At least one cairn burial is dated as late as 1600 AD.

There is a great deal of evidence to suggest that these East African pastoral communities originated in the Ethiopian highlands. Stone bowls and cairn burials are found in Ethiopia, although their distribution, contexts and dates are uncertain. (Stone bowls associated with pottery at North Horr near the border of Kenya and Ethiopia have very recently been dated to the second and third millennia BC.) Skeletal evidence from the cairns and cremations was, at one time, considered to demonstrate that the pastoralists were not Negroid but Caucasoid. This seemed an even more certain indication of northern origins, for the Ethiopian peoples are Caucasoid. However, a more recent reassessment of the bones places them within the range of Negroid physical variation. The Cushitic languages are centered in Ethiopia. The present inhabitants of the Kenyan and Tanzanian highlands speak Southern Nilotic. They displaced Southern Cushites from the area about two thousand years ago. The southern Nilotes show evidence of profound Cushitic cultural influence. The interaction between the two communities probably occurred in southwest Ethiopia before the Nilotic speakers moved south. Small communities in the Rift Valley today speak Southern Cushitic dialects. They are near extinction and survive only as isolated islands in a sea of Bantu speakers. Their distribution, age, economy and the traditions that they have concerning their origins and history – all suggest that they are the survivals of the first pastoralists.

On archaeological evidence the East African pastoralists never moved beyond the highlands. There may have been good environmental reasons for this. The woodlands of inland Tanzania afford poor grazing and are liable to infestation by tsetse fly. It is also very possible that alien habitation was a more significant factor limiting expansion.

The warm lowlands around Lake Victoria, with fertile volcanic soils, now support dense populations, based on plantain cultivation. These areas have yielded several collections of a distinctive type of pottery – Kantsyore ware. The makers of this pottery are still very shadowy figures but its contemporaneity with the pastoralists seems assured on stratigraphic and absolute dating evidence. In its style and motifs this ware is very like the "dotted wavy line" wares of the northern Sudan and Nile valley. It could well be a variant of this ceramic complex.

It may be that the makers of Kantsyore ware were again primarily fishermen. The distribution of their sites lends weight to this. But the lands on which they chose to settle were also very fertile and lake sediments, dated to 1000 BC, from Lake Victoria, contained pollens of grasses that are particularly associated with land regeneration after cultivation. Thus the makers of Kantsyore ware may have been farmers. In this case, East Africa three thousand years ago may have seen an interaction between cultivators and pastoralists. The varied topography and vegetation would have reinforced these specializations. Interaction between the two was also to be the key to so much of East Africa's more recent history.

Looking further afield for evidence of the earliest

cultivation in southern Africa, one must at present be content with tantalizing and isolated glimpses of unexplained "anomalies" in the archaeological record. In rock shelters in Rhodesia, scraps of a thin-walled pottery, quite unlike the better-known later wares, have been found in later Stone Age horizons. From its very rarity this "Bambata ware" cannot have been a regular product of these Stone Age hunters. The sherds were probably strays from other contexts. Perhaps they came from temporary encampments, whose surface indications, like those of their Stone Age contemporaries, are so slight that they are now unrecognizable. For amicable survival with the hunters, the economy of the pot makers must have been very different. This would suggest that the makers of Bambata ware were farmers.

In South Africa, some Late Stone Age people certainly made pottery. Mounds of shell along the shores of the southwest Cape Province of South Africa are the debris of nomads who lived mainly off fish and mollusks that they caught in river estuaries or shallow intertidal waters. They have been named "strandloopers," beach wanderers. They made pottery of a pattern so consistent that some archaeologists believe that it must represent the end of a long ceramic tradition. If so, one must look for its origins outside South Africa. There are no signs of its earlier development in the local cultural sequence.

Late Stone Age deposits in the South African coastal caves at Nelson Bay, Bonteberg and Die Kelders in the Cape Province, dated between 135 BC and 15 AD, contain

Opposite: a mixed stand of the staple African cereals. Sorghum, the taller plant, is the most important indigenous crop. Bullrush or pearl millet – *Pennisetum* – with the dark, dense head, was grown in Dhar Tichitt in the late second millennium. By 1000 BC it had spread to India.

Below: a bowl, covered by fallen *daga*, exposed on the floor of a hut in the Early Iron Age village of Dambwa in southern Zambia, dated to the 8th century AD. Scale in inches.

bones of domesticated sheep. They must also have been a foreign introduction to South Africa. It is difficult to see pottery and sheep as introductions by sea from Madagascar or Indonesia, though this has been suggested. A closer point of origin, within the continent, is more probable. It has yet to be demonstrated.

As will be seen later in this chapter, there are linguistic indications of a widespread early farming population throughout eastern Africa. They may well have preceded the Bantu-speaking farmers, who clearly represent a later phase of the prehistoric record. Perhaps the first farmers were the makers of Kantsyore ware in Kenya and Bambata ware in Rhodesia and introduced pottery and sheep to the Late Stone Age people of the southern tip of the continent.

The Early Iron Age. Evidence for the first experiments in farming in eastern and southern Africa is doubtful, fragmented and incoherent. Its very validity is debatable. In comparison, the changes that followed were swift, comprehensive and widespread. They represent the Early Iron Age. Everywhere it is readily recognizable. The new societies and economies that were introduced were completely different from their Late Stone Age predecessors. The changes affected every aspect of life. Indeed the break with the past was so abrupt and complete that one can only suppose that it reflects a change in population. This, however, was not necessarily rapid or total. In some areas Late Stone Age hunters coexisted for a long time with the later farmers and were only gradually assimilated by the more successful societies.

The Early Iron Age has been the subject of intensive research from 1960. Before that, most archaeologists in Africa had studied either the Stone Age or the great and controversial monuments. The Early Iron Age was perforce entirely undocumented and too remote for traditional histories to be precise or enlightening. Therefore archaeology seemed the only relevant discipline for its investigation. This gave it a particular scientific purity that appealed to many fieldworkers. The Early Iron Age also laid the cultural foundation of African traditional life as it is known today. Almost certainly it also equates with the rise of the Bantu-speaking peoples, who now populate all of Africa south of the equator. Its fundamental importance to the prehistory of African societies was very clear.

Despite the name, iron itself is a minor element in most Early Iron Age archaeological assemblages. Even taking account of the corrosive effect of acid soils and tropical rainfall, many early sites contain very little ironwork. Throughout this period iron was still a scarce material, difficult to produce. It was considered attractive and valuable enough to be used for beads, bracelets and other jewelry. It was used primarily for small cutting tools – razors, arrowheads and spearheads. Large objects – hoes, axes and adzes – consumed so much of the metal that they represented considerable investments. They were used for as long as possible, and worn to stubs. The remnants were then resmelted. Iron technology was never sufficiently developed for the manufacture of large items – be they swords or plowshares.

Usable iron ores could be dug from the soil almost anywhere in Africa, though the best ores were sufficiently rare to allow some areas to specialize in working and trading iron in much later periods. Iron smelting is an extremely complex process. The ores have to be crushed and, often, roasted. Charcoal must be burned. The furnaces have to be charged with precise amounts of these materials. Furnaces must be designed so that, at the end of the smelting process, the metal and the waste are separable. Firing temperatures are high and must be carefully controlled and sustained for hours or even days. Most important, the air supply to the furnace must be manipulated so precisely that the chemical action that reduces the oxidized ores to the pure metal can take place.

The spread of ironworking. Ironworking is so complex a process that the technology must have reached tropical Africa from other areas. There seem to be two possible sources. One is the kingdom of Meroë, on the Upper Nile. It owed much in its culture to Rome and pharaonic Egypt. It therefore appears alien and exotic in African terms. Its iron-smelting industry was both efficient and prolific from about the 4th century BC. Alternatively, a knowledge of iron smelting may have spread from the Phoenician cities of North Africa, carried by caravans across the Sahara desert or by Phoenician sailors on coasting voyages down the Atlantic seaboard. Or perhaps the knowledge traveled west across the Sudan. Certainly the technology had reached the forests south of the western Sudan by the 4th century BC. The Nok culture of central Nigeria was producing iron by this time. This traditional African society, with village-based communities dependent on farming for their subsistence, may have been the first center of ironworking technology for black Africa. It may have spread from the Nok people eastwards through the Sudan to East and southern Africa. Confirmatory evidence is entirely lacking for any of these speculations. Little in the investigations of Meroë, North Africa or Nok has so far touched on the technology, origins, furnace types or other aspects of ironworking technology. Until this happens, speculation is a fruitless exercise.

Iron smelting represented an extremely significant technological advance. It provided efficient tools and weapons for protection, hunting, land clearance and tillage in every sort of country – forest, wood or grassland. The Early Iron Age economy was based on mixed farming. Every community had sheep or goats. Cattle were not unknown, but they played little part in the economy of many areas, particularly in the east. Direct evidence for crops – grain impressions or the carbonized grains themselves – is seldom found. Nonetheless, their presence cannot be doubted. In the areas selected for settlement, villages could not exist without planting crops. Querns, mullers, cooking vessels, storage pits and stone foundations of bins for seed storage demonstrate that grain crops were harvested and eaten.

The most telling evidence for farming is the way regional patterns of settlement were distributed to take advantage of good farmland. This has been particularly brought out by archaeological research in Zambia. In the thick deciduous forests of the north, which cover comparatively infertile sand soils, sites are few and far between. Where they exist, their deposits are sparse. In dense woodland, sites only occur on the edges of fertile natural clearings, called *dambos*, where impermeable clays keep the soils damp and inhibit tree growth. Anthills, with their enriched earth, particularly attracted individual settlements. On the higher grasslands of the watershed, villages were comparatively close together. Many were occupied for so long that mounds of ash and rubbish mark their sites. In Rhodesia villages were sited at the foot of granite hills, where the light soils derived from the granite are easily hoed, even if they do not remain fertile for long.

All Early Iron Age villages had very much the same general character. Huts were made of rings of thin,

The distribution of Early Iron Age wares in eastern Africa, showing the possible sequence of their spread. After Phillipson.

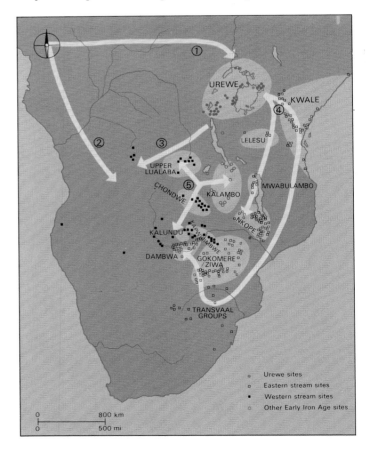

upright poles, set in the ground and plastered over with clay or *daga*. They were presumably thatched. Most were very simple structures. All were probably used as dwellings, several huts to a family. There were no specialized or public buildings. There is no sign of any differences in the layout or size of the buildings. There is no indication of differences in occupational specializations, wealth or status. The huts had none of the elaborate molded clay decorations and furnishings that are found in houses of later periods. Villages covered many acres. Many were established in the open country of the plains. They rarely, if ever, needed to seek the seclusion and protection of hilltops or caves. There seems to have been no reason to take defensive measures.

Archaeological evidence. Archaeologists recognize the Early Iron Age by its pottery. There is a clear unity of style everywhere, from Uganda to the Transvaal. Fabrics were thick and gritty and were fired to produce a uniform red color. The most characteristic vessels were squat, with short necks, curving outwards and decorated with grooves gouged from the damp clay in horizontal lines or curvilinear patterns. Detailed analysis of pottery assemblages have been used to define regional variants. At least 16 are now recognized, seven of them in Zambia. Several attempts have been made to group these variants in broader complexes, in order to discern patterns of change and spread. This is made particularly difficult by the extraordinary and universal lack of change through time in most Early Iron Age pottery. The potters were so conservative that, in many cases, assemblages a thousand years apart are indistinguishable. Only in one Rhodesian and one southern Zambian industry can temporal phases be distinguished by pottery style – three in each case.

Early Iron Age villages were almost entirely self-sufficient and there was little economic necessity to establish systems of exchange. Nonetheless, there was some trade in luxuries. A few copper trinkets turn up in almost every Early Iron Age excavation. Copper ores in eastern Africa are a great deal more limited in their distribution than iron ores. By 700 AD the rich and easily accessible copper ores of southern Zaire and northern Zambia were being mined. The metal was traded from them in ingots and as wire.

There is some sign that contacts with foreign traders existed in southeast Africa almost from the start of the Early Iron Age. Occasional seashells, particularly cowries from the Indian Ocean, and glass beads have been found on even the earliest Iron Age sites in Rhodesia. By the end of the first millennium AD a regular pattern of imports of glass beads is recognizable. To judge by the uniformity of the beads, they all came from a single source. This must have been outside Africa, probably in India. But the quantities that were imported were very small. The local independence of the economy of every village was scarcely affected. Specialization in production, distri-bution or trade lay in the future, with the later Iron Age.

At present, the most complete and convincing study of the origins and spread of the Early Iron Age has been made by David Phillipson. Taking 163 radiocarbon dates that have been obtained from excavations of Early Iron Age sites throughout eastern Africa, and using a statistical patterning of these, which minimizes those dates most likely to be anomalous and misleading, Phillipson has demonstrated that there is a clear chronological sequence of Early Iron Age industries. Using typological analyses of pottery styles, he has produced a pattern of stylistic relationships in the pottery covering the whole area. A correlation of these two sets of data gives a detailed picture of the spread of the Early Iron Age. The earliest sites, dating to about 300 BC, are from the northern and western shores of Lake Victoria. The wares that are closest in style to these are found down the eastern seaboard, starting near the Tanzanian border in about 150 AD, and passing through Malawi, the Transvaal and probably southern Mozambique in the succeeding two centuries. The Early Iron Age reached Rhodesia very slightly later. The Rhodesian wares look similar in style to those of the eastern stream. Westwards, in the far interior, a slower-moving, more diverse and heterogeneous "western stream" is dated to about 480 AD in Zambia. It met the furthest expansion of the eastern stream in the vicinity of the Victoria Falls, less than a century later.

Following this pattern, the origins of the Early Iron Age must be sought to the north and west of Uganda – probably in Tchad or the Central African Republic – areas that are archaeologically largely unexplored. The Sudanic grasslands of these countries are the natural home of many indigenous African grains. They form a belt of easy communication that stretches from the west to the Upper Nile and Ethiopia. The Sudan is also an area that received the remnants of the Saharan pastoralists when their homelands became dry and uninhabitable desert. It seems that a single overall pattern is beginning to emerge, which traces the start of village life in Africa back to remote antiquity in the Sahara in a single continuous sequence of related developments.

Linguistic evidence. The Early Iron Age can be brought more to life when one realizes it probably equates with the first Bantu-speaking peoples in eastern Africa. Without documents and inscriptions, a correlation between a prehistoric culture and a language group can never be demonstrated directly. It can never be more than, at most, a very strong supposition. Nonetheless, in this instance, there are many suggestive indications. Social forms, economies, architecture seem to have been identical. On internal evidence, linguists would give the Bantu languages a similar age to those of the Early Iron Age. The distribution of both is identical. Since the Early Iron Age, there has been no change in population or culture on the scale represented by the Early Iron Age. There is no later event in the archaeological record that can be equated with a spread of Bantu-speaking peoples. Both the prehistoric cultures and Bantu languages exhibit a similar diversity within unity. In both, there is a wide range of regional variants, between which a complex series of inter-relationships can be traced.

In tackling questions about the relationships between archaeological and linguistic groups, prehistorians have been forced to use very incomplete information. Archaeological data, in particular, are almost entirely derived from research programs that rarely consider linguistic implications. They are generally concerned with very different questions. This means that the data contain all sorts of unintended and hidden biases. To show how much caution is needed, one can instance the widely accepted model of Bantu expansion which accepted Malcolm Guthrie's linguistic hypothesis of a Bantu-speaking origin or early nucleus south of the equatorial forests, in southern Zaire. It took the first six or eight radiocarbon dates for the Early Iron Age and suggested that these showed a spread radiating from southern Zaire. Cynics could point out that origins of both the Early Iron Age and the Bantu-speaking people were thus con-veniently placed in an area that was archaeologically blank and unexplored. (Sadly, the key areas for Phillipson's hypothesis also lie in territories that are unknown archaeologically.) Not only has Guthrie's hypothesis proved untenable; the archaeological data with which it was correlated were woefully inadequate to be manipu-lated in this way.

From linguistic evidence, it is now undisputed that the Bantu languages originated somewhere close to the border of Nigeria and Cameroun, on the edge of the tropical forest at the extreme northwestern corner of their present distribution. The tropical rain forests of Zaire probably proved an impenetrable barrier to the southern expansion of early Bantu farmers. They would have skirted the forest to the north, moving east through the Sudan. This is in excellent accord with Phillipson's suggestions.

Linguistic studies by Christopher Ehret have an important bearing on the Early Iron Age-Bantu cor-relation. In a detailed study of loan words, Ehret has shown how the Bantu languages of eastern and southern Africa have borrowed successive sets of alien words. Ehret believes that the source of these was a Central Sudanic linguistic group, now almost entirely extinct, whose language is today only identifiable through the small groups of words that survive in living Bantu languages. Such linguistic borrowing must connote cultural inter-action. If a set of loan words is connected with a specific technology, this must indicate that the technology was acquired from the same source as the loan words. The words that the Bantu people borrowed from the Central Sudanic groups are all words related to cattle and cereal agriculture. If Ehret is right, it seems that there must have

been a widespread early population of farmers, growing millet and sorghum, herding cattle and sheep and milking cows, who gave knowledge of these practices to the Bantu-speaking groups. Ehret believes that these in-teractions took place within eastern Africa. Various stages in the process are marked by successive sets of loan words, shared by wider or narrower groups of Bantu speakers.

Bantu speakers are not the only people who borrowed words connected with food production from Central Sudanic speakers. Khoi is the language of a Bushmanoid people, the undisputed descendants of the Late Stone Age hunter-gatherers of southern Africa. It also contains Central Sudanic words for various farming practices.

If the two language groups did share a prolonged association, one can envisage that the Central Sudanic grain and cattle economy was best suited to the high open grassland; while Bantu-speaking farmers lived in a hotter, wetter environment, with an economy based pre-dominantly on vegeculture – the cultivation of yams or plantains. As Bantu speakers obtained cattle and cereals, they could adopt a mixed farming economy. This enabled them to spread over the whole of eastern Africa and extinguish the Central Sudanic speakers.

Attempts to make a detailed correlation between regional archaeological industries and Bantu languages and dialects must remain speculative until more ar-chaeological data are available. But prehistorians are already asking the sort of questions that will prepare the way for the next stage of research. Do the two Early Iron Age streams correlate with the two major divisions within the Bantu languages, Eastern and Western Bantu? Do the Central Sudanic languages, which Ehret believes were established in eastern Africa before Bantu, equate with the Early Iron Age and Bantu with the later Iron Age? Is the Early Iron Age to be equated with Eastern Bantu and the later Iron Age with Western Bantu? Did the Central Sudanic-Bantu interaction, discussed in such detail by Ehret, take place, as he supposes, throughout eastern Africa? Or did the interaction occur on the present frontier between the Bantu and Sudanic speakers, and spread from there south? Is the Sudan the place where the Early Iron Age obtained the agricultural expertise that powered its expansion?

These questions cannot yet be answered. Nevertheless, the contribution of studies of the Early Iron Age to African prehistory are of key significance. The Early Iron Age provided Africa with the fundamentals of a social organization, based on autonomous, self-sufficient vil-lages, classless and kin-based, that survived over vast areas of the continent until colonial times. Their economy was based on mixed subsistence farming. Their crafts were centered on simple pottery and metalworking. On this basis, in a few fortunate areas with mineral resources and communications with the outside world, much more complex social organizations were to develop: the kingdoms and states of the last millennium.

Traditional Architecture

The traditional buildings of Africa reflect the history of the continent. Some seem no more than shelters, responding to a harsh environment in the simplest way. But there is always more to it. Buildings enclose space. Spatial qualities reflect the philosophy of a society, its history, ideals and beliefs. Traditional structures are imbued with symbolism. New social forms develop a new aesthetic.

Patterns of settlement reflect man's relationship to the land. Clusters of thatched homesteads exemplify the peasant farmer – egalitarian and self-sufficient. They continue an Early Iron Age pattern. Villages grew into capitals. *Zimbabwe* or the tombs of Buganda kings

manifest the new power – and a continuity with ancient structures. Islam brought new values. Mosques represented more than worship: refuge, charity, learning, social intercourse – the urban virtues. The forest peoples of western Nigeria are among the most social in Africa. Courtyards intensify and promote the public intimacy they prize, while the labyrinthine complexities of their palaces reflect a divine ruler's multifarious responsibilities.

Below: a circle of homesteads, covered in mats and hides, of the Samburu, nomadic pastoralists in the desert scrub of northern Kenya.

Above: Ganvie, in Benin, is a village of Akan fishermen, originally refugees from 19th-century wars, who have developed a unique adaptation to the resources of Lake Nokwe. Houses have a mangrove pole framework and open sides to allow ventilation to alleviate humidity.

Left: a village of Karamojong pastoralists in northern Uganda, palisaded against predators and raiders, with their most valuable possession, cattle kraaled in the center of the settlement.

Opposite below: a small village of Nupe farmers on the edge of the Nigerian forest. Millet is the staple food and grain bins are an important architectural element. The continuous outer enclosure reflects a need for protection and privacy as well as a strong sculptural sense.

Above: the tomb of the last three Kabakas, kings of precolonial Buganda. It was protected and cared for until very recently by women of the royal court – "wives" of the Kabakas. The fabric is continually maintained and renewed. For Bugandans, it epitomized the majesty and continuity, the enduring presence, of their kings.

Below: in northern Tanzania, *tembe,* large, communal houses with flat roofs, covered in earth and supported on a grid of posts, are built – as expedients against raiding – by various groups who usually live in detached, round, thatched huts. These are near the shores of Lake Manyara in the eastern Rift Valley.

The mosques of the western Sudan reflect the urban commercial character of the Islamic trading states. In the dry climate, flat roofs and mud walls are possible but they need constant renewal. Designs may be ancient if the actual fabric is new. Thus the Friday Mosque at Jenne (*above*) goes back to the 14th century, when the city was at the height of its prosperity. Zaria mosque (*left*) reflects the Fulani conquests in the Sudan in the early 19th century. New architectural forms – domes, vaults and arches derived from the Roman remains of North Africa – consciously sought to express the new state system. But these forms were no longer expressed in stone but in flexible timbers bent into curved shapes, embedded in the earth and encased in clay.

Swahili civilization in eastern Africa finds architectural expression through different materials and in a very different climate from its contemporary in the far west – though both share the same values. Coral and its products induce a sense of coolness, unity and calm. Hospitality is promoted in reception rooms of imposing size and elaborate decoration. The Djombe Palace in Domoni in the Comoro Islands (*above*), probably an 18th-century building, is a reminder of what life on the mainland was once like. Small mosques, with no architectural pretensions, are to be found in every ward of a town. The Msangani Mosque in Moroni, capital of the Comoros (*below*), is an example.

Ethiopia has been Christian since the 4th century. Each church has a completely enclosed inner sanctuary, entered only by priests, with a richly frescoed exterior; an inner ambulatory; and an outer space or veranda for the mass of the congregation – mirroring, it is claimed, the threefold division of Solomon's Temple. Circular churches like the monastery church on the shores of Lake Tana at Zeghie (*above*) are comparatively recent (post–16th-century) innovations. *Tankwas*, papyrus boats of ancient design, lean against the outer ambulatory wall of St Gabriel on Kebran Island in Lake Tana (*left*). The church roof incorporates the same material. Windows in the outer veranda at Zeghie (*below*) are a pale external reflection of hidden internal riches.

The churches of Gondar broke with the imperial style of Aksum and evolved a rigid style of court painting inspired by Portuguese missionaries in the 16th century. The winged seraphim that cover the ceiling of the 17th-century church of Debra Berhan Selassie (*left*) reflect this while retaining their own strong and individual Ethiopian flavor.

A series of churches were cut into the living rock at Lalibela in the early 13th century. The church of Abba Libanos (*below*) has a carved facade that imitates many features of the architecture of Aksumite palaces. The surrounds of the lower windows in particular reflect the interlocking and projecting timbers that were a characteristic Aksumite structural device to reinforce ragstone walls.

Far left: a courtyard within the palace of a Yoruba ruler, the Ogoga of Ikere Ekiti, in western Nigeria. The posts are carved with figures of Yoruba kings and deities. The seated figure is the Ogoga, wearing a beaded crown. Each courtyard has an altar dedicated to a different deity and is the scene of regular ceremonies and sacrifices. A palace will have a great many such courts while in a lineage compound life is centered in a single large courtyard, the scene of every domestic task and all social relationships.

Left: shrines, particularly among the Yoruba, can be a tree, natural or carved rock or the flimsiest structure. They are by no means necessarily monumental. The shrine of Ogun Laadin – god of iron – in the palace of Ife includes a stone carving of a fish and a large block of forged iron, shaped like a tear drop.

4. Mines and Courts of the South

Between the Zambezi and the Limpopo rivers, just within the southern tropics, rises a core of granite. It is high land, from 3,000 to 5,000 feet above sea level, cool and fresh for most of the year. Millennia of erosion have reduced it to open plains. The northeastern part of it, with 30 inches of rain a year, is covered in light deciduous woodland. The lower, southwestern half of the country is drier and its rainfall uncertain. It bears a rich grass cover, ideal for cattle. The plateau is an island of fertile country, rich in minerals. It is surrounded by much less hospitable regions. To the north, the Zambezi river flows through a valley tens of miles across and up to 2,000 feet deep. The valley sides are cut by ravines and difficult to climb. Its floor is hot and waterless. It bears a shallow, infertile, sandy soil. Human settlement here has always been sparse and transient. The Limpopo river and its tributary, the Shashi, bound the plateau on the south and southwest. On the west the plateau gives way to the dry grasslands of the great pastoral communities of the present Tswana people. These in turn eventually give way to still drier lands – the deserts of the Kalahari and Namib. The northwest of the plateau supports teak forests, which grow on wind-distributed sands of the former Kalahari desert, country difficult to clear and one whose coarse soils rapidly lose their fertility. Its agricultural potential in no way matches that of the plateau. The warm, humid lowlands of the coastal plain, between the plateau and the Indian Ocean, were an ideal habitat for tsetse fly, carrier of trypano-somiasis. This prevented any cattle breeding.

The plateau and the coastal plains to the east of it are today the home of people who speak Shona, a cluster of some seven separate dialects, whose distinct identity suggests that they developed independently of other Bantu languages for about the last thousand years. Archaeology and oral tradition suggest a similar time scale for Shona settlement on the plateau. This then is the setting of the development of kingdoms and empires during the last 800 years of southeast African history.

The end of the Early Iron Age. Though Early Iron Age farming communities were entirely self-sufficient, towards the end of the first millennium AD almost all of them possessed glass beads and shells that had come from the Indian Ocean. Their trinkets of copper often came from equally far-distant sources. In exchange an export trade in gold was starting to develop. In the 10th century the Arab geographer al Masudi first recorded the metal reaching the Sofalan coast from the interior. This gold was probably panned from the gravel and alluvia of the many rivers that flowed through the plateau goldfields. Panning is a simple process, one that many villagers still practice today to eke out their farming income. Foreign colonists in the 19th century found that old, roughly cut, open mine workings

Previous page: granite hills are the basis of the underlying structure, spectacular scenery and sandy soils of the Zambezian plateau. Stones split from exposures like this were an ideal building material.

Above: these stopes, dug to follow narrow reefs or veins of gold-bearing quartz, are part of the most extensive system of "ancient workings" on the plateau.
Opposite: in panning, the traditional method of gold recovery, the crushed stone is washed so that the lighter material is swirled away, leaving the heavy metal behind in the pan.

riddled almost every goldfield on the plateau. To the inexperienced prospector they were a certain indication of the presence of gold. Most of them were destroyed in a feverish renewal of mining activity. Consequently it will never be possible to investigate their dates or history. However it is unlikely that any were of Early Iron Age date. Certainly no mining or milling tools survived on Early Iron Age sites, nor does the pattern of Early Iron Age settlement coincide with the goldfields.

Nonetheless, towards the end of the Early Iron Age, there are hints that the goldfields were being developed and that there was some competition to control them. Some settlements were now established on hilltops. One of these, on Maxton Farm, a few miles northeast of Salisbury, is entirely surrounded by a stone wall – though this was too low to have provided adequate fortification. This site, which has given its name to the last phase of the Early Iron Age on the northern side of the plateau, looks toward Tafuna Hill, a notable outcrop of gold-bearing deposits, where there were once many early mine workings. On the slopes of Tafuna stood the village of a different Early Iron Age group. Rock hollows made by milling gold ores abound around it.

The later Iron Age. In the early centuries of the present millennium, the Early Iron Age ended. Its broad cultural unity dissolved. Later Iron Age societies were more complex and diverse. They seemed to have developed in greater isolation from each other. Each society reflected its own distinctive responses to local opportunities in agriculture, industry or trade. The change from the earlier condition was rapid, universal and complete. It affected every aspect of life. Such a process must indicate the entry of a new people and a substantial change in population. The area where the later Iron Age of southeast Africa originated is unknown. There are, at present, very slight hints – stylistic comparisons between two or three meager and isolated pottery assemblages in western and northern Zambia – that it may have grown out of the Early Iron Age cultures of neighboring southern Zaire.

The later Iron Age was fully established in the dry southwestern grasslands of the plateau by the 11th century AD. A small hill, Leopard's Kopje, near the town of Bulawayo, first excavated in 1947, has given its name to the culture.

Cattle now became, for the first time, an important economic and social force. Cattle pens in many villages, miniature figurines of long-horned humpless cattle and ceremonial burials of cattle horns, all manifest the importance of the animal. They would have reinforced and ratified group identity and cohesion. They were

probably exchanged as bridewealth. They demonstrated prestige and were a means of creating patronage and obligation. They enabled wealth to be accumulated, manifested and exchanged. Anthropologists have often speculated that cattle herding can be associated with the start of centralized forms of government. Cattle need wide grazing lands. Often herds are cared for by children and receive little supervision. Inevitably disputes over grazing arise and there are pressures on grazing lands. From these come a need for arbitration and hence for an authority with the power to adjudicate and to enforce its decisions.

Sites of the earlier (Mambo) phase of the Leopard's Kopje industry, like their Early Iron Age predecessors, are to be found on easily tilled soils between granite hills. The later (Woolandale) phase is notable for its many villages in the heavy soils of the gold belts – an area difficult to till and never settled before. Several small villages have been found close together in one goldfield, many of them permanent enough to have produced mounds of ash and rubbish so large that they encroached on the villages themselves. By this time gold was certainly being mined. Woolandale sherds have been found in several early workings and a crucible bearing traces of melted gold was excavated from Woolandale deposits. The earliest dated gold workings are in the southwest of the plateau. Wood used in fires lit to crack the gold-bearing rocks has given three radiocarbon dates, two of the 12th or early 13th century and one of the 13th or 14th century. These mines did not yield any cultural material.

Glass beads found in early Leopard's Kopje sites are no different in form, manufacture or quantity from those of Early Iron Age sites. Woolandale sites normally yield very many more glass beads – small, regular spheres of translucent or nearly translucent glass in a variety of colors. They are quite different from earlier varieties of

Gold-bearing rock was crushed and ground in deep, circular "dolly holes" formed, largely by wear, on flat granite outcrops. The rubbing stones were of dolerite – a harder stone than granite.

bead. This must mean that bead manufacture had been improved, or that merchants were getting their trade beads from new sources abroad, or that new trading groups had established themselves on the coast.

In the south, away from the gold sources, in poor agricultural country, suitable only for extensive cattle grazing, striking changes in society took place. Mapungubwe is a great isolated sandstone outcrop surrounded by cliffs, close to the Limpopo river. Its flat top covers several acres. It can only be reached through two steep, narrow crevices in the cliff. The village that grew up in this situation is one of the richest sites of the Leopard's Kopje culture. Several people were buried here wearing necklaces of gold beads, with golden dishes and wooden sculptures sheathed in gold beside them. Dishes of Chinese celadon, made in the 14th century, reached the site, as well as glass beads in abundance. The deposits of Mapungubwe were almost entirely removed in excavations during the 1930s. The prejudices of the period and the lack of any knowledge of the context of Iron Age society impaired any rational interpretation of the site at this time.

A site very like Mapungubwe was found in 1967, about 50 miles upstream, on the bank of the Shashi river, a major tributary of the Limpopo. Here too a flat-topped, cliff-girt hill, Mapela, had been settled about the 12th century. The village contained sharply distinct types of dwelling. The edge of the settlement gave evidence of thin-walled huts of wattle and daub with floors that were little more than stamped earth. On the summit, on terraces supported by stone-faced walls, a succession of buildings was erected, with clay walls so thick that they needed no timber reinforcement. Their floors made lavish use of the same material. Decorative curbs surrounded the dwellings. There were probably molded clay hearths, seats and pot

Above: the richest grave on Mapungubwe contained a wooden bowl and staff covered in sheets of beaten gold. A carved rhinoceros, 6 inches long, was also encased in gold.

Opposite: the slopes below the cliff-girt summit of Mapela Hill were defended and made habitable by terraces faced in much rougher and less accomplished walling than that of any *zimbabwe*.

Left: the distribution of *zimbabwes* on the Zambezian plateau.

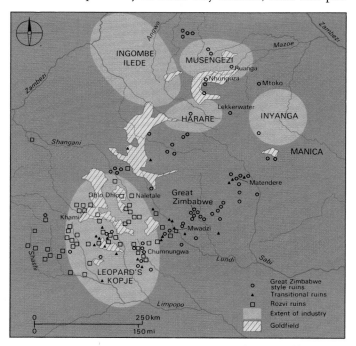

stands within them. The long, steep slopes of the hill below the summit were terraced. Stone walls retained the soil and provided level building spaces. Walls controlled the paths up the slope. The scale of this work and its uniform planning show that it must have been carried out by a large labor force, organized by a single authority.

In many ways, then, the Leopard's Kopje tradition shows significant cultural developments. Cattle acquire a new social and economic significance. Gold is mined and exported. Foreign trade takes on new dimensions, probably under the stimulus of contacts with new coastal trading centers. Settlements occupy diverse environments and exploit them in specialized ways. Large, nucleated

Farming and mining. Mixed cereal agriculture formed the economic base of every community. Sorghum, millet, beans and squashes were the staple foods. Cattle were individually owned. They may often have been, as they were for the Shona chiefs of the Rozvi in the 18th century, a basis for power and patronage, particularly as they were essential elements in marriage settlements, funerals and sacrifices. Land was the common property of the entire community and available for use by every family. Iron, for tools, agricultural implements and weapons, was worked by part-time smiths within most villages. This did not prevent villages close to particularly good ores from establishing a wide-ranging trade in iron, as the Njanja, living near Mount Wedza, did. Copper from the north and cotton cloth from the lower Zambezi valley were two items that formed the basis of regional trading networks. Otherwise, there was little incentive to break down the autonomy and self-sufficiency of the local communities.

Gold was the basis of foreign trade. It is difficult to trace the changing patterns of its production or organization through time. Archaeology and traditions give little information. One is forced to synthesize passing references in the Portuguese chronicles and administrative reports, written between the 16th and 19th centuries. Most of these show an uncritical acceptance of hearsay, often coming from biased sources to ignorant, gullible clerks.

The granites of the plateau are ancient intrusions into even more ancient and much-altered lavas and sedimentary rocks. The latter weather to dark red clay soils, rich

Below: the sandstone hill of Mapungubwe, its extensive flat top almost entirely surrounded by cliffs, is an outstanding feature of the middle Limpopo valley.

settlements grow up on sites chosen specifically for defense. Their fortification is on a scale that entails large-scale group cooperation with the entire community organized and put to work. Competition, war and threats of war become governing factors in siting settlements. Social differentiation is evident in the very different forms of dwellings, whose structures cannot be explained in terms of function or environment. The largest sites – Mapungubwe and Mapela – are sited on major rivers in otherwise inhospitable country. Perhaps this indicates that foreign trade was centrally controlled and routed along a few major arteries. The amenities of rank are probably reflected in the large number of highly polished and very decorative shallow pottery bowls found at Mapungubwe, and especially designed for serving food. Mapela and the Woolandale sites also developed their own idiosyncratic forms of bowls. These changes all point to a very different and more complex social formation than anything that had gone before. This is most apparent at Great Zimbabwe. Before looking at this in detail, one should consider traditional Shona economy a little more closely.

but heavy and difficult to cultivate without draft animals or plows. These areas, enclosed within or lapping the edges of the granite core of the plateau, contain gold. Borne by the granite intrusions, the metal was extruded, as the granite cooled, into the surrounding rocks in veins of quartz. These veins are narrow, from a few inches to four feet thick, discontinuous and difficult to follow. Many are heavily faulted, fractured and fissured. Their yields vary sharply and arbitrarily. Sources of gold on the plateau are thus widespread, sparse and unreliable. As a consequence mining has always been difficult and costly. All development work was a gamble.

Gold production was a subsidiary, seasonal activity of farmers. July, August and September, when the crops were in and there was no work on the land, were lean months, especially in drought years. Food was in short supply and people sought non-agricultural supplements. By this time, too, the water level of rivers had fallen and only pools remained in the riverbeds. Now the gravel and alluvia, deposited by rivers that flowed through the gold belt, were panned for free gold. Whole communities would move as a body to the banks of major rivers and, working in family teams, pan for gold – a system suggesting overall control, although it was conducted for individual gain. The Angwa, Ruenya and Mazoe rivers, which all flowed north to the Zambezi (and were used by traders to travel from the Zambezi valley trading settlements to the plateau) were particularly important sources of alluvial gold. The scale of activity could be considerable. Pools were dredged, or baled dry, or men would dive for the alluvium deposited on the river bottom. Alluvium on the banks was dug and, as all gold was normally to be found at the base of the deposits, shafts were sunk into the deeper deposits.

Prospecting skills could be readily developed by experienced farmers. Outcrops of gold-bearing ore are easily recognizable to trained eyes, through soil and vegetation changes. Yields could easily be checked by trial panning. Development work often entailed removing considerable depths of soil overburden or cutting shafts through hard granite rocks. The shafts were often 80 feet deep or more. With simple equipment it was difficult to expand them along the reef. Ventilation was a problem, made more difficult by the necessity of fire-setting – lighting fires to crack and loosen the quartz. Tunnels or adits needed propping and shuttering. Removing the waste rock was laborious. The work was hard and frequently dangerous. Flooding was an insuperable problem – further incentive for mining to become a seasonal occupation, undertaken late in the dry season when the water table was at its lowest. On the surface, the ore was often roasted over fires, before being milled and ground. Finally it was panned in rivers or pools, to recover the gold. The processing of the ores was more time-consuming than the mining itself. The tools needed were simple. The iron agricultural hoe developed into the pick

and the gad. Dolerite hammer stones were used to break up the ore. Grindstones, of the same shape as domestic querns, were used to mill it. Baskets and gourds served to transport and wash the ore.

Mining, like panning, was communal work, undertaken by families. The skeletons of women and girls have been recovered from the collapsed shafts of early workings. Milling resembled the usual domestic tasks of women in preparing cereal foods, and was therefore probably considered their responsibility. There is little evidence to suggest that specialist groups of miners, working full-time for themselves or for others, ever existed. Many early records reiterate that mining was an unpopular activity. It was a poor and miserable occupation, done reluctantly when one was "very hungry." It is a common fantasy that gold production means riches. Like us, the Portuguese were often surprised to find that it was generally as unrewarding as it was unpleasant.

Although the profits from gold production were so uncertain, nonetheless it did produce disposable wealth. It was soon recognized that the price of gold was dependent on the amount produced. Therefore, production was to some extent regulated by major rulers from outside the mining communities – the Munhu Mutapa, on the northern plateau, and the Changamire Mambo in the southwest. Their rights to do this were well established. Nonetheless, these were by no means absolute. New mines had to be reported to the rulers; but they controlled few mines directly. Incentives to encourage local mining operations were often necessary. There are records of the Munhu Mutapa presenting cattle to the mining communities as an indication that production should start.

In response, foreign traders, both Swahili and Portuguese, adopted consistent strategies to obtain gold at a favorable price. They often showed their eagerness to gain direct access to the mines, to engage in mining operations themselves or, if need be, to gain political control of production policy. They sought to introduce new concepts of status, measured in wealth in consumer goods. Foreign manufactured goods were imported and used to stimulate new demands. They were given presents in a system of credit, devised to exploit traditional obligations of reciprocity in order to create an indebtedness among the miners that could only be met by trading gold.

Trade. Trade was not monopolized by the central authorities. Markets or "fairs" were established, often near regional capitals. One of the earliest of these centers may have been near Great Zimbabwe. The later Portuguese fairs of Dambarare and Luanze have been located and investigated archaeologically. Every subject of a kingdom was permitted access to the fairs and could trade at them. They were under the authority and jurisdiction of local chiefs, who fixed the prices – often arbitrarily, with no necessary relation to demand or supply.

At times foreign traders were allowed access not only to the fairs, but to the capital and the ruler. Swahili traders exerted considerable political influence over at least one 16th-century Munhu Mutapa. During the 17th century the Portuguese were to turn him into a virtual puppet. As the Munhu Mutapa lost his power, the Rozvi ruler, the Mambo, gained it. In 1693 he drove the Portuguese from the plateau. Recognizing the political threat that they posed, he forbade foreigners to enter his territory. The Portuguese then employed specialized African traders, the Vashambadzi, as their agents. However, the Vashambadzi did not form a full-time trading class. Trading, like mining, was a seasonal occupation undertaken in the dry season when travel was easy. The rest of the year the Vashambadzi farmed and herded their cattle on the plateau. The Mambo may have restricted travel to certain routes and markets to certain towns but traders were not subject to any greater controls.

Rulers nonetheless appropriated a portion of the surplus produced by mining in kind and tribute. One way this was established was by the stipulation that all nuggets of gold, as opposed to dust or "impure" gold, were the property of the ruler.

The scale of trade in gold was remarkable. There is concrete evidence of it still to be found at the fair of

Luanze fair was protected by ditches and banks that were probably palisaded. Excavations in 1965 yielded quantities of 17th-century Chinese ceramics. The soil still contains gold dust spilled in trade.

Luanze. Here, far from any goldfields, visible gold – both alluvial and reef – can still be recovered in any panning of the surface soil. Great Zimbabwe gave similar puzzling and unnatural yields in the late 19th century. The source was not recognized. This led to rumors that the ruins were built on a peculiar deposit of gold-bearing hill wash.

Gold was exported to the towns of the Indian Ocean coast and from there to Arabia, the Gulf ports or India. The economy of the interior was thus integrated in the world economy. In the 11th century the Muslim world had adopted a gold standard. The first gold coins were struck by the Almoravid rulers of Morocco. The Christian king of Toledo followed this example in 1173. Through the later 13th and early 14th century the trading states of Europe did the same. Medieval Europe had a passion for the metal. It was fashioned into jewelry, hoarded and accumulated as treasure. While silver and copper were the currencies of merchants, gold was the currency of governments, princes and the Church. It financed wars and rectified political follies. The Mongol conquests of China, India and Persia in the first half of the 13th century united Asia; at the end of the century, the conquest of the Crusader kingdoms enabled an uneasy peace between Christianity and Islam to be established. Europe's trade with the east revived. The demand in Europe was for eastern silks and spices. In return, Europe could only offer gold, for the east was otherwise almost entirely self-sufficient. Many other goods were, in any case, too bulky to make their transport economic. Until the riches of

A view from the Hill Ruin at Great Zimbabwe showing the Elliptical Building and some of the smaller enclosures between it and the Hill.

America were integrated into the European economy, after the Spanish conquests of the 16th century, West Africa had been the most important source of gold, providing two-thirds of the world's supply. But India's demand for gold was insatiable. There was a steady and irreversible drain of the metal from Europe to the east. East Africa also played a considerable part in supplying this demand.

The Indian Ocean trading network had its center in the Gulf and India. East Africa and, more especially, Rhodesia stood at the periphery of this system. The ports of Mogadishu or Kilwa marked the furthest extent of free and equal trade relations. People in the interior, whatever local initiatives they might take, could not comprehend their own place in the world economic system. They were the subjects, the passive partners. They lacked an international perspective and could not see the dangers in the exploitative relations that were being established if not imposed. They were exchanging rare and precious raw materials and wasting assets, gold and ivory, for manufactured luxuries, trinkets and prestige goods.

Opportunities for internal, independent development were being extinguished. The relationship gave no stimulus to or prospect of developing local industries or economic growth. The exchange was unequal. From the start of their relations with the outer world, the East African states were locked in a cycle of underdevelopment. The formation and expansion of kingdoms and states, new institutions, new social awareness and cohesion cannot hide a fragile, unstable and unbalanced economy, at the mercy of external economic pressures.

Great Zimbabwe. This then was the economic context in which Great Zimbabwe developed. It stands in a uniquely favorable area on the southeastern edge of the plateau. Here the scarp captures the moist southeast trade winds from the Mozambique coastal plain. Consequently, it receives unusually constant and reliable rainfall. Many different ecological zones meet at Great Zimbabwe. Not far off is one of the plateau's gold belts, but the ores of this field are unusually poor and were probably never exploited in prehistoric times. The heavy, fertile soils of the gold belt meet the light, granite soils of the hills. Heavily wooded and broken hunting grounds open onto the wide grazing land of the lowlands. Great Zimbabwe also stands in a strategic position for travel to the coast. The headwaters of the Lundi river flow past the site down to the Sabi river valley. The Sabi outflanks the eastern mountain range of the Chimanimani mountains and leads directly and easily to the lowlands and the sea. Indeed there are persistent rumors of harbors, wharves and iron-mooring rings on the river's banks, where it crosses into Mozambique.

Great Zimbabwe includes several separate complexes of walls. A single enormous enclosure, named the "Temple" by European antiquarians and now known, less romantically, as the Elliptical Building, dominates a wooded valley. It is surrounded by about 12 much smaller enclosures that echo its basic shape. Across the valley a cliff of granite is capped by another high-walled enclosure. The boulders on the adjoining summit are enclosed in a maze of smaller walls, the "Acropolis" or Hill Ruin.

The Shona word, *zimbabwe*, means venerated house, the dwelling of a chief. This is what Great Zimbabwe was. The extent and grandeur of the great ruined stone walls, which so impress everyone who sees them rising, isolated and alone, through the now empty African bush, should not be allowed to mask their purpose. While they now serve as a monument to the power and prestige of an ancient kingdom, they once also had a more private and domestic role. Within the enclosures, short lengths of wall now look a meaningless jumble. Excavations and careful architectural analysis reveal that all these walls originally stood against circular clay-walled huts. Each group of walls and huts formed a family dwelling complex, with huts for wives and children, for sleeping, cooking and entertaining guests, separated by courtyards where women could perform domestic tasks in some seclusion and other areas where craftsmen could work. In the largest enclosures, some spaces and structures were probably designed for ceremonies. But they were set in an essentially private domestic context.

It is a striking feature of Great Zimbabwe that the layout is always concerned with domestic spaces and structures, designed for ordinary living and working and for sheltering animals and people. There are no streets, simply paths between private houses; no public gathering places, no monumental public buildings, no markets or barracks, no commercial or industrial areas. The buildings grew haphazardly in response to the demands of living, not to an overall, imposed design. There were no town walls (beyond a late, rudimentary boundary wall) or fortifications. Not even the most imposing buildings

responded to military needs. Entrances were undefended. There were no outworks. Wall tops had no access or protective cover. Buildings were not sited to give support to each other. The only use made of natural features for defense was in the Hill Ruin, built on the edge of a cliff. This siting obviously reminds one of Mapungubwe and Mapela and it was probably contemporary with them and the earliest building at Great Zimbabwe. But here the cliff does not encircle the settlement. The further slopes of the hill can be easily climbed and are unprotected by walls.

The building techniques of Great Zimbabwe are a response to the abundant supply of stones that had split and fallen from the bare granite hills that surround the site. This exfoliation is a natural process, the product of the crystal structure of the rock and of sharp changes in temperature – but one that can be imitated artificially by lighting and quenching fires on the bare rock outcrops. The parallel-sided slabs of stone could readily be cracked to produce manageable building blocks. Laid with some care, they give fair outer faces to walls whose cores are of more loosely piled blocks. The absence of mortar and the thickness of the walls give a flexibility, that allows the structures to adjust to subsidence or movement without cracking or collapse. The walling methods have their roots in many centuries of local experiment and adaptation.

During the Early Iron Age the boulder-strewn hills that are such a feature of the plateau landscape were chosen for shelter. Gaps between the boulders were closed with fallen stones, to improve their natural protection. Later, stone walls were still seen simply as external screens. They were not treated as load-bearing structures. They carried no roofs. They were not an integral part of dwelling houses. Walls were not bonded together but loosely abutted against each other. Wall faces were not tied back to the interior fill. The entire planning basis of the buildings rests on continuous and continuously changing curves. They reproduce the forms of the screens and fences found in all traditional African compounds. They show no regularity or repetition. This basic and extraordinary concept of stone walling, so difficult for a western mind to comprehend, reflects the complete cultural isolation of the builders.

Although there was little change in the technical sophistication of the masonry, an increasing elegance and growing mastery of the material are apparent. In later walls the blocks were carefully matched and laid in courses that run regularly and horizontally for considerable distances. The faces of these blocks were dressed to give an entirely regular outer surface. Each course was stepped slightly back from the one below so that the walls sloped gradually backwards in an elegant curve. Steps were formed in a refined and entirely local and idiosyncratic system of progressively increasing composite curves. Terraced display platforms were built in the corners of courtyards. Towers and low cylindrical stone "altars" were erected. Entrances were lengthened and made more restricting by the addition of low, semi-circular "bastions" inside them, frequently grooved to take timber doorposts. A few walls were decorated with lines of sloping blocks to form dentil or chevron patterns. One entrance had courses of different-colored stones. Cylindrical turrets and upright monoliths of natural and carved stones were erected on top of the outer walls. Dwelling huts had thick walls of clay, and were faced and molded with a hard, glossy clay skin. The hearths, platforms, seats and pot stands inside the hut were made in the same way. So were the rounded curbs that protected the foot of the outside walls against damage and erosion. Clay was used as prodigally and to the same effect as stone. In both, the aim was more to impress than to protect or shelter.

The inhabitants of the stone buildings of Great Zimbabwe could be numbered in hundreds, not thousands. If the Elliptical Building, by far the largest and most imposing structure, was the palace of the ruler, the other enclosures can be seen as the dwellings of his immediate court: relatives, governors, priests and bureaucrats, the restricted administrative circle closest to him. The rest of the settlement, covering about 100 acres, housed farmers, artisans and craftsmen, living in wattle-and-daub huts that have left no surface trace. Only their rubbish dumps of ash, bones and household debris remain. The extensive excavations away from the enclosures, that could elucidate the demography, economy, farming practices and social structure of the complex, have not yet been undertaken.

Industry and trade. Archaeological reconstruction of development at Great Zimbabwe rests almost entirely on the records of the people who ransacked the site in the late 19th century. Their finds show that Great Zimbabwe was a center of crafts and industry. Gold, copper and iron were worked. Crucibles and the tools used in drawing metal into the thin wire needed for bangles and bracelets have been found in deposits in the Hill Ruin and in the Elliptical Building. Gold beads, gold wire and thin sheets of gold, used to cover wooden carvings, were found in abundance. Nodules of iron ore were found on the floor of a cave in the Hill Ruin. There were the remains of smelting furnaces close by. Soapstone was carved to make flat, wide dishes. Their sides were decorated with carved interwoven cable patterns or friezes of long-horned cattle, zebras or baboons. Monoliths were surmounted by carvings of stylized birds. These represent a sculptural style in the process of formation. It had no apparent antecedents and no issue. Terracotta figurines of cattle are like those from Leopard's Kopje sites. Cotton was spun and presumably woven, to judge by the many spindle whorls cut from potsherds. It is unlikely that cotton was grown locally. It may have come from as far afield as the Zambezi valley.

Indeed, Great Zimbabwe may have stood at the center of a considerable regional trading network. Products from the whole plateau were collected and reworked at Great Zimbabwe and many of them then sold to foreign traders. A unique hoard of the most diverse and bizarre goods was unearthed in 1902 in an enclosure just outside the Elliptical Building. It exemplified the contact between the regional and overseas trading system. It contained a great quantity of locally made iron hoes – a widely used form of tribute and religious offering among the Shona. There was a great quantity of coiled wire of iron, copper, bronze and gold; sheets and beads of gold; ingots of copper; and copper jewelry. Three iron gongs, each made of two sheets of metal welded together around the edges, were found. These are characteristic musical instruments of West Africa. They are also insignia of chieftancy among many Bantu-speaking peoples. The local artifacts thus included

The dozen or so carved soapstone dishes and columns found at Great Zimbabwe show few signs of technical or artistic accomplishment. The dish, *above*, depicts zebra, baboons, a leashed dog and bird. A crocodile rests below the bird, *opposite*.

Below: pottery figurines of cattle, like these from the Leopard's Kopje type site, have been found on many later Iron Age sites. They may have been children's toys. Many clearly represent a humped Sanga breed.

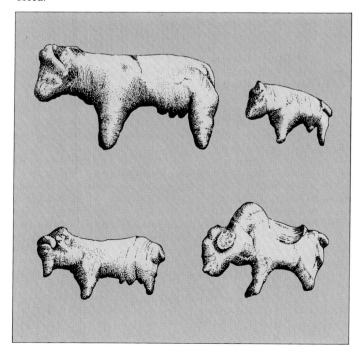

extravagant jewelry, rare insignia, prestige items and characteristic tribute goods.

With them was a small but extraordinary group of foreign baubles. Many of these are of types that have never been found anywhere else in the interior. There was an iron spoon, an iron lampstand, bits of coral, bronze hawk bells, copper chains, cowrie shells, engraved and enameled Syrian glass, a Persian faience bowl bearing an Arabic inscription, Chinese celadon and stoneware vessels. There were also tens of thousands of glass trade beads. It was a strange array indeed, but one whose intrinsic value scarcely matched that of the gold for which it must have been exchanged. This hoard, originally considered to be a cache that had been hidden by a foreign trader, was, more probably, tribute received by the ruler of Great Zimbabwe. Whatever it was, it is a striking illustration of Great Zimbabwe's preeminence as a center of trade, of tribute and of industry on the plateau.

The first permanent settlement at Great Zimbabwe was established in the 11th century and continued through the 12th century. From the little that is known of it, it was very similar in many ways to the earlier (Mambo) phase of the Leopard's Kopje culture, which is securely dated to this period. A single radiocarbon date of 1075 AD ± 150 marks the end of this phase of settlement at Great Zimbabwe.

The first stone walls at Great Zimbabwe were comparatively crudely built. Their stones were laid in rudimentary courses and the faces were left rough. A timber lintel, supporting a drain under such a wall in the Elliptical Building, was one of the earliest samples to be

Imported vessels from Great Zimbabwe included celadon dishes, top and right; an inscribed Persian bowl, center; and Syrian glass, bottom left. Scale in inches.

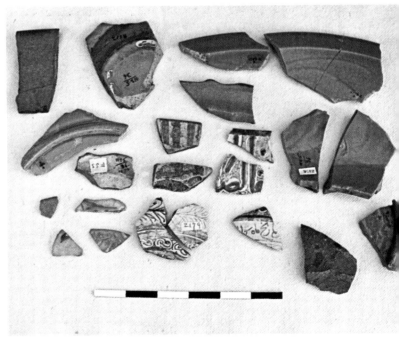

submitted to a radiocarbon count, at a time when the laboratories were still pioneering the method. The three 7th- and 8th-century dates that resulted were disturbingly early. One would expect this phase to be contemporary with the later (Woolandale) phase of the Leopard's Kopje culture, which is dated to the 13th and 14th centuries. This sample has now been redated and has produced two dates of the late 13th or early 14th century. Another timber, from a lintel in a similar wall in the Hill Ruin, has a similar date. There are two 14th-century dates from occupation deposits – one of them certainly of the same period as the early walls. The context of the other remains unpublished.

The later walls at Great Zimbabwe show a mastery of masonry techniques. They were regularly coursed and their faces were dressed. They probably coincide with a great increase of building work in the late 14th and early 15th centuries. This was the period of Great Zimbabwe's greatest prosperity. All the celadons, faience and enameled glass that were imported can be placed in the 14th century. Great Zimbabwe must have ceased to have any economic significance some time in the 15th century. It was the only site in the interior to obtain Chinese celadons in any quantity, yet it has yielded no more than two or three sherds of Chinese blue and white porcelain. This ware was imported to the coast in equal quantities to celadon by the mid-15th century. It had almost entirely supplanted celadon by the end of the century. As porcelain is not found in significant quantities at Great Zimbabwe, Great Zimbabwe must have ceased its trading contacts with the coast by the mid-15th century at the latest. One of the last huts in the Hill Ruin is dated to 1440 AD ± 150. This date coincides with the evidence of trade goods, but the standard deviation is so large that it reduces its significance to almost nothing.

Other zimbabwes. Great Zimbabwe did not exist in isolation. Stone-walled enclosures were built over the whole granite plateau. A few, in goldfields or beyond the granite, are built of sandstone or schists. At least 80 enclosures, in their masonry styles, dwelling types, ceramics, metalwork and imported beads, show that they were contemporary with Great Zimbabwe and closely related to it in culture and purpose. Many of these were pillaged by gold prospectors and treasure hunters in the late 19th century. Few have been investigated archaeologically. No more than seven have walls showing the full range of masonry techniques found at Great Zimbabwe and therefore can be supposed to have had as long a history and development. Those that do, include the Lekkerwater, Mtoko and Chumnungwa Ruins.

The Lekkerwater Ruin was extensively excavated in the early 1960s but the full results have never been published. It is one of the few sites that have yielded a sequence of radiocarbon dates. The 12 dates obtained range from the 12th to the 16th century, but only five – of the 13th and 14th centuries – are said to relate to the main occupation of

the stone enclosures. Excavations at the Mtoko Ruin in 1929 yielded a sherd of 14th- or 15th-century celadon – the only stone enclosure other than Great Zimbabwe to produce such a find. The Chumnungwa Ruin, 100 miles southwest of Great Zimbabwe, and like Great Zimbabwe on the southern edge of the plateau scarp, may have been the capital's nearest powerful neighbor and perhaps rival. Rich finds of gold from burials inside its enclosure were made in 1898.

Most of the smaller ruins tend to have walls in the latest style of masonry found at Great Zimbabwe. They probably belong to the period of Great Zimbabwe's maximum prosperity in the late 14th and 15th centuries. They may well represent a colonial expansion of the capital during this period. Dates have been obtained from small excavations inside five of them. They range from 1340 to 1580 AD, with one date of 1695 AD ± 55. Probably all the later radiocarbon dates can be equated with 15th-century calendar dates. There is no evidence to suggest that any of these stone enclosures was inhabited after the 15th or early 16th century.

The distribution of the stone enclosures is very wide but it is certainly not random; nor, at present, can it be related in any direct way to gold outcrops, trade routes or particular environments. This is a field that demands close study and analysis. Many small sites, often up to six, were built within a day's walk of a major site – like Chumnungwa or Great Zimbabwe – or of each other. This suggests either that they housed the dependants – family, kin or courtiers – of the ruler; or that successive rulers in each area built their own enclosure, so that no enclosure was inhabited for more than a generation. The thin occupation deposits in many enclosures would support such a hypothesis.

A distinctive new style of stone building was developed in the southwest. All enclosures of this group are within about 60 miles of the Khami Ruin, the largest example of the type. This phase of the Great Zimbabwe tradition is named after it. Their stone walls were, like those of their predecessors, regularly coursed with carefully dressed faces. However, they were almost all built to face and retain earth terraces and platforms, on which dwelling huts were erected. Few had free-standing walls. Thus the original functions of stone walls, to provide privacy and shelter, were now entirely superseded. But the prime purpose of every stone building remained: to manifest a ruler's opulence, power and prestige. Many walls were elaborately embellished. Chequer patterns, formed by omitting alternate blocks in very regularly coursed walls, occur with great frequency and are the characteristic decoration of this phase. With this pattern are found friezes and panels in the stonework of zigzag, herringbone and oblique patterns. Lines of colored stone, usually ironstone slabs, were frequently inset in the walls.

The ceramics of these sites show a similar stylistic coherence. They are also clearly distinguishable in style from the pottery of the preceding phase. Their decoration elaborated the basic Great Zimbabwe motifs, to produce increasingly complex patterns, heightened by polychrome finishes.

Ruins of the Khami phase of the Great Zimbabwe tradition have given six radiocarbon dates, from the late 14th and 15th centuries into the 17th and 18th centuries. The more important excavated sites, the Khami and Dhlo Dhlo Ruins, have also produced 17th- and 18th-century Chinese blue and white porcelain, European glass, jewelry and silverware and Portuguese firearms and cannon. These were the presents, tribute and dues of a new ruling dynasty and center of economic power, successor to that of Great Zimbabwe. They came from the Portuguese, the new trading power of the Indian Ocean, who had driven their Swahili predecessors from the plateau.

Many of the changes that characterize the Khami phase, particularly in architecture, certainly owe something to influence from the Leopard's Kopje culture. Stone walls, which terrace and retain the fill of artificial building platforms, are first found on many later Leopard's Kopje

The walls of the Manekweni *zimbabwe* are unprepossessing, but excavations in 1976, shown here, revealed clay floors spanning five centuries and many building elements and artifacts characteristic of the Zimbabwe culture. Scale in 50 cms.

sites, most obviously Mapela. Ruins in the Khami style cover the same territory as the Leopard's Kopje culture. The two groups coexisted at least for a time. The nature of the interaction between them is considered later. The influence of Leopard's Kopje building tradition is, however, manifest in the new forms of stone-built courts.

On the furthest edge of Shona settlement, close to the sea in southern Mozambique, recent excavations have shown that the courts and capitals of the ruling Shona dynasties here also followed the pattern of prestige building and courtly sophistication established on the plateau. Manekweni is a simple, stone-walled enclosure of limestone blocks – the only stone to be found on the coastal plain and one that has none of the excellent fracturing qualities of granite. Stone walls and thick-walled clay dwellings proclaim authority here as they do on the plateau. Traditional items of Shona chiefly regalia – iron gongs and conus shell pendants – have been found. Pellets of gold, whose nearest source is the mines of the eastern mountains of the plateau, some 250 miles away, confirm economic links with the interior. Glass, Chinese blue and white porcelain and beads demonstrate foreign trade. Local wares bear new variations of Great Zimbabwe motifs and show a clear autonomy within a general unity of ceramic style.

Manekweni is as old as Great Zimbabwe. Twelve radiocarbon dates indicate that its walls were built about the 12th century and that it was inhabited until the 16th or 17th century. From its situation alone, it is clear that Manekweni, more than any other stone-built court, can only have prospered through its long-distance trade. In the sandy, low-lying plains that surround it, uncertain rainfall, a thin infertile soil and a complete lack of surface water for many months of the year make subsistence farming a difficult, even impossible, task. Even today agriculture cannot sustain more than a dispersed scatter of homesteads. Today there are no villages in the area, let alone such densely populated permanent settlements as Manekweni once was.

The fall of Great Zimbabwe. Great Zimbabwe fell into sudden economic decline in the 15th century. Many reasons have been proposed for this. There are emotional and psychological ones: the expansionist ambitions of a ruler, stemming from no more than his own personality or implanted in his mind by foreign advisers. Economic motives can be seen in an interference in Great Zimbabwe's external trade bringing about a determination to control the mines and export routes that were being developed on the northern edge of the plateau. Social causes can be suggested in the friction and tension generated by increased cattle herds and grazing disputes. A general environmental degradation – with game, forests and wood supplies, grazing and fertility nearing exhaustion as a result of unusually large and permanent settlement – can also be suggested. None has been tested archaeologically. All are still entirely speculative.

For this period one must now start to look at evidence from outside archaeology. Shona traditions, supported by near-contemporary Portuguese accounts, tell that in the mid-15th century the first Munhu Mutapa left his home in the south and settled in the Zambezi valley, "because of a shortage of salt." This colorful phrasing can be taken to imply that either agricultural or economic difficulties at the capital had proved insoluble. It is an event which correlates convincingly and closely in date with Great Zimbabwe's sudden commercial end. Great Zimbabwe may well have been the capital that the Munhu Mutapa abandoned when he moved north. This event may indeed simply reflect tensions, perhaps a succession dispute, within the ruling dynasty of Great Zimbabwe. This may have caused the dynasty to split, with a dissident faction led by the Munhu Mutapa moving north. Succeeding Munhu Mutapas rapidly subjected all the Shona groups between the plateau and the coast to their rule. Princes of the dynasty were installed to rule the states of Manica, Teve and Sedanda. This was the "empire of Munhu Mutapa," whose fame rests largely on descriptions written by the Portuguese who became its trading partner in the 16th century. They knew and said much less of the kingdom that arose at the southwest end of the plateau.

Here the tradition of stone-walled capitals, started at Great Zimbabwe, continued. From these roots a new Shona state grew up, that of the Rozvi, ruled by the Changamire dynasty. It grew to power on the particularly rich gold and cattle resources of the southwest. In 1693 the Changamire ruler, the Mambo, swept the Munhu Mutapa and his Portuguese allies from the plateau. Until it fell to the Nguni invaders in the 1830s, the Rozvi state remained the real heir of Great Zimbabwe and the unchallenged power of the plateau.

Interpretations. This then is an outline of the history of Great Zimbabwe and its successor state. Many general questions still need answering. How was the state structured? How did it originate? On what authority did it rest? Where did its power come from?

Many misunderstandings of the Great Zimbabwe culture have stemmed from an old-fashioned view that all archaeological assemblages must represent a cultural totality, the artifacts of an entire tribe or people. They do not. At Great Zimbabwe one is looking only at a small section of society, a ruling class that held power through its control of the products sought by foreign merchants. The specialized nature of the society is not only apparent in its buildings. It can also be seen in ceramics, household utensils and diet. Finely finished pots, suitable for drinking, and large storage vessels, designed for brewing or storing liquids, entirely dominate all pottery assemblages. There are no bowls for serving cereals or relishes and few vessels suitable for cooking these items. Querns for preparing grain have very seldom been recovered. Analyzed assemblages of food bones consist almost entirely of cattle bones. Every excavated *zimbabwe* tells a similar story. No other later Iron Age sites have anything like this restricted range of items. No others show such specialization or reflect such a restricted segment of society.

In this discussion it is particularly significant that many outposts of the Great Zimbabwe culture were much too small to have had an independent existence. Most can have housed no more than one family. They were clearly not viable units in economic terms. They must have depended on a larger population in the immediate vicinity for their protection and support. They must, indeed, have been the recipients of considerable outside resources in labor and produce. Who provided this? Who, besides the ruling class, made up the later Iron Age communities?

Besides the Leopard's Kopje people in the southwest, at least three distinct later Iron Age archaeological groups have been recognized. They occupied distinct territories in the northern half of the plateau. They differed from each other only in the styles of their ceramics. They are best interpreted as separate ethnic groups – "tribes" – within the Shona people. All lived in extensive villages in open, agricultural country. The lack of any imported goods, besides a small selection of trade beads; the poverty of their jewelry; the simplicity of their huts; the absence of

John Senex's map of Africa of 1720 shows the Shona states of the preceding century. It includes the Munhu Mutapa's capital, the *zimbabwe* of Teve and Tonge, and possibly the Manekweni *zimbabwe*.

any suggestion of differences in wealth, status or specialization in the architecture or layout of their villages – all these are apparent in excavation. All suggest that these villages represent egalitarian communities dependent on subsistence agriculture. They are all dated to between the 12th and 16th centuries and are thus contemporaneous with the stone enclosures. Stone enclosures were dispersed over the territories of all three groups (as well as the territory of the Leopard's Kopje culture). There can be no doubt that they all coexisted. These people were presumably the peasant farmers and miners on whom the rulers depended for their food, manpower and wealth.

They represent the stable, near-autonomous, food-producing sector of a traditional African dual economy. Relations between the peasant farmers and their rulers have yet to be studied.

Only two excavated settlements show evidence of the two sectors of society living in close proximity. The Ruanga Ruin, a building dated to the 15th or 16th century, near the Mazoe river, stands on a hill occupied by one of the peasant communities from the 12th century. The distribution of the artifacts suggests that they coexisted. Manekweni, the stone enclosure in southern Mozambique, has a variety of ceramics, whose styles and distribution at present suggest a similar situation.

The contrast between rulers in their stone-built courts and their subject tribesmen of various groups does not represent the whole story. Some people were more than simply farmers. The people who lived on the northern edge of the plateau exploited the copper ores of the Urungwe hills. The ingots that they made, ridged and shaped like the "sails of a windmill," as the Portuguese described them, have been found stretching south towards Great Zimbabwe. Graves of this group at Ingombe Ilede, on the banks of the Zambezi, contained tools used to draw out the copper wire that could be used to fashion bracelets and anklets. The ingots, bars and rods that mark the successive stages of this process were also found. The high status of these metalworkers is shown by the welded iron gongs and conus shell pendants found with some burials. Their power is represented by collections of hoes, of a form used more for giving in tribute than in agriculture. Their wealth is shown by the gold beads that they wore as necklaces and the gold settings of their pendants.

Copper ingots of the distinctive Ingombe Ilede shape have also been found, with their molds, near the copperfields and early mines of southern Zaire. Welded iron gongs are also generally accorded a northern origin. This suggests that the Ingombe Ilede metalworkers may have derived their strength from joining two of the main copper-producing areas of central Africa in a wide-ranging regional commercial network that stretched from Zaire to Great Zimbabwe.

This group seems to have disappeared after the Munhu Mutapa moved north. Their trade is mentioned once by the Portuguese at the start of the 16th century and never again. It is tempting to see a causal connection between these events. It may even be that the copper trade of the Zambezi valley attracted the Munhu Mutapa northwards. Urungwe may indeed have been one of his commercial rivals and he may have destroyed it.

If the Great Zimbabwe dynasties ruled over several distinct groups, from small defenseless outposts many miles apart, one must consider how they achieved this control, how they maintained their security and how they appropriated men and produce for their purposes. The

Pendants, $\frac{3}{4}$ inch to 3 inches across, cut from conus shells, are found only in the most important settlements. Like the iron gongs (*opposite*), they traditionally denote chieftaincy. After Livingstone.

courts are too small and defenseless to have been part of a military system. Military coercion can have played no significant role. Control of long-distance trade is unlikely to be the whole answer.

The role of religion. In an African context, political and economic power is seldom divorced from religion. Both are almost invariably closely linked and frequently personified in a single individual – the king. Archaeology at present allows no precise interpretation of the role of religion in Great Zimbabwe's growth and power structure. There is no doubt, however, that many structures reflect it. Turrets, towers, monoliths, altars, and a series of soapstone sculptures of birds that were set both on walls and altars, must all have had a supernatural significance. The central role of ritual in confirming political authority within the Great Zimbabwe culture can, at present, only be illustrated archaeologically from finds in excavations at the Nhunguza Ruin, a minor enclosure not far from the Ruanga Ruin. Its interior was dominated by a very large, circular, clay building – one of the largest known from any stone enclosure. This was divided into a large hall, which led to a small room, containing only a large seat. Walled in behind this "throne" were a stepped platform and a low stone cylinder, encased in clay and grooved to hold a vertical monolith or carving. This was the sort of altar and display platform that early antiquarians' records of Great Zimbabwe describe. Whatever objects were set out in this sealed and hidden chamber, they gave literal as well as symbolic backing to the person who sat on the "throne" before them and exercised authority from this *zimbabwe*. Analogies between the structures and artifacts of the Great Zimbabwe culture and traditional Shona religious or chiefly practices cannot at present be traced.

Traditional Shona religion is a complex amalgam of successive layers of practice and belief. The earliest Shona religious forms were territorial cults. These were widespread, locally independent and completely decentralized. They were concerned with fertility and rain-making and the welfare of local communities. They appear to be relics of the beliefs of early farmers, who lived

The pottery of Ingombe Ilede is among the most delicate and sophisticated. It is stamped with a fine comb and burnished with graphite.

in self-sufficient communities with no strong or permanent forms of leadership. Possibly they began in the Early Iron Age. Certainly they predate the centralized forms of government of the later Iron Age.

The cult of Mwari, the sole high god, himself remote from human concerns but whose priests manifest him in oracular statements from his shrines, dominates the plateau. It is a centralized cult with a single, clearly defined hierarchy of shrines, priests and officers. The Rozvi rulers took advantage of the unity of the Mwari cult and used it as a major source of political support. The cult's priests provided the Rozvi Mambo with a network of information and influence that covered the country, though the autonomy of the priests was always respected by the Mambo. This cult now has its main shrine in the Matopo Hills, south of the Khami Ruins. Traditionally it was centered at the Rozvi court. Traditions also link it with the Khami Ruins and Great Zimbabwe.

On the northern edge of the plateau, and in the

Below right: an iron gong, about 10 inches long, cut from sheets of iron and welded together.

Below: a young man buried at Ingombe Ilede wore copper bangles, a necklace of gold and nine conus-shell pendants (four are numbered here). Copper-working tools and ingots lay beneath his head.

Zambezi valley beyond it, the territory of the Munhu Mutapa state, *mhondoro* cults have considerable power. *Mhondoro* are the spirits of ancestral kings, founders and hero figures, who have become semi-divine. They possess and speak through mediums. This participation of the spirits of former rulers in important contemporary decisions is the sort of adaptation that enables religious practices to fulfill a clear political role. Spirit possession is harnessed to the requirements of society or the state.

If authority had its origins in priestly office, and derived its rights from religious beliefs, and adapted religious practices to support its validity; if ritual kingship was the source of authority from which the state grew; if the institutions of the state were established on a religious base, nevertheless the state derived its power from economic controls. Government on the plateau was supported by surplus derived from gold production. This surplus was not so much extracted from village-based, part-time mining communities in tribute, as realized from foreign traders through controls over external trade.

The kingdoms that ruled on the plateau followed the pattern of many states based on commerce. When its power was firmly established, Great Zimbabwe appears to have sought to control not just its markets but the trade routes and centers of production. Through its many colonies and outposts, it sought to dominate the economy of the plateau. In many ways the pressures of its very success may have threatened its future. People would have been attracted to live permanently in the capital. A large permanent population would cause rapid environmental degradation. Colonies could grow to become rivals. Administration could become overextended. One group eventually moved away to establish the Munhu Mutapa kingdom in the north, where the Zambezi river and its tributaries, the northern goldfields, the Ingombe Ilede metalworkers and their trade network, and the Urungwe copper mines could be brought into its economic system. Following this, the Munhu Mutapa reduced the eastern Shona states – who had been commercial rivals standing between him and his foreign trading partners – to subservient provinces. These states had always lacked the resources and economic strength of the plateau. But this

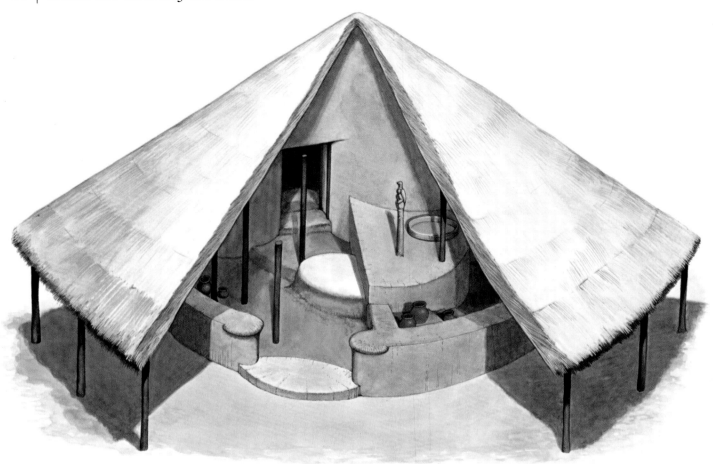

Above: the main building at Nhunguza demonstrated the public functions of its occupants. Behind the seat dominating the small room in the foreground was an "altar" holding a decorative column. The door from the "throne room" led to a room that could hold large assemblies.
Below: excavations in 1969 of the main building within the Nhunguza Ruin.

brief imperialism could not be sustained. It was followed by subversion of the empire's periphery by foreign merchants, seeking better terms of trade. They encouraged the provinces to reassert their independence. A fragile and artificial unity was fragmented.

The southwest fared better. Here the Rozvi kingdom grew from the Khami phase of the Great Zimbabwe culture. Here, it has been suggested, alternative sources of economic wealth were developed. The dependence of the state on long-distance trade was minimized. The rich grazing lands of the southwest increased the economic role of cattle. Ownership of all cattle gave the Rozvi Mambo an alternative source of wealth, of patronage and of rewards and inducements for loyalty. Developed agricultural technology rendered the kingdom relatively free of alien commercial pressures. In the 18th century the military organization and prowess of the Rozvi, and the establishment and maintenance of a standing army, enabled officers of the Mambo to travel his territories and collect tribute direct from all dependent centers. Tribute no longer passed through a hierarchy of village and provincial chiefs. It became an independent and significant source of income that went directly to the central ruler. Thus the pattern imposed by commerce – of growth, territorial expansion, conquest, subversion by foreign traders and fragmentation – was no longer inevitable.

Ruins of Zimbabwe

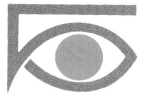

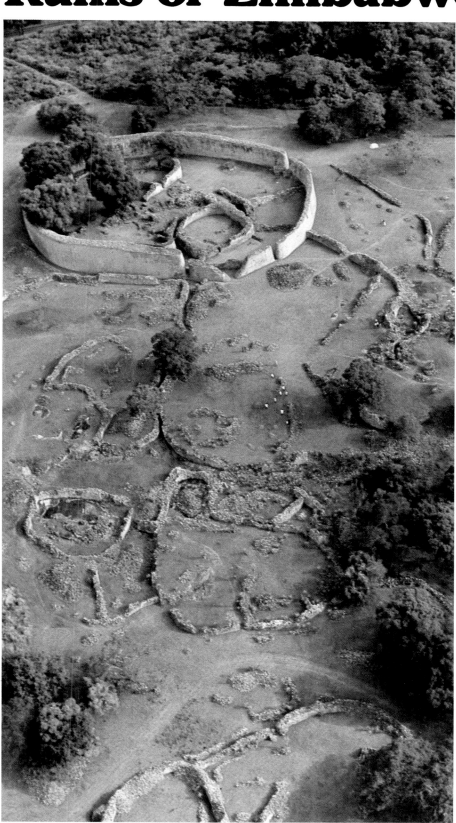

The architecture of the stone enclosures of the southern plateau – the *zimbabwe* of Shona kings – is a creative human response to a marvelous natural building material. But the enclosures had a new purpose: they were designed and built as political symbols. They embodied power over people. Their very building was a means of political control: through work, the courts could share out their wealth: rewards for labor, largesse for loyalty. The needs of society, environment, history and technology were thus united in a single indigenous response to an overriding political purpose.

The curved patterns of the walls of Great Zimbabwe seem an incomprehensible labyrinth. But when the clay houses that they adjoined are restored in the mind's eye, they form a coherent series of domestic living spaces for a numerous court. The ruin field has three main areas: the Hill Ruin, the small Valley Ruins and the great Elliptical Building.

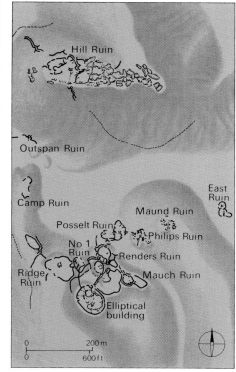

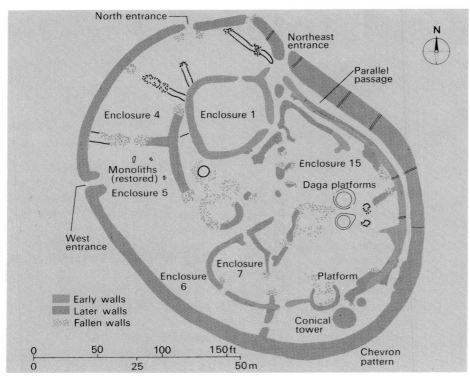

North entrance

Northeast entrance

Parallel passage

N

Enclosure 4

Enclosure 1

Enclosure 15

Monoliths (restored)

Daga platforms

Enclosure 5

West entrance

Enclosure 6

Enclosure 7

Platform

Conical tower

Early walls
Later walls
Fallen walls

Chevron pattern

0   50   100   150 ft
0   25   50 m

Above: the Elliptical Building marks the period of Great Zimbabwe's greatest power. It started with the small circular enclosure, probably built early in the 14th century. The area outside it was enclosed with an encircling wall. When prosperity was at its peak, in the early 15th century, this was superseded by the great outer wall. Building started at the north end, progressed anticlockwise and grew in size and grandeur, passing outside the old encircling wall.

Above right: the passage formed between the old and new outer walls. As it approached the area of the Conical Tower, it was narrowed by "bastions" or "buttresses." They were not even bonded into the main walls but lean loosely against them – one of the many technical details that demonstrate that the builders did not learn their craft from developed foreign traditions. The bastions were slotted and their sole function was to hold the timber frames of a low wooden door.

At its most magnificent, the outer wall (*below left*) is 35 feet high and 17 feet thick. Great Zimbabwe is replete with symbols, which doubtless continue the theme of the entire complex: royal majesty. The Conical Tower (*below*), focus of the interior of the Elliptical Building, appeared to Victorian antiquarians to be a phallic symbol, suggesting barbarous orgies. Its shape is more like a Shona farmer's granary – perhaps symbolizing tribute or largesse.

Right: early walls of the Hill Ruin ride over natural granite boulders and incorporate some in their fabric. Together they form an integrated whole. Stone walls were developed to improve natural shelters in the granite hills. On the Hill the earliest evidence of settlement at Great Zimbabwe has been found.

Below: a juxtaposition of the peripheral walls of the Elliptical Building shows how masonry skills changed. The old outer wall (right foreground) has short, uneven wavy courses. The new outer wall behind has regular horizontal courses.

Right: the Hill Ruin seems a natural defensive strongpoint. It surmounts a cliff above the Valley Ruins. But from the other side, it is easily approached. The slopes were terraced to take dwellings.

Below: the builders of Great Zimbabwe developed their own beautiful and idiosyncratic method of incorporating steps in a wall's thickness. The system of multiple curves of decreasing radius continued the flow of the masonry.

The Hill Ruin (*left*), looking
westwards. The Eastern Enclosure,
in the foreground, originally contained
the majority of the carved soapstone
columns, dishes and small stylized
human figurines found at Great
Zimbabwe. Low stone cylinders, once
covered in *daga*, were built on terraced
slopes leading to the boulders. These looked
like "altars." All this suggests that it was
an area of particular religious significance.
The Western Enclosure, in the
background, contained most of the
dwellings in the Hill Ruin. Here
successive deposits of hut debris, 15 feet
deep, were excavated in 1958. They
spanned the whole period of continuous
settlement. The earliest levels, of the 11th
and 12th centuries, predated all stone
walls.

Monoliths of natural granite and small cylinders of masonry – "turrets" or "altars" – capped the outer walls of the Elliptical Building (*left*) and the Western Enclosure on the Hill (*right*). Many monoliths had fallen and were recovered in clearance work by the first curators. What now remains is largely their reconstruction and restoration. The meaning of these embellishments is lost. Perhaps they were no more than decorative. Perhaps each item had a precise and defined role in manifesting and commemorating a dynasty's history. Systematic collection and study of Shona oral traditions is now the only hope of realizing the range of possible reasons and of starting to answer such questions.

Little survives of the *daga* buildings at Great Zimbabwe. The Lekkerwater Ruin (*above left*) shows how the builders mastered clay as a material as they had mastered masonry. It was used as lavishly as stone, to express the same magnificence. The smooth hard surface was often decorated with intricate, molded geometric patterns.

After Great Zimbabwe went into decline in the 15th century, Khami (*above*) was the largest capital. Walls now supported rubble platforms on which the houses were built. Privacy and shelter were sacrificed to the old western traditions of terracing – going back to the rough walls of Mapela. The visual effect was enhanced by a lavish and inventive use of decoration. The new trends reached perfection in the Naletale Ruin (*left*), where the decoration has the lightness, gaiety and interest of a pleasure pavilion of the European rococo.

This platform at Mwadzi on the banks of the Lundi river, 40 miles southwest of Great Zimbabwe, is a typical example of a small provincial capital of the Khami phase of the Zimbabwe culture.

This ruin, on the Bumboosie river, is built of sandstone. It lies 175 miles northwest of Khami, far beyond the granite plateau and separated from it by teak forests and infertile Kalahari sand soils. It is known to have been built and occupied by Zanke, a member of the Rozvi Mambo's dynasty, in the early 19th century: the last of the centuries-old Shona tradition of stone courts.

Matendere is 80 miles northeast of Great Zimbabwe, on the edge of the Sabi river valley. It looks as if it is built in the earliest style of stonework developed at Great Zimbabwe, but it is probably a late manifestation of this. Caton-Thompson's excavations in 1929 revealed only sparse evidence of occupation. The few finds – glass beads in particular – suggest that Matendere belonged in the Khami phase. Like so many *zimbabwe*, it lies on the very edge of the disease-free high plateau. This pattern of distribution – together with faunal evidence of diet – suggests that cattle herding was an important element in the *zimbabwe* economy. From the capitals, cattle could be driven into the lowlands to new pasturage during the dry months when risks of disease were slight. This transhumant pastoral economy, aimed at intensive beef production, enabled the fullest range of environments to be exploited.

5. Cities on the East African Coast

The gold and ivory of the Zambezian plateau were sold to Swahili or Arab traders living along the East African coast. The producers of the interior and the traders of the coast were linked in an economic system on which the prosperity and survival of both were almost entirely dependent. Neither could prosper without the other. The bonds were, however, entirely commercial. The Shona states were a completely indigenous response to the stimulus of foreign commerce. Their social and political forms and institutions developed from indigenous cultural roots and owe nothing to foreign forms. Their architecture, regalia, weapons, domestic crafts and buildings are as unaffected by alien examples. Great Zimbabwe is striking and vivid evidence of how little cultural interaction there was. Only a limited range of imported beads and ceramics gives concrete evidence of foreign contact. Nothing in the architecture, building techniques or technology shows any suggestion of alien influence.

There is little evidence that any traders settled far inland. None of their towns existed away from the seashore, except in the lower Zambezi valley. For many years their contacts with the indigenous peoples were probably very limited. Even at an early and important capital of a Shona kingdom near the coast, like Manekweni, there is very little evidence that traders themselves ever entered the town. However, by 1560, Swahili traders were living at the Munhu Mutapa's capital. Historians have spoken of their "subtle and pervasive political influence" on the ruler at this time. They instigated the murder of their first foreign rival, the Portuguese priest Silveira, in 1561. But reports of "10,000 Moors" in the interior, related by the captain of Sofala in 1511, seem scarcely credible. They suggest the exaggerations of frightened bureaucrats, reporting to the Portuguese crown, as the trade they had captured slipped through rigid and incompetent hands back to the people that had generated it.

The coastal towns may have owed their prosperity to the gold that they obtained. They were otherwise oriented entirely towards the sea. Their traffic came from Aden, at

Previous page: the dhow trade between East Africa, Arabia and India has withered in the last decade. Now only a solitary, motor-driven *boom*, the tramp of these seas, reminds one of the former fleets.

the entrance to the Red Sea; and from Oman, at the entrance to the Persian Gulf; from Siraf, the port of the towns of Fars and Shiraz in southern Persia; perhaps joined by Dabul and other ports on the Kutch coast of northwest India. Thus, East Africa was integrated into the commerce of the Muslim world, stretching from the Mediterranean to India, China and Indonesia. The culture of the coast was urban, commercial and Islamic.

Were the East African towns then alien to the continent? Colonies of one or more of the great Muslim states of the Near East? Exotic, artificial transplants, with no place in an account of African culture and only a marginal one in a history of Africa? Or, if the African element is recognized, was East Africa a stagnant backwater, the passive recipient of foreign initiatives?

In every case the answer is no. The language of the coast was Swahili, a language with many Arabic words and first written in Arabic script, but whose grammar, structure and basic vocabulary are entirely Bantu. The first Arab immigrants found a Negroid population settled on the coast and intermarried with it. The physical appearance of the majority of the inhabitants was always Negroid, as the many descriptions of foreign visitors make clear. However, the most telling evidence that this was a fully autonomous, living culture can be seen in the architecture of the coastal towns, an indigenous creation of considerable originality, skill and charm. Some elements, particularly the more ornate stone tombs, are quite unlike structures anywhere else in the world.

It was a complex and heterogeneous society. Different towns had their own particular overseas connections. These are reflected in the different goods that each town imported. Each town had its own potting industry, each showing very different local styles, reflecting an underlying ethnic diversity.

Merchants formed a distinct class, which included the sultan, his family, courtiers and bureaucrats. They built and lived in small groups of fine stone houses at the center of each town. They were supported by a large subservient population living in wattle-and-daub huts on the edges of the towns. Dependent entirely on trade, no town controlled any significant territory inland. Colonies on the coast were unusual and generally short-lived. Each town

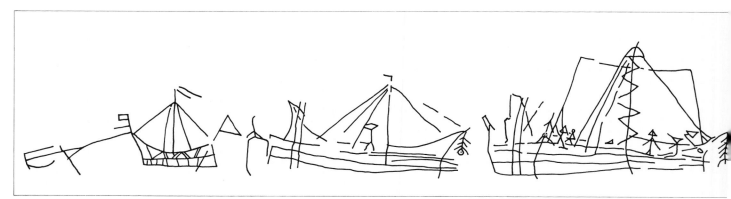

was autonomous. Some acted as suppliers of agricultural produce and as collection centers for goods destined for the major ports. Thus some urban economies were linked and complementary, but commercial competition between the towns was a more general pattern.

The geography of the coast. The cities of East Africa spread down a thousand miles of coast from Somalia to beyond Kilwa in southern Tanzania. Coasting voyages took traders almost another thousand miles further south, to the vicinity of the present Sofala. Arab geographers divided the coast into three distinct regions. The southern portion of the Somali coast is known as the Benadir. Though the word means "ports," this coast offers only the occasional small rocky headland as protection against the

Below right: coasting dhows, *jahazi*, careened at low water at Faza in the Lamu archipelago. The sandy foreshore is an ideal harbor.

Below: graffiti of ships occur on many early buildings. Some depict the square sail of the *dau la mtepe*, others the complex tiller rigging and curved prow of the true *mtepe*, decorated with oculi and amulets.

The last *dau la mtepe*, the archaic vessel of East African waters with a square matting sail and its hull timbers sewn together, disappeared early this century.

force of the sea. Still, it is more habitable than anything to the north. The narrow coastal plains of southern Somalia are backed by barren, high sand dunes. Inland is the flat, dry alluvial plain of the Shebele valley, supporting sparse acacia thornbush and some cultivation. This coast is made hazardous by reefs and islets. The anchorage of Mogadishu, the most important town of the Benadir, is entirely exposed to the sea and hazardous for many months of the year. The drowned river valley of Bur Gao is the only sizable natural harbor in Somalia. It has been searched, so far unsuccessfully, for signs of early settlement. Southwards stretches a string of coral islets, a mile or so offshore, the Bajun. They provide a protected coasting channel between themselves and the mainland. At their southern end is a second great drowned valley, an old mouth of the Tana river, on whose estuary are the islands of Lamu, Pate and Manda, separated from the

mainland by a narrow channel, fringed by mangroves. Each island has, at various times, supported important towns.

The Lamu archipelago, with greater rainfall and tropical vegetation, marks the start of the Zanj coast. From here southwards the offshore coral reef is continuous enough to provide a protected inshore channel leading to many small, safe creeks and harbors. Shores are sandy and shelve very gradually. Though the tidal range is small, the sea may retreat many hundred yards at low tide. Small vessels can therefore be beached and unloaded almost anywhere. Coral islets with fresh water offered ideal sites for settlement. The sea was a natural defense against marauders from the mainland. Settlements on the mainland were usually built on sand spits or coral headlands, separated from the interior by small *jangwa*, shallow creeks that only filled at spring tides; or by streams flowing parallel to the coast, seeking a break in the coastal sand dunes; or by low-lying, seasonally flooded marshland. The large ocean islands of Pemba, Zanzibar and Mafia were obvious sites for trading cities. From them the mainland can be reached in a daylight voyage. Drowned river valleys provide deep-water harbors, such as Mombasa and Dar es Salaam and Kilwa.

The Sofala coast begins south of Zanzibar. Beyond Kilwa it saw few permanent settlements. Frequent coastal voyages carried goods to the major ports from the south. The name Sofala, "shoals" or "low-lying country," may point to the problems of navigating in the Mozambique Channel. The Kerimba archipelago and Mozambique Island are the last islands of the coral reef. South of the Zambezi estuary the sea is too cold for coral to grow. The great dunes and sandstones of the Sabi estuary and the Bazaruto islands, lying not far from the Shona capital of Manekweni, are waterless and infertile. They have no building materials. Their channels and harbors are made hazardous by shallow water and shifting sandbanks.

The immediate hinterland of the East African coast is known as *nyika*, "wilderness," dry semi-desert, covered in acacia scrub or thorn thickets. There is little cultivation, surface water, grazing or food for man or beast. It is a formidable barrier to communication with the interior. This is why the fertile highlands of western Kenya and Uganda were never visited by traders until the 19th century. Only the Zambezi and Sabi river valleys offer easy access to the interior. Physical geography reinforced the cultural predisposition to look across the sea for sustenance.

Life was dominated by another force: the seasonal monsoon winds. These governed the timing and length of trading voyages. The changing winds also determined where the main entrepots and collecting centers of the coast could flourish.

The northeast monsoon, blowing from the Persian Gulf and India towards East Africa and down its coastline, starts in November and reaches its full strength and southward

A tomb in Gedi with the carved coral, paneled decoration and pillar characteristic of the coast. It is one of the few with an inscription or date surviving: 802 AH (1399 AD).

extension in January. It generates a current that also flows southward along the coast as far as Lamu. These winds are reliable as far as Kilwa. However, dhows generally traded in the Gulf and Red Sea at the start of the season, to accumulate cargo for Africa. This and the fear of early gales off Somalia meant that dhows sailed for Africa late in the season. They could usually only reach Mogadishu or northern Kenya before the winds fell away. The lull between monsoons is also the only period when Mogadishu is free of onshore swells. In the south, light and unreliable winds blow down the Mozambique Channel reaching as far as Sofala in January, the limit of all northerlies. They are assisted by the strong southerly set of the Mozambique current. But December and January are a season of cyclones in the Mozambique Channel.

In April the southwest monsoon starts. By June or July it is boisterous everywhere and produces very frequent gales off Somalia. From the start of this monsoon a strong northerly current flows up the Somali coast. Dhows therefore seek to leave East Africa as soon as this monsoon is established. Those reaching Arabia and the Gulf first are also able to get the highest prices for their East African goods. In the south the contrary southerly current is weakest from May to July. During this time an inshore counter-current can also be used to travel north; however, coastal traffic sailing north from the Sofalan coast cannot reach the major ports before the oceangoing craft have left on the early monsoon.

This pattern of voyaging goes far to explain the position of many of the major coastal towns. Mogadishu is the nearest port of call to Asia, ideal for voyages made late in the season and only safe for sailors making a brief halt between monsoons. As boats and navigation improved and voyages could be made more quickly and timed more reliably, the Lamu archipelago, Zanzibar and Kilwa successively became the most efficient ports of call. Kilwa represents the maximum range of oceangoing craft that do not wish to winter in East Africa and spend a year on the round trip. Light winds and contrary currents mean that voyages to Sofala cannot be timed with any certainty. Small coasting craft, sailing throughout the year, are the most efficient means of travel and communication in the Mozambique Channel. The goods that they collected and brought north had to be stored in warehouses to await transport in oceangoing vessels to Asia in the trading season of the following year. The first buildings at Kilwa included exactly such great warehouses.

This pattern of navigation and settlement was disrupted when Portuguese ships, traveling from Europe to India, had to plan voyages that took best advantage of both the Atlantic and Indian Ocean wind systems. Portuguese fleets also had to restock with food and water in Africa. Mozambique Island, well south of Kilwa, and a strategically unimportant site for voyages within the traditional Indian Ocean cycle, met these new needs.

Architecture. The culture of the coast is expressed most vividly by its architecture: an original, creative synthesis of the opportunities of African climate and resources and the heritage of styles and methods developed in the Arabian homelands. The surviving buildings of all the towns show a coherent, evolving unity of style. There is a clear relationship between all the coastal buildings. It is visible not only in the plans but in details of building techniques, moldings and carvings.

Though no systematic comparison of the architecture on the coast and in southwest Asia has been made, it seems clear that elements of the coastal style can be found in many different places and periods. The plan of one of the earliest major buildings, Husuni Ndogo on Kilwa Island, echoes the Roman *castra* and Umayyad desert palaces of early 8th-century Syria. The layout of a neighboring palace, Husuni Kubwa, resembles the mid-9th-century Abbasid palace of Samarra on the Tigris river. It also includes elaborate geometric forms, found in 13th-century Mamluk Egypt. Its dome shapes and vaulting systems echo 12th-century Seljuk forms. The characteristic, simple, pointed mosque arch, with an ogival or nicked apex and no keystone, is unlike the two-centered or horseshoe forms of most of the Arab world. It is derived from Bahmanid India. Mosques are many-pillared, rectangular halls, rather than the great arcaded courts,

pavilions or *iwans* of the Muslim homelands. The internal arrangement of all coastal houses is based on identical suites of rooms ranging back from a reception court in the front. This reflects a characteristic African social form, with ordered degrees of privacy. Similarly, the form and medium of much of the decoration inside houses and mosques may be Arabian but the content is African.

Stone tombs, grouped outside many mosques, have tall, octagonal or cylindrical pillars of coral masonry at their heads. Some pillars are inset with decorative ceramic bowls. These pillars are a feature unique to the coast. Their origins and meaning are unknown. The stelae of the Aksumite kingdom of the northern highlands of Ethiopia and the pillared graves of the Sidama in southern Ethiopia have been seen as possible sources. On the other hand, the pillared tombs may be a carry-over from local coastal pagan practices.

The simple, restrained architecture of the coast was created by accepting the restrictions imposed by the only available timber – mangrove poles – and by fully exploiting the potential of coral and its derivatives. The main building material was a coarse, vesicular coral, broken into rough irregular blocks. This is soft and easily cut and dressed when it is taken from the living reef. When exposed to weather and rain, the pores of the rock fill with salts, so that it becomes hard, impervious and crystalline. This need for the stone to weather meant that buildings were often erected in stages over several years. Fine-grained coral was cut and dressed to form all moldings. Each such ornamental block was carved for a particular position and fitted into the whole as part of an intricate jigsaw. This ornamentation was the work of individual craftsmen. There was no repetition or standardization of the components. Coral was also burned to provide the lime needed for mortar. A very fine-textured plaster was applied as a thin finishing coat to the

A bank of niches decorating the reception room of a house in Faza. They are formed in plasterwork and probably date to the 18th century.

stonework. Less than one-tenth of an inch thick, it was so hard that it survived for centuries.

Wooden ceiling beams, usually squared, carved and painted, supported thick, flat roofs. These were made of a concrete of coral chips in a lime mortar. The module that governed the whole architectural system was the span of the mangrove poles used to support the roofs: a dimension very close to eight feet. This means that all rooms were rectangles eight feet wide; the largest long and narrow, the smallest almost square. They were arranged on axial plans, in rigid and complex geometric compositions.

Decoration was sparse and reticent. Often a cornice of timber was set below the ceiling beams. Carved friezes of wood, or carpets, or textiles hung down the walls and decorated the main rooms. Rectangular niches, framed by simple moldings, were built into pilasters on each side of the more important doors. They held lamps. Recesses were also used more decoratively: to display porcelain and break up the wall surfaces into paneled patterns. In the 18th century the walls of important rooms in rich houses of the Lamu archipelago were decorated with a diaper work of geometric and floral patterns in plaster, around banks of niches.

Houses often had impressive entrances: large arched doorways, flanked by seats and approached by a flight of steps. They probably framed carved and studded timber doors like those that made 19th-century Zanzibar famous. They led to private courtyards, surrounded by high walls that were blank and windowless like the outside walls of all the houses. A wide raised bank usually ran around three sides of the courtyard and provided space to sit. Here visitors could be received, business transacted and domestic chores, including cooking, done. A long, narrow reception room, with wide doors and large windows, faced onto the court. Private rooms, often beautifully decorated, led off the reception rooms. Larger houses frequently had an entirely private courtyard in the rear. Here women could cook and wash. Small, stone-lined pits, capped by a perforated slab of coral, were built beneath the centers of the reception rooms. These drained the floors. Beads, coins and gaming pieces – disks cut from potsherds – frequently disappeared into the soakaways, to await an excavator's trowel.

At the center of the larger towns, stone houses were grouped in rectangular blocks, separated by narrow alleys. The outside walls of many houses and courtyards interlocked with their neighbors in a complex arrangement. They must have been built at the same time to an agreed plan. Such planning enabled some features, like yards and wells, to be shared by several houses. It was so flexible and individual an arrangement that it is clear that the plans were not derived from a central authority or a standardized pattern. Groups of kinsfolk must have built and lived together, acting in unison as distinct social units.

The so-called "palaces" of the coastal cities differed very little from a set of ordinary houses. The residential unit at the core of a palace was no different in its components, layout or decoration from a merchant's house. A rare example of palatial grandeur occurs in a vaulted arcade that surrounds a deeply sunken reception courtyard in the palace of Songo Mnara.

Husuni Kubwa. One group of buildings on the coast stands out as unique. Husuni Kubwa (a Swahili name meaning the "large fortified house," probably attached to it centuries after it was built) is built on a cliff-girt, sandstone headland, in a commanding position overlooking the approaches to the roadstead of Kilwa. It stands in isolation, a mile outside the town. On the tip of the headland is a symmetrical and spacious courtyard, surrounded by arcades, with ornamental alcoves in each corner. Overlooking the sea is a group of pavilions containing a unique series of elaborately inscribed and carved stone moldings. At the other end of the court, a double suite of domestic rooms leads to a domestic courtyard at the rear. The private quarters also contain a great sunken pool, an octagon with apsidal recesses on four sides. Its elaborate plan indicates the love of geometry characteristic of much of the coastal architecture.

Beyond this was an audience court. Facing its public entrance were tiers of seats, lit at night by lamps placed in a chequerboard of niches on the flanking walls. Above these rose a pavilion, almost entirely open, where the ruler must have held court. Above the arcade that ran along one side of the audience court, and looking down on it, was a suite of vaulted rooms. Only remnants of their roofs now remain. These included a variety of barrel vaults and a conical dome fluted on the inside and outside. The vaults were supported on pendentives, carved friezes or quarter-

Opposite : plan of the stone buildings of the 15th-century town of Songo Mnara. All houses share the same basic plan.

Below : the court of the palace at Gedi differs little from that in a merchant's house: the platform provided seating; the monumental arched doors led to the reception rooms.

vaults. They must have embellished a series of reception rooms. Immediately beyond this, off the headland itself, is a courtyard many times larger than any other. Each side of it was lined by identical sets of store rooms or magazines. Wide corridors connected them. A separate outer wall enclosed the warehouse courtyard, the most vulnerable part of the complex. It also enclosed a well and was entered from a set of rooms that may have incorporated a guard post. On the shore, at the foot of the headland, are the remains of a small mosque. The palace was reached from the mosque by a monumental stairway, a fitting public and ceremonial approach.

Many features of Husuni Kubwa are unique: the pool, the vaults, the size of the courtyards, the complexity of the plan, the refinement of decoration and finish, the warehouse and magazines. This building incorporated many different social and economic functions, integrated in a single plan. It is concrete evidence of the dominance of one man; of complete, centralized economic controls; of wealth and of luxury. These do not recur in any coastal city. The social and historical implications of the building have not yet been fully studied.

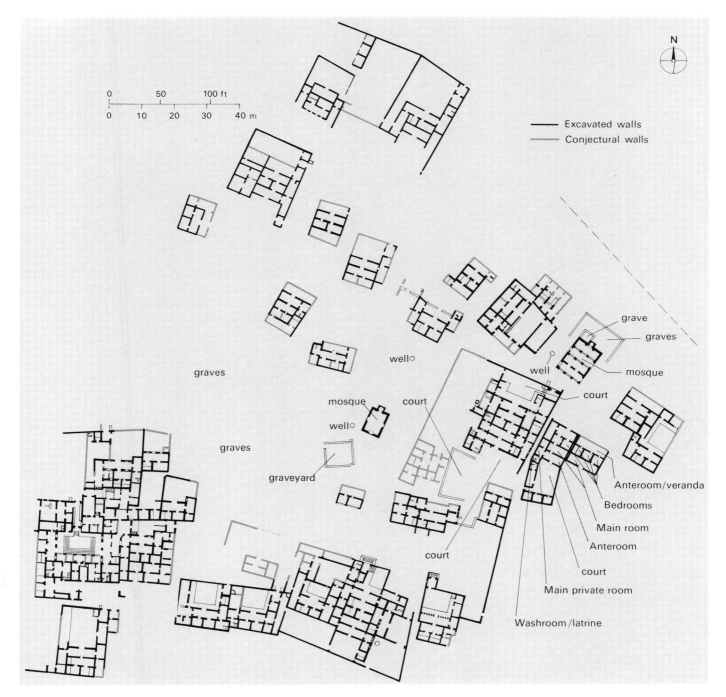

The Husuni complex is made more remarkable by a second building, across a small gully from Husuni Kubwa. Husuni Ndogo (the "small fortified house") is a rectangular enclosure, 230 feet by 170 feet across. It is surrounded by a wall of greater height, thickness and strength than any other on the coast. This is defended by 14 symmetrically placed bastions. No other building on the coast was fortified on such a scale, with such regular outworks or with such forethought. There is a single entrance. Short wing walls, scarcely more than buttresses, divide the interior into equal-sized portions. Otherwise, there is only the slightest evidence of buildings within the structure. Husuni Ndogo is an enigma. It may have been a market, with the wing walls demarcating separate stalls. Finds of many copper crucibles indicate that some industrial activities took place within its walls. It could equally have been a caravansaray or a barracks. There is no way of elucidating this because there is no comparison that can be made with any other East African building.

Mosques. Mosques were built in the center of each town. They were simple, rectangular chambers, divided by one, two or three rows of columns, which supported timber beams and mangrove rafters. The majority had flat roofs of coral concrete. The planning module and planning system were those of the domestic buildings.

The wall facing the entrance contained an apsidal recess, the *mihrab*, indicating the *qibla* or direction of Mecca. In the coastal architecture, the *mihrab* was surmounted by a simple pointed arch, its apex nicked and its moldings of fine coral blocks. It was framed by pilasters, each containing a recess to hold a lamp. The spandrels of the arch sometimes contained coral roundels, generally carved with complex interlaced and geometric patterns, or inset glazed Chinese or Persian bowls.

A detailed study of the coastal *mihrabs* shows a gradual development in style. There is a progressive elaboration of the moldings. In the 17th century, for instance, one innovation was the addition of a multi-lobed inner arch to the *mihrab*. In the 19th century the quality of building declined. Moldings were formed in plaster rather than carved in stone. Heavy, arched, masonry arcades were built across the halls, to replace the simple columns and beams. Long, rectangular halls gave way to squarer rooms.

Minbars, the stairs and platform beside the *mihrab*, from which preaching took place, are rare on the coast, even in a town's main congregational mosque. Where they exist, they are small, simple masonry structures. Wooden *minbars* are very rare. The only minarets on the coast are found in two early mosques in Mogadishu. They are stout, fortress-like, free-standing, cylindrical towers. Other mosques simply had a flight of stairs leading to the roof, from which the *muezzin* would make the call to pray.

Some minor regional differences in style are distinguishable. Mosques in the north tend to have a central row of square piers. In the south, two rows of octagonal columns are more common. Some groups of towns show a set of distinctive local architectural features, presumably indicative of a particular cultural stimulus or the individual genius of a single architect or architectural school. In Kilwa and nearby towns there is an unusual group of mosques with domed and vaulted roofs of unique elegance. The Friday Mosque, the Great Mosque

Opposite: this impression of Husuni Kubwa attempts to convey the unique elegance of the architecture, the complexity and variety of domes and ordered progression of public and private courts.

Below left: the palace of Husuni Kubwa, looking inland. The pool is visible (right front), with the audience court beyond and the warehouse court – here still overgrown and unexcavated – in the background.

Below: the audience court of Husuni Kubwa showing lamp niches, and the flight of steps and seats leading to the ruler's pavilion. The harbor entrance is visible in the background.

of Kilwa, was originally a small chamber with a flat roof supported on timber columns. A large, arcaded courtyard was added to it – the only one ever built on the coast. Its arcades were supported on a unique series of columns carved from a single block of coral. Off the arcade was a large, domed chamber, its dome faced inside with carefully cut and fitted stonework – another unique feature. Later, the whole court was roofed with alternating barrel vaults and hemispherical domes, supported on groined squinches – i.e. arched segments of dome built across each corner of the square bays to convert them to octagons. This is a significantly different vaulting method from the flat-faced, false pendentives of Husuni Kubwa. The vaulting system of the Great Mosque was reproduced in two mosques in the town nearby, in a mosque on the neighboring island of Sanje Majoma and in the arcades surrounding the courtyard of the palace on the adjacent island of Songo Mnara.

In Mogadishu, the Mosque of Fakhr al Din, founder of the ruling dynasty of the town, has an outstanding and unusual design. A complex and decorative system of timber beams divides the roof into nine bays. The central bay has a plain, tall dome. Above the main door is a conical vault – an octagon supported on plain pendentives, its surface decorated inside and out. This mosque is a careful, centralized composition, forming a single, unified space that is very uncharacteristic of the coastal architecture.

It is difficult, in a brief description of some of the important buildings of the coast, to give the full flavor of the architecture; to emphasize its individuality, without a tedious number of comparisons; or to illustrate the vigor and directness with which the culture responded to the potential of the East African climate and materials. It is a creative achievement rooted in a particular local social structure. It has a unity, homogeneity and longevity that deserve recognition. This recognition has been held in check because the society was urban and commercial. Its most obvious cultural sources appeared to be Islamic. Its outlook was maritime. Such things have been considered alien to Africa. But beneath the surface, the African origins, roots and values of the coastal culture are easily discernible.

Evidence of the past. The earliest foreign record of the coast is the *Periplus of the Erythraean Sea*. This is a description of the topography, inhabitants and commerce of the African coast from the Red Sea to Rhapta, "two days' sail beyond the island of Menouthias . . . the last mainland market town of Azania." Giant pirates lived there, who recognized a south Arabian hegemony and exported ivory, rhinoceros horn and tortoise shell. The origins, purpose and date of this document have been much argued over. It has often been considered a compilation, written from hearsay, and intended for sea

Above: the 13th-century minaret of the Friday Mosque in Mogadishu. The rest of the mosque and the surrounding buildings are much later – probably 19th century.

Below: the rectangular, bastioned enclosure of Husuni Ndogo. The excavations expose the stone foundations of insubstantial and unexplained buildings.

captains and merchants. The latest and most convincing analysis concludes that it is the eye-witness report of an agent of imperial Rome, written for government use in the early 2nd century AD. Though no material evidence has yet been found, most interpretations of the *Periplus* place Rhapta on one of the major river estuaries in Tanzania, probably the Rufiji.

That most remarkable traveler, Ibn Battuta, described his visits to Mogadishu and Kilwa. He was one of many. Such works are complemented by local dynastic histories. Only one, the Kilwa Chronicle, written about 1520, survives in an early form. De Barros incorporated it in his *da Asia*, published in 1552. A second version exists in a 19th-century copy, once owned by the sultan of Zanzibar. The many discrepancies between the two make for considerable uncertainty in any historical reconstruction.

Historical studies have been supplemented by archaeological fieldwork. Scientific archaeological work started on the coast in 1948, when James Kirkman began a ten-year excavation campaign in the city of Gedi, not far north of Kenya's present main port, Mombasa. In 1958 Neville Chittick initiated excavations at Kilwa on a very considerable scale. They were continued every year for seven years. Chittick spent the subsequent three years excavating a much earlier town on Manda Island in northern Kenya.

Archaeologists have probed a dozen or more sites on a much smaller scale. A great deal of this effort has been devoted to the clearance (and conservation and restoration) of major buildings: palaces, mosques and the most substantial merchants' houses in the town centers. No one would claim that these areas are representative of a whole settlement or society. This bias has inevitably produced a somewhat distorted and incomplete view of coastal society.

Kilwa, Mogadishu and Zanzibar minted their own coinage: small, paper-thin copper disks, bearing a sultan's name and, on the reverse, a rhyming couplet of praise or exhortation. They were of little intrinsic value and were presumably intended for use in small everyday transactions. Twelve sultans of Kilwa are named on these coins. The most recent analysis of the Chronicle suggests that all but one ruled in the 13th or 14th century. One sultan not mentioned in either version of the Chronicle is placed after 1520.

Coins recovered from stratified deposits have extremely inconsistent associations. The degree of wear that they bear shows no consistent pattern. It varies greatly and randomly. The weight of the archaeological evidence suggests that the names the coins bear do not denote the reigns in which they were struck. Their value as chronological indicators is therefore very slight. Hoards of foreign coins have been found up and down the coast, many of doubtful provenance and authenticity. Roman coins have been found in hoards that also contain much later coins. A gold dinar, struck in 798 by the wazir of Harun al Rashid (the caliph of Baghdad, who instigated the *Arabian Nights*), was unearthed in Zanzibar in 1896. It is the earliest object on the coast to confirm foreign contacts.

Foreign ceramics were imported in considerable amounts. A blue-glazed Sasanian-Islamic earthenware is the earliest. It was produced in southern Persia in the 7th to 10th centuries, and exported, particularly from Siraf. It has been found on the islands of Manda, Zanzibar and Kilwa. There is still considerable uncertainty about the precise date of manufacture of many of the later imported ceramics. Islamic and Chinese wares, found together in coastal deposits and clearly made at much the same time, have been assigned dates up to a century apart in their homelands. Excavators on the coast have, not surprisingly, arrived at equally discrepant attributions of date for contemporaneous sets of finds. Precision in this field has not yet been attained.

Very few inscriptions in mosques or on gravestones survive. Even fewer bear dates: a further disappointment for fieldworkers. The earliest inscription found on the coast is a dedication, dated 1107, incorporated in the *mihrab* of a mosque on Zanzibar, that was rebuilt in the 18th century. In Mogadishu, three mosques incorporate 13th-century inscriptions. There are grave-stones in Mogadishu of the same date, commemorating Shirazi

Above: the arched entrance – with a nicked apex characteristic of East African buildings – to the minaret at Mogadishu. The dedicatory inscription records the start of building on 1 Muharram 636 AH (14 August 1238 AD).
Below: the *mihrab* of the Friday Mosque of Gedi in the style of the early 16th century. A cable-patterned molding surrounds it. Ceramic bowls were inset in pilasters and spandrels.

Above: one of a small group of vaulted and domed buildings built on Kilwa and nearby in the 15th century.

Right: coins and beads from Kilwa. Glass cane beads predominate. Others include large remolded beads, top; carnelian, left; snail and ostrich shell disks, right; wound glass, lower center; and aragonite, bottom. The coins are about $\frac{3}{4}$ inch across.

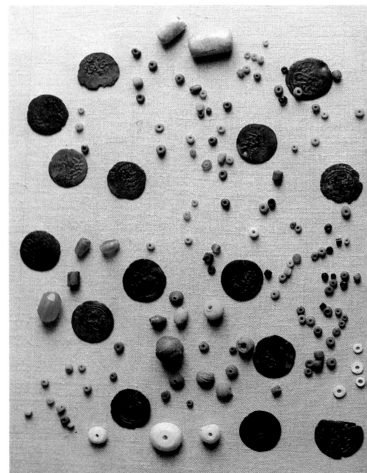

immigrants. The palace of Husuni Kubwa on Kilwa Island had three inscriptions. Two of them were simply pious exhortations. One named the sultan visited by Ibn Battuta in the 14th century. Four gravestones from Kilwa bear dates: they range from the 14th to the 18th century.

Growth of the first cities. The origins of the coastal society lie with the Zanj, the name by which East Africans were known by the first foreigners to meet them. It survives in the names Azania and Zanzibar and, hence, Tanzania. The Zanj enter history in the 8th century with the insurrection of many hundreds of Zanj slaves, who were employed in draining the marshes of the Tigris river in Mesopotamia. The Zanj institutions and system of government were African. Their belief and practices were invariably described by Arab visitors as "pagan." They lived on the northern fringe of the Bantu-speaking peoples and were themselves probably Cushitic speakers:

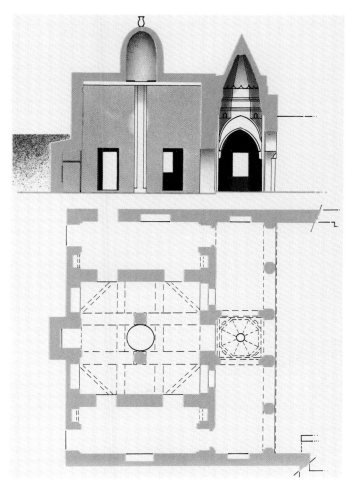

Above: the Mosque of Fakhr al Din in Mogadishu, with its domes and centralized plan, is a unique survival of the early architecture, reminiscent of Husuni Kubwa. The *mihrab* bears the date 667 AH (1269 AD).

Above right: the *mihrab* of the Friday Mosque on Manda Island is carved of coral. The foliate or lobed inner arches are characteristic of 17th-century designs.

"Ethiopians," as al Masudi described them in the 10th century. (A northern influence on the culture has already been suggested as the source of the pillar tombs.) The Zanj had no boats and did not voyage themselves, but their control of the earliest markets was absolute. Their initial resistance to Islam was strong.

Civil wars, conquests and sectarian persecutions rent the Arab homelands from the 8th century. They caused many to flee. But the refugees are unlikely, as all traditions would affirm, to have traveled far. Certainly, they did not emigrate in great numbers to tropical Africa. In the 10th century the first group of distinct Muslim immigrant people in East Africa is described. They lived in one of several settlements near a Zanj town on the island of Zanzibar. Only in the 12th century did systematic Arab migrations introduce substantial permanent foreign elements into coastal society. This initiated the cultural amalgam that is characteristic of the coastal civilization:

one whose roots were African, but whose many foreign elements were synthesized in a unique and distinctive whole.

Manda Island, in the Lamu archipelago, has yielded the earliest archaeological evidence of a substantial settlement on the coast. A small collection of Sasanian-Islamic wares and early Chinese celadons and porcelains show that it was founded about the 9th century. The site faces the mainland and is separated from it by a narrow, mangrove-choked channel. Pottery is spread over 47 acres. A massive sea wall, of squared coral blocks up to three feet across, ran along the shores of the settlement. It is the only such structure on the coast. From the beginning, important buildings were of coral and lime mortar. They exist in only a small part of the town. Burned clay bricks, set in a mud mortar, were used for some buildings. So far, little detail has been published of the Manda buildings and town.

Manda is the only town of its kind so far discovered on the coast. It showed no signs of change, before it fell into decay in the 13th century. Many of the ceramics suggest that it was a trading partner of Siraf, the great port of southern Persia. In this, as in its date, it is very much the archeological equivalent of the town that al Masudi, in the 10th century, called Qanbalu. It is tempting to equate the two but, if descriptions are reliable, this seems unlikely. Qanbalu seems to have been a much larger island, further to the south and further from the mainland.

Scatters of foreign pottery like those on Manda have been found near Mogadishu, at Unguja Kuu on Zanzibar, at two sites on the mainland opposite Zanzibar and in the earliest deposits on Kilwa. Burned clay bricks like those of Manda have been found below a mosque in Ungwana. Cut and squared masonry blocks were used in building the first mosques on Kilwa and the nearby islands of Sanje ya Kati and Kisimani Mafia. These buildings are all dated to the 12th century. The use of squared coral blocks and mud bricks is a survival of building traditions alien to the coast. They ignore the potential that coral offers as a building material. Such building methods were soon abandoned.

Mogadishu, the northernmost important port of the coast, rose to prominence in the mid-12th century, when a Yemeni clan settled there and took power. By the early 13th century it was the most important town on the coast, deriving its wealth from control of Sofala and the southern gold trade. Yemeni control was interrupted, here and in the other towns of the Benadir coast, when migrants from Shiraz became powerful. (This change is illustrated by the gravestones of Shirazis in Mogadishu that bear dates of this period.) It is from the Benadir coast that the Shirazis, in de Barros's words, spread "like a slow plague" south, to establish and rule many of the towns of the Zanj coast.

Kilwa came under Shirazi rule in the late 12th century. It had already existed for three centuries or more. For much of this time it was simply a fishing camp. A collection of wattle-and-daub huts was built by sailors on a low-lying sandspit on the edge of the sea. Once Islam was established, congregational mosques were built at Kilwa using squared coral blocks and wooden columns. The first coins, of copper and even some minute silver specimens, were minted in the town. The new and growing town may, as the Chronicle describes, have taken some time to establish its independence from the island of Kisimani Mafia. The much nearer island of Shanga, with extensive mainland territories, was a rival. Eventually, it was Kilwa's first conquest.

Traditionally, it was the commercial venture of another Yemeni family, the Mahdali, that made Kilwa preeminent on the coast. A younger son of the family had established himself far to the south, on the Sofala coast. Eventually Kilwa ousted Mogadishu and gained a monopoly over gold exports. This was a development to which Kilwa's position in the navigation cycle clearly lent itself. About 1300 AD, backed by his family's Sofalan interests, Hasan bin Talut took the Mahdali dynasty to power in Kilwa. Thirty years later, his grandson, Hasan bin Sulaiman, had such wealth that he could build the palace, warehouses and barracks or market of the Husunis. His palace was isolated from the town and dwarfed it and its society. He held a position of power that no subsequent ruler matched. Even

Ibn Battuta was impressed by Hasan's piety and generosity and the wide-ranging connections of his court.

As Kilwa flourished, Mogadishu declined. The Great Mosque and the Mosque of Fakhr al Din were built in Mogadishu early in the 14th century. These were the last achievements of consequence in the town. Kilwa itself had its setbacks. The mint ceased operating before about 1375. At the same time, the Great Mosque fell into ruins. Only the dome of Sultan Hasan survived. There was a revival of fortune early in the 15th century. At this time, the courtyard of the Great Mosque was covered by vaults and domes. Several small mosques, in the same elegant style, embellished different quarters of the town. South Arabian connections remained. The sultan had studied in Aden as a young man. Later, he was visited by the ruler of that town. But the ruler's monopolies had gone. The sultans abandoned Husuni and occupied a house in the town, little grander than that of any prosperous merchant. Though the titles and offices suggest an ordered hierarchy, the associates of the sultan were no more than a small commercial oligarchy of near equals. Succession disputes and revolts started. Factions within the ruling dynasty intrigued for political power. In the process, Sofala became independent and was lost. Kilwa developed no further, until it started to participate in the slave trade during the 18th century.

Prosperity and decline. Many towns were established on the coast in the 13th century. But almost all significant building in stone – evidence of solid, commercial substance – came in the 14th and 15th centuries. In the north, not far from Manda Island, Ungwana, with its ornate mosques and tombs, saw a great deal of building that can be dated archaeologically to between 1350 and 1450. Its connections with Egypt are mentioned in Swahili chronicles. This evidence of local individuality is borne out archaeologically by a distinctive range of imported Mamluk glazed wares recovered from excavations. Further south, Gedi, the most complete remaining town of the coast and the most extensively excavated, was rebuilt in the 15th century. Many of the smaller mainland towns – where only the ruins of a mosque or *mihrab* now remain – were collecting centers for ivory and depots for small coasting dhows. Probably they were also centers where food, especially grain, could be grown or bought to supply the larger towns. Kilwa, on its near-barren island, may have imported rice from Mafia Island or even Madagascar. All the coastal towns retained their autonomy and cultivated their own distinctive trade connections. They were not colonies of a major town but independent polities. The idea of an "empire of Zanj" is even more of a fantasy than the "empire of Munhu Mutapa."

The rise of Kilwa at the start of the 14th century and its decline in the mid-15th century reflect a worldwide trade cycle that was particularly significant around the seaboard of the northern Indian Ocean. They mirror events in the interior even more closely. Great Zimbabwe's rise and decline are closely contemporary with Kilwa's: so close that they are the firmest evidence so far available of the commercial interdependence of the kingdoms. The later 15th century saw a series of upheavals throughout eastern Africa. The abandonment of the Great Zimbabwe, the fragmentation of its ruling dynasty, the wars and conquests of the Munhu Mutapa on the north of the plateau, the extinction of the copper traders of Urungwe and the revolt of Sofala against Kilwa's hegemony probably all happened in these decades. They left the coast weak and disunited. It quickly succumbed in the face of Portuguese attacks in the early 16th century.

Swahili traders had responded with understanding and sensitivity to local commercial opportunities. They had acted in consort with local rulers. They may have tried to increase production, particularly of ivory and gold, by trying to enter into direct and exploitative relations with the producers. But they were free of all military, territorial and political ambition.

The Portuguese were very different. When they first landed in East Africa, they were concerned solely with participating in the spice trade of the Indian Ocean. In Africa, their initial aims were simply to protect their flank from attack by the Turkish navy, which operated out of the Red Sea. However, as soon as they realized the potential wealth of the gold trade, they were determined to take control of it. Using sophisticated vessels and weapons of war, they sacked Kilwa and other towns. Forts were built at Kilwa and Sofala and a rigorous control of all sea traffic was established. Portuguese trade was a royal monopoly. It was delegated by the Crown to the viceroy and then bought and sold down to the fort captains. Within this system, fraud and corruption became institutionalized. The Portuguese had little organizing ability. They combined an ignorance of their trading partners with an inherent contempt for them. With a few ruthless and inflexible men, they destroyed a centuries-old commercial system. The Swahili trade died or dispersed to become a clandestine traffic passing through new ports free of Portuguese knowledge and interference, like Angoche, north of the Zambezi estuary. The Portuguese sent out expeditions to penetrate the interior and seek the mines. They established new trading fairs. Ultimately they demanded political control of the gold mines from the Munhu Mutapa. This was largely granted by 1634.

By then, the general prosperity of the coast was gone. Even towns in the north beyond direct Portuguese interference were very weak. Internecine warfare had caused great strain. The Galla were pressing down from the north. Refugees from northern towns that they had threatened or overrun gave Gedi a brief new lease of life. The refugees reoccupied a small part of the old town and enclosed it in a defensive wall. Several other towns – Songo Mnara near Kilwa was one – were probably also surrounded by defensive walls at this time. Gedi was probably destroyed soon after by Mombasa in revenge for its help, and that of its ally Malindi, to Portuguese expeditionary forces. Ungwana, like Kilwa, was sacked by the Portuguese in 1505. Further disruption came from the south, as the Zimba moved north from their homelands near Lake Malawi in a wave of slaughter and pillage. The civilizations of the coast and the southern plateau were almost entirely extinguished.

Events in the interior. The economic links between the East African coast and the Zambezian plateau initiated important social and political changes in both areas. North of the Zambezi, the interior of East Africa received none of the benefits. It played no part in the trading economy of the coast. Not a single foreign import earlier than about the 18th century – not a sherd, shell or bead – has been found on an archaeological site inland from the coastal cities.

There are some obvious geographical reasons for this isolation. The thorn scrub, the *nyika*, that separates the coast from the interior, is dry and sparsely settled. There are no natural routes through it. No great rivers provide direction and sustenance for long distances inland as they do on the Sofala coast. The highlands of the far interior had none of the mineral wealth of the Zimbabwe states. The ivory, rhinoceros horn and skins that they could provide were obtainable more easily and abundantly nearer the coast. Only in the mid-19th century, when Zanzibari slaving caravans started raiding as far inland as the Great Lakes, did the East African interior feel the effects of foreign contacts.

The lack of long-distance trade did not preclude change. Kenya and Uganda are on the northern borders of Bantu settlement. They adjoin the territories of Central Sudanic, Nilotic and Cushitic speakers. Encounters between people speaking very different languages and with centuries of different cultural development behind them, would inspire all sorts of changes, through many different means. This was especially true in the relationships between cattle herders and settled farmers. Their interaction was encouraged by local topography. In the East African highlands, dry open pasture lands alternate with pockets of well-watered fertile agricultural land. Environmental factors, geographical isolation, ethnic and linguistic diversity and different subsistence economies acted as spurs to development. Change in the East African highlands has also been seen as determined by the single factor of race. As we have seen, many theories assume that pastoral Caucasoids, the tall, light-skinned, fine-featured Hamites of the north, imposed government and order on backward Bantu agriculturalists, usually through the institution of "divine kingship."

As in the south, the later Iron Age, around the Great Lakes of the highlands of East Africa, represents a deep, widespread and sudden transformation from the Early

Iron Age. This happened in the early second millennium AD. Throughout these parts of East Africa, later Iron Age sites can be identified by pottery vessels that are covered with patterns that were made by rolling plaited and knotted cords over the damp clay. These "rouletted wares" are not found south or west of the Great Lakes. But this decoration masks a regional diversity greater than that of the later Iron Age of the south. Regional typologies and temporal changes in pottery styles have not been studied or compared in any systematic way. Their social implications are little understood. The origins of the later Iron Age of East Africa are obscure.

High grasslands stretch west of Lake Victoria to the lakes and mountains of the western Rift Valley. Rolling downlands, with few trees and punctuated only by great euphorbia plants, are covered with the short tufted grass on which cattle thrive. In this "interlacustrine region" the pastoral and tribal kingdoms of Nyoro, Toro, Nkore and Rwanda grew up and lasted for some seven centuries, until they were extinguished by the demands of national unity that came with independence from colonial rule in the 1960s.

The largest prehistoric site and the ancestor of these states is Bigo, in the grasslands of Nkore, west of Lake Victoria. The Katonga river and its tributary, the Kakinga, are now sluggish or stagnant streams, choked in papyrus. Much of the land on their banks is swamp. Further back, low-lying water meadows are covered in lush pasturage. Two square miles of this land between the rivers have been enclosed by earthwork banks and ditches. In all there are some seven miles of ditches, up to 13 feet deep and 35 feet wide. Considerable stretches of ditch had to be cut through rock. Altogether, over seven million cubic feet of rock and earth were dug. (This represents an operation on a far greater scale, for instance, than any single building project at Great Zimbabwe. The massive outer wall of the Elliptical Building of Great Zimbabwe is only a fortieth of the volume of the Bigo banks.) The soil of the ditches was generally piled outside them to form the banks. This reversal of normal defensive measures destroyed any military value the earthworks might have had. The ditches provided no protection for defenders and the banks no obstacle to attackers when built in this order. There is further evidence of their military weakness. The earthworks and their interiors are overlooked by high ground outside them. The outer walls are broken at least 12 times by wide, undefended gaps. It seems, indeed, that this great work was devised solely to control cattle. The enormous area inside the banks shows very little evidence of habitation. On rising ground at the center, there is a smaller system of ditches, banks and mounds, that was more readily defensible. It resembles the royal enclosures of later courts and capitals – the *orireremba* of Nkore capitals. Even inside these structures, there were few finds at Bigo. Carbon samples date Bigo to between the mid-14th and end of the 15th century (the period

Above: Fort Jesus, Mombasa, built in 1593 to the designs of Joao Batista Cairato, architect of fortifications in Milan and Malta, Chief Architect of India. It is a textbook example of European military buildings of its time.

Below: Fort St Sebastian on Mozambique Island, the principal Portuguese captaincy in eastern Africa. The early 16th-century chapel of Our Lady of the Bulwark, beyond the ramparts, is the earliest surviving European building on the coast.

when Great Zimbabwe and the coastal cities were also at their height).

Five miles away, on both sides of Bigo, on the banks of the Katonga river, are two smaller earthworks. A few miles up the Katonga river is Ntusi. This site, unlike Bigo, shows very considerable evidence of habitation. There are spreads of potsherds and middens covering over 500 acres. At the center of the settlement, two water reservoirs have been constructed by scooping out a stream bed and piling the soil into two large earth dams.

Bigo and its related settlements were the product of organized labor forces, so large that they could only have been collected and administered by a centralized authority with considerable power. The origins of the Bigo state are obscure. Its successors are better known. Bweyorere, a Nkore capital, is one of many courts where earthworks were built around the king's residence in a style whose ancestry in Bigo is readily apparent. The kingdoms of Uganda have retained many traditions about their founders and their ancestry. The Chwezi feature in many of them. Consequently they have achieved a certain historical credibility. They are usually interpreted as a dynasty that ruled for a short time, two or three generations, about 20 generations (say 500 years) ago. They were pastoralists. Long-horned cattle were a central element of their culture. They are credited with introducing a sophisticated technology, a centralized monarchy, its institutions and appurtenances, to the interlacustrine area. Their empire – Kitara – disintegrated as a result of strife, misfortune or epidemic. Prehistorians credit the Chwezi with building the earthworks of the Bigo culture. The dates of the archaeological sites and the time span of the traditions coincide. They make this a tempting correlation. It also seems to give useful confirmation to the validity of the relationship between the evidence of archaeology and oral tradition. Some anthropologists have been more cautious. Some have even doubted the historical existence of the Chwezi entirely. For them, Chwezi traditions are best seen as expressions of the cultural values attached to kingship. Kingship is an abstract concept. Its concrete meaning and implications have been embodied by different people at different times in ideas of the Chwezi as gods, devils or ancestors. The association of the Chwezi with the earthworks of the Bigo culture looks as if it is a recent, popular fantasy. One can compare it to local superstitions in Europe that give so many earthworks names like "Devil's Dyke."

Kingdoms of cattle-herders and farmers. From about 1500 the history of the interlacustrine kingdoms is on surer ground. About this time, groups of nomadic, cattle-herding Nilotes entered Uganda from the southeast of the Sudan Republic. These were the Luo. In the north, they established the Nyoro kingdom. They became assimilated into the existing Bantu-speaking population. The retreat of other Bantu groups in the face of the Luo gave rise to the southern kingdoms of Toro and Nkore. The Luo threat was a strong incentive towards the formation of centralized governments. In some areas the Luo settled into an uneasy symbiosis with the Bantu agriculturists. In Nkore the ruler became a neutral broker between the two groups. His capital became a meeting place for both. Government was largely shared by both groups on terms of equality. In other states – particularly Rwanda – the Nilotic invaders established an aristocracy, an exclusive minority that held the Bantu farmers in subservience. They used cattle as a means of buying Bantu wives in a one-way system of exchange that reduced the strength and size of the original Bantu population. They also used cattle as a means of patronage to reinforce permanent client relationships. This was a system that bore many resemblances to the feudal societies of Europe.

The view of these pastoralists as a sharply distinct and all-powerful racial group is mistaken. Physical differences can be seen as the result of the high-protein diet and distinctive life-style of endogamous pastoral groups over several centuries. The figure of the tall, lithe members of the Tutsi ruling aristocracy of Rwanda that has so often been contrasted with the stocky Negroid appearance of their Hutu Bantu-speaking clients and servitors is largely a distortion, a legacy of colonial outlooks.

The effect of the Nilotic migrations can be exaggerated.

They represent the final and most dramatic episode in a long history of interaction between pastoralists and agriculturalists. Their relationships were more often than not creative and stimulating. They did not evoke stereotyped responses. Economic diversity destroyed village self-sufficiency. It created systems of interdependence that encouraged more complex systems of government. It was the situation that provided the stimulus, not the innate character of any particular ethnic group.

Environment also played its part. The emphasis has so far been on the kingdoms of the high grasslands. In the humid lowlands, on the western and northern shores of Lake Victoria, the Buganda kingdom arose. It was perhaps the most powerful and famous of all the interlacustrine states. Rich volcanic soils, an equable climate, good rains and warmth enabled the population to subsist almost entirely on the plantain or banana. These trees provide a certain yield. They can be cropped throughout the year and need little labor to tend them. Half an acre of planted land can support one person. With subsidiary crops a family farm can be established on between two and eight acres. The land can be kept in permanent cultivation. A surplus is easily achieved and accumulated. In Buganda, land can be owned outright by an individual. It can be sold or inherited. This is a most unusual situation in sub-Saharan Africa. Its potential for creating obvious differences in wealth, and hence a stratified society, is obvious. With this stimulus, it is not surprising that the origins of the Buganda kingdom date back to before the arrival of the Nilotes.

From this review it can be seen how the interior of East Africa holds a mirror to the economic complexities of the coast. It shows how kingdoms can develop without the stimulus of rich resources, external trade, foreign intervention or "civilized example."

Below left: one of the outer ditches of the Bigo earthworks, cleared and excavated in 1960.

Below: plan of the earthworks of Bigo. After Posnansky.

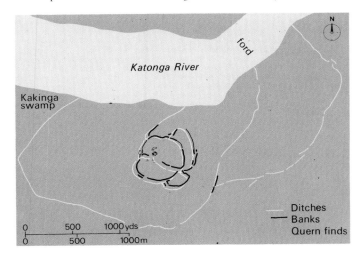

Sculpture of Ife and Benin

The early kingdoms of the Nigerian forest are known almost entirely from their sculpture. These are objects of such striking technical accomplishment and aesthetic quality that they have distracted scholars from any real search for their human contexts. The refined realism, repose and serenity of Ife sculptures have led many to assume that this is an "aristocratic" art associated with gods or kings – or both. The elaborate jewelry, beadwork and headdresses depicted on some statues are used to support such ideas, but they remain entirely speculative. There is no doubt that the art of Benin – at least in bronze or brass – was a manifestation of the royal court. Plaques had covered the pillars and beams of the palace. Life size heads adorned the shrines. The guild of brass smiths worked almost exclusively for the king.

Our knowledge is so much greater and more precise for Benin than for Ife that it is tempting – but dangerous – to interpret the one from the other. Some art historians derive the brass-casting and sculptural traditions of Benin from Ife. Traditions seem to support them: many motifs are common to both. Other art historians, equally authoritative, disagree. So far, few excavations that will place the art of Ife in its social surroundings and help understand it have been undertaken. All the Ife terracottas shown here have been deliberately chosen to come from one such excavation – on Obalara's land. They are all dated to the 14th century and all belong together, dedicated to a single shrine. Despite our incomprehension, the art offers enormous aesthetic pleasure. Some, with President Senghor, will identify the art of Ife with the spirituality that he sees as the essence of negritude. Others will find in Benin an earthy, secular force, an energy and directness that have no peer and are infinitely more African.

A group of human skulls (*right*) was placed beside the Obalara shrine; with them were three sculptures. The half-life-size head (*previous page*) expresses obesity, malevolence and horror with such force that the very anatomy is distorted. It far transcends the accepted canon of Ife art in emotion and power. The miserable creature (*left*) with bags under his eyes, swollen lips, a running nose and a goiter lay close by. Both heads are broken from larger statues. The torso and arms of the sickly figure were modeled in thin clay in a far more rudimentary fashion and to a different scale from the head. With these was a sculpted pot with a leopard's head, depicting human sacrifice (on p. 115). The theme of each piece thus correlates in some way with the emotions generated by the skulls.

Left: this head, half-life size, typifies the common conception of Ife art: natural, serene, classic. It and all the terracottas on the facing page were found in a careful arrangement beside the Obalara shrine. Seemingly, damaged, "dead" terracottas were treated as carefully as the human skulls and dedicated to the same shrine. The vertical striations on this head may not represent scarifications but a means of emphasizing modeling and shadows. Traces of red paint remain on the face. The eyeballs were painted white.

Opposite: this head with its conical top is strongly reminiscent of the beaded crowns of Yoruba kings.

Below: the elaborate facial markings on this head probably represent scarifications.

Left: the three small keloid scarifications on the temple of this head can be matched on many sculptures in Benin.

Right: this superb bronze, 20 inches high, is larger, more complex and more dynamic than any found in Ife itself. It is one of 11 bronzes kept in shrines at Tada on the Niger river directly north of Ife and associated with Tsoede, founder of the Nupe kingdom. Its history is otherwise unknown. The others are quite different in style.

Below: this simple standing figure, 15 inches tall, was one of a pair, buried together a short distance away from the other offerings at the Obalara shrine. The body proportions, with the exaggerated size of the head, are characteristic of most African sculpture.

Left: this head from Benin is one of six or seven very similar pieces depicting a queen mother. She wears a collar and headdress of coral. Like all such life size Benin heads, this would have been placed on a royal altar. The casting is extremely thin, the regalia comparatively simple and subsidiary to the facial features. The appearance is, for Benin, realistic. Such features place it in the "Early Period" and closest to the Ife tradition, for those who accept the Ife connection. The artistic tradition of Benin clearly differs greatly from that of Ife. It has an energy, simplicity and emotion that imply a fundamentally different approach to art. The sculpture of Benin is almost certainly later than that of Ife. It probably started about the 16th century.

Right: only some 27 so-called "bronze" sculptures – in fact almost all are brass – are known from Ife – a minute fraction of the Benin opus. Most of these were found in building work near the royal palace in 1938 and 1939. Seven were found in builders' diggings on the outskirts of the old town, at Ita Yemoo, in 1957. They included this figure, 19 inches high. It is generally believed to represent an Oni, because it is bedecked in elaborate beadwork and jewelry. The proportions are distinctively African. In his left hand he holds a horn. Similar horns – in pairs – adorn both the sculpted cult pots from Obalara's land (*opposite*). In Yoruba traditional medicine, horns filled with magic are extremely powerful instruments – for curing or cursing.

Left: this Ife "bronze" is unique in several respects. It has, as long as is known, been kept in the royal palace. It is the only sculpture of almost pure copper, and it is the only mask known from Ife. Slits beneath the eyes enabled the wearer to look out. Like several of the other full-size bronze heads, it has been pierced so that hair and beard can be attached to it. It is traditionally said to represent Obalufon II, the third Oni of Ife, who usurped the throne of his uncle Oronmiyan, youngest but most powerful son of the Creator Oduduwa.

Above: three terracotta heads, each about $1\frac{1}{2}$ inches high, are depicted on this pot. The central one is naturalistic, striated and has a crested headdress. It is flanked by conical heads with rudimentary faces which resemble royal beaded crowns. One of them has protuberances on top reminiscent of the birds perched on the apex of many crowns. The heads stand in an open case, under a cover of cloth or palm fronds hung from a rope. A snake coils around the pot and rests its head on the cover. This pot from Obalara's land is thus a unique and contemporary record of sculptures in their functional context. The snake is reminiscent of the great brass pythons that curled their way down the gables of the palace of Benin (*right*). Plaques of Portuguese heads adorn the palace columns and leopards guard the entrance. The feet of a bird remain on the gable's apex. Such birds are shown on the palace gables in an engraving of 1668 (see frontispiece).

Another pot (*left*) showing cult objects – many identical to the ones above – lay with the skulls and the two terracotta heads showing disease and horror, beside the shrine on Obalara's land. It shows a human sacrifice in the form of a decapitated head with a rope gag (to stifle curses) through its mouth. Beside this stands a leopard. The vessel's mouth also takes the form of a leopard's head. Leopards were an important symbol of royalty in Benin. The Oba is said to have kept a menagerie of the animals and is depicted overcoming them on several plaques. These superb ivory examples (*right*) are both carved from five tusks. The treatment of the fur is stylized in the same way in both Ife and Benin. The symbols shared by Ife and Benin may point to a common fund of beliefs more than to a direct artistic connection.

A Benin head of an Oba attributed to the "Middle Period." It is more coarsely and less naturalistically sculpted than its predecessors. The coral bead collar is now much larger and covers the chin. The casting is thicker. In this typology the Benin plaques are all placed in the same period, which is dated to the 17th or 18th century. Many of these typological features may however have a functional or social significance rather than a chronological one. We still have no independent means of dating the Benin pieces.

One of the three altars erected by the present Oba of Benin to his immediate predecessors. This one is dedicated to his father, Eweka. Before the palace was destroyed in 1897, it is said that 13 separate courtyards had altars dedicated to different royal ancestors. In the small group of figures, the Oba is flanked by guards and leopards. He holds an *eben*, a ceremonial sword, and a gong. At the front of the altar are ground stone axes, believed to be thunderbolts and, hence, symbols of supernatural power. Behind are carved wooden rattles or staves that signify authority transmitted from previous Obas. Bells surround the altar, which is stained with blood from sacrifices. The bronzes all date from the 19th century. The heads of Obas, holding carved ivory tusks, have elaborate coral headdresses characteristic of the "Late Period." The size and shape of the altar are like those of ancient Ife.

Perhaps more than anywhere else in Africa, trade played a key role in the development of the kingdoms of the West African savanna. Exchanges between groups within West Africa have a long prehistory. They can be traced back to the time men first settled in villages. Early settlements on the Upper Nile obtained beads of amazonite from the Ennedi mountains in the eastern Sahara. In the tropical forests the stones that were commonly ground and polished to form ax heads occur in only a few areas. The Bibiani hills of southern Ghana are, for instance, an important source of greenstone. Axes of these stones are found considerable distances away from their sources. Though some ground-stone ax heads are known to have been made centuries after permanent agriculture had started, their manufacture and exchange may well have begun with the first farmers. Kintampo farmers, who lived on the edges of the forests of modern Ghana, traded their characteristic rasplike stone tools of a distinctive form of dolomite. They also had regular mines where grindstones were made in considerable quantities, presumably for distribution well beyond the local communities.

In the 8th century BC the Phoenician port of Carthage was established. Other Carthaginian towns grew up along the Mediterranean coast: the Roman towns of Sabratha, Tripoli and Leptis Magna were all Carthaginian foundations. There has been a great deal of speculation on the extent of Phoenician knowledge of black Africa. No doubt the Phoenicians established some contacts with the nomads of the desert fringes. It is possible that a knowledge of ironworking was transmitted to the Negro inhabitants of the southern savanna through such intermediaries in the mid-first millennium BC. Travel by sea through the Pillars of Hercules – the Straits of Gibraltar – and south along the Atlantic shores of West Africa was a more difficult venture, even for sailors as skilled and intrepid as the Phoenicians. The African coast north of Senegal is barren, waterless and without shelter. Though boats were technically capable of the voyage south, beating back northwards against the constant north-easterly winds of this region would have been impossible for craft with square sails and only oars for steering. Nonetheless, in 480 BC, a Carthaginian captain, Hanno, is said to have sailed, with 60 vessels, down the desert coast of Africa. Eventually they reached tropical marshland and a high mountain belching fire, the "Chariot of the Gods." This was presumably a volcano. In this case, it can only be identified with Mount Cameroun, visible from the sea deep in the Gulf of Guinea. It is impossible to identify any of Hanno's other landmarks. Indeed his report has a distinct air of unreality. It is now widely considered to be a forgery.

Previous page: Benin figures, in different styles, whose helmets, pendants and staffs suggest they are the royal messengers from Ife who ratified the Oba of Benin's succession. Their unusual scarifications also occur on Ife terracottas.

In about 450 BC Herodotus described the Garamantes, who lived in desert oases beyond the settled farmlands of the Mediterranean coast. He described their four-wheeled chariots. Engravings of such vehicles have been found deep in the desert, particularly around the prehistoric copper mines of southern Mauritania. Paintings of light two-wheeled chariots, with the horses that pull them spread-eagled in a distinctive "flying gallop," have been recorded from the Fezzan, through the mountains of the Tassili, Ahaggar and Adrar des Iforas, almost to the Niger river. They suggest that regular communications and a fixed route had been developed across the Sahara. Nonetheless, these flimsy vehicles, designed for warfare or hunting, can scarcely have transported much in the way of trade goods. This scanty and uncertain evidence scarcely goes as far as establishing that there were significant commercial links between the Mediterranean and black Africa.

After the Punic wars and the Roman conquest of North Africa, the Mediterranean coastlands became the granary of the Roman empire. Beyond the *limes*, the inland frontier of Rome, the oases of the Fezzan were settled and farmed. On occasion, Roman military expeditions had to be sent to subdue them. Further afield again, there lived nomadic tribesmen of the desert. Their only contact with Rome was a trade in precious stones – "carbuncles" – described by Pliny. (Carbuncles were probably worked chalcedony. However, this is uncertain enough for it to be possible to hold that they were the "aggrey" beads that were coveted centuries later in many of the forest kingdoms of West Africa.) While the earlier Mediterranean towns may have traded with their immediate hinterlands, the Roman cities that succeeded them became wealthy on the produce of local farmers, not on strangers bringing exotic riches from across the desert.

In the last half of the 7th century AD the armies of Islam gradually overcame the peoples living along the southern Mediterranean shore. The economic system of the southern Mediterranean that had been developed by Rome was swept away. Large parts of southern Europe were forced back to a subsistence economy. What was a disaster for Europe became the start of a new era for West Africa. In 734 AD the first Arab expedition traveled from the Maghrib to Mauritania, seeking gold. Nine years later, a second expedition returned with the precious metal. By the end of the century, the Islamic world knew of Ghana, the earliest kingdom of black Africa, established in the lands south of the desert.

Products of West Africa. The trans-Saharan caravan trade that now grew up depended on four products: gold, copper, salt and slaves. There were four main gold-producing areas in West Africa. Each came to economic prominence at different times. The Bambuk goldfields, between the Senegal and Faleme rivers, were the source of Ghana's wealth. The goldfields of Bure, further south, on the headwaters of the Niger river, in northeast Guinea, financed the later empire of Mali. Further south still, on the edges of the tropical forest near the Volta river, are the Lobi fields. Deep in the forest, the Akan goldfields exported primarily to the trading posts that were established by the European powers on the Guinea coast in the late 15th and 16th centuries.

None of these fields was rich. In the Bambuk fields, the gold was alluvial, weathered and washed from the rocks of ancient reefs. It lay near the bottom of deep deposits of river sands and gravels. To get it, shafts up to 60 feet deep had to be sunk. Even with this effort, the chances of finding worthwhile concentrations of the metal were extremely uncertain. Mining was difficult and dangerous work. Yields were uncertain. Only the hope of a lucky strike made the effort worthwhile.

Documented studies of gold production in West Africa in the precolonial period reveal a situation very like that already encountered in the goldfields of Zimbabwe. People were farmers and gained their living from their crops and lands. However, the soils of many goldfields were infertile and their yields were poor. Many months of the year are rainless. There is no work in the fields during these months. Farmers then turn to mining, gambling with the hope of a lucky strike. Single families or small temporary groups came together in a mining venture. There was no large-scale cooperation, specialization or centralized organization. Gold mining was the result of agricultural poverty, not of a beneficent supply of easily accessible riches. Perhaps because mining was only marginally worthwhile, the mines were not monopolized by any single authority. Anyone could mine: local villager or foreign specialist. The only form of control rested with the ritual specialists of nearby villages, who intervened to appease and reward the spirits of the earth. Some local rulers employed slaves to mine on their behalf. This gave them marginal advantages over villagers who were engaged in seasonal mining activities, in terms of organization, scale and regularity of supply. Their rights over the mines were no different from those of a local villager.

A painting in the Tassili mountains depicting a light two-wheeled chariot drawn by galloping horses.

The people who grew rich on the proceeds of West African gold were the middle men who interposed themselves between the miners of the forests and the traders of the desert caravans. Markets were established. The men who controlled them grew in wealth and power from market dues, tolls, customs duties and fees for adjudicating in commercial disputes. Thus the foundations of the kingdoms of the West African savanna were laid. The rulers soon learned that attempts to control gold production at its source were certain to fail. They led to immediate decline in production or total cessation of mining. Attempts to extract a surplus from the miners in the form of tax or tribute meant that mining simply ceased to be worthwhile. People abandoned the mines and went back to their farmlands.

Contacts between traders and miners were often so tenuous and indirect that legends of a completely "silent trade" grew up. In this, goods for exchange were laid out in a forest clearing. When the traders withdrew, the producers would examine these goods and leave what they considered an equivalent value of gold in exchange. When they in turn had withdrawn, the traders returned. If they accepted the bargain, they removed the gold and withdrew. Each side viewed the goods alone. They never met.

While gold was exported, copper was imported into the West African forest. It was not used for weapons or tools, but to make the elaborate regalia of kings, the insignia of office, vessels used in ritual and the jewelry of the wealthy. It was a metal that indicated rank and status in much the same way as gold. The main source was the mines around Akjoujt in southern Mauritania. Far to the east, at Azelik in the Air mountains of the Niger Republic and at Nioro in the Republic of Mali, there may have been other centers of copper production. Ibn Battuta wrote of copper smelting at Takedda, in the Air. Evidence of smelting has been found here, though no bodies of ore have been located. The mines of Mauritania had been in production for many centuries before the caravan trade of Islam developed. Copper arrow, ax and spearheads have been found lying in the desert at many places nearby. They are undated, but their forms resemble those of the Maghrib and Iberian peninsula of the first millennium BC. Indeed,

Mauritanian copper workings have produced radiocarbon dates of the mid-first millennium BC.

The most dramatic archaeological evidence of the copper trade of the desert caravans was made by Theodore Monod in 1960. Deep in the desert of southern Mauritania, 26 days' journey from the nearest water, at a site known as Ma'den Ijafen, he unearthed the remains of a small camel caravan that had met with disaster. It was carrying copper bars of a standard size and weight. Each was two feet long and weighed one pound. They were tied in bundles, each of 100 rods. The dry sand has preserved their wrappings, baskets and bindings. Specimens of these have been radiocarbon dated to the 11th or 12th century AD. The use of copper rods as a currency in the kingdom of Mali was described by Ibn Battuta in the early 14th century.

Another source of the metal was bronze and brass vessels. Several such vessels have survived in villages in modern Ghana. In many instances, they are reverenced. Large brass basins bearing inscriptions in Kufic, an Arabic script that fell into disuse in the 14th century, have been recorded in village shrines around the trading town of Begho on the edge of the Ghanaian forest. A bronze ewer, bearing an inscription, the arms of England and the badge of King Richard II, dated to 1399, was found in the royal palace of Asante by the British military expedition that occupied it in 1896.

Crystalline salt, of a purity, hardness and durability that made it greatly valued throughout West Africa, was mined, under conditions of great hardship, at Taghaza. This oasis, in the desert of the central Sahara, is an important stopping place for caravans crossing the desert. It suffers a climate so dry that the houses can be built of salt blocks. Here Ibn Battuta halted on his journey south and watched slabs of salt of standard weight being loaded for transport to the savanna kingdoms.

In the caravan with which Ibn Battuta returned from Mali, 600 men were being carried into slavery. The significance of West African slaves in the economy of the Maghrib is difficult to determine. Slaves were used in dangerous and unpleasant work, such as mining or cutting salt. They acted as porters to transport trade goods from the forests to the caravan towns of the southern edge of the desert. Some early Arab chronicles describe the slave villages or even provinces within the early kingdoms of the savanna. The produce of their fields and labor went to the king as tribute. The rulers of the Akan kingdoms, within the forest, used slaves to mine gold. They also used slaves as soldiers in raiding parties seeking to capture slaves. The personal loyalty of these men to the king was assured by their knowledge that their children would become free citizens, equal with their captors. In the 19th century the king of Dahomey used slaves to develop a new economy based on the products of royal plantations.

The forms of slavery within Africa were, of course, very different from the slavery of the West Indies and

Above: a brass basin with a Kufic inscription, kept in Nsawkaw, a village on the old trade route between the Akan goldfields and the Niger. The broken egg is an offering to the vessel. Scale in cms.
Opposite: the western Sudan and Sahara, showing early states and caravan routes.

Americas. This is no place to discuss the effect of the Atlantic slave trade on West Africa's history. Before this developed, about 1500, it is certain that slavery never molded the economy of a West African state. It was never the main way of supporting a ruler or a state, or of achieving a surplus that could be appropriated for centralized government.

Other goods were also carried by the Saharan caravans. Kola nuts, ivory, skins and furs were sent north. Horses, weapons, textiles and other manufactured goods were imported to the savanna and forests. Cowrie shells from the Indian Ocean were probably used as currency: 3,000 of them were found among the goods of the caravan excavated at Ma'den Ijafen.

The caravan trade. From Carthaginian times, if not before, the lands of North Africa beyond the Mediterranean littoral were inhabited by people who spoke Berber, one of the Afro-Asiatic languages. In the Fezzan, they farmed the banks of the rivers that stretched into the desert. Further into the desert, nomadic pastoralists were dominated by the Sanhaja tribes. These veiled horsemen and warriors were as aggressive as their relatives, the Tuareg, have been reputed to be in much more recent times. With the introduction of the camel at the beginning of the Christian era, the Sanhaja were able to move across the desert and settle on its southern edges. Between the 2nd and 5th centuries, the Sanhaja tribes came together in a confederation that controlled the oases and camel pastures of the Maghrib. But the Sanhaja were essentially tribal and nomadic peoples. Unity beyond the tribe was a temporary and fragile occurrence.

Sanhaja pressure forced the Negroid farmers who still survived in the mountains of the southern Sahara desert to move south into the savanna. Under the threat of the Sanhaja, they consolidated and united their communities. These pressures preceded the stimulus of foreign commerce. Commercial development only consolidated earlier indigenous movements towards centralization. This process resembles the interaction that we have already traced between farmers and herdsmen in East Africa. An increasing complexity of social integration and political cohesion was not necessarily the result of foreign conquests. Often it was an indigenous reaction to foreigners who posed a threat simply as a result of their sophisticated, streamlined and authoritarian forms of organization and administration. The alien threat provided a stimulus. It did not necessarily provide an example or diffuse knowledge of administrative skills.

There is no indication that the kingdoms of West Africa had foreign origins. The Sanhaja could offer little in the way of statecraft or political sophistication. They were tribesmen, not state builders. The members of the ruling dynasties of West Africa were black and Sudanic like their subjects.

The Sanhaja were neither town dwellers nor traders. Nonetheless, they filled roles of fundamental importance in the caravan trade, as guides and protectors. Caravans set out across the desert from towns in the southern Maghrib. Here finance for caravans could be arranged, camels and provisions bought and camel drivers, guards and guides hired. Sijilmasa was perhaps the most important northern caravan terminus. Towns grew up in the same way on the southern edge of the desert. Camels could not travel south from here without discomfort and danger of disease. Goods had to be transferred to donkeys and porters. Awdaghust was the most important savanna caravan town. These towns were controlled politically by the Sanhaja; but they cannot be considered the capitals of states or kingdoms. These were concepts alien to the Sanhaja.

A network of caravan routes crossed the desert. Parties of traders traveled together in large convoys. The dangers of the journey have been described vividly and many times. Fears of raids and robbery were matched by the rigors of great extremes in temperature and lack of water, shelter and provisions. Some of the oases in the desert, where caravans rested and replenished their stores, became major markets. Some were meeting points for separate caravan networks. In them goods were transshipped. The oasis of Taghaza was, of course, not only an important

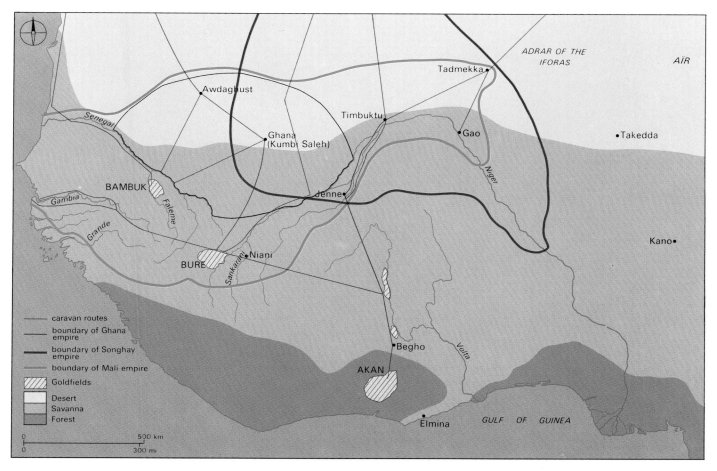

economic center but also a most important source of salt production. The traders were frequently from Berber groups other than the Sanhaja, often dissident or at least unorthodox Muslim sects, such as the Zanata from the coastlands of the eastern Maghrib.

The kingdoms of the savanna. By the time of Muhammad, the kingdom of Ghana, as it was known to Islamic scholars, or Wagadu, as Soninke traditions recall it, had existed for 20 generations. Its territory extended west of the upper reaches of the Niger river. This area is now desert. A thousand years ago there was enough grass and scrub to support at least a pastoral economy. Early Arab travelers leave no doubt that Ghana was an African kingdom. The capital had a cosmopolitan, commercial section. This contained the houses and mosques of wealthy Berber merchants. In sharp contrast, the royal court was built in traditional style. Around it were the sacred groves and shrines of traditional religion. The royal tombs stood nearby: large earthen tumuli covering burials with rich grave goods of weapons and jewelry. All reflected traditional beliefs. The kings of Ghana did not engage in trade themselves. Few Soninke did. They grew rich on the dues paid them by foreign traders. Nonetheless, the

The quays of Gao on the river Niger. Here goods were transshipped between canoes bound for the western kingdoms, desert caravans and porters traveling to the forests.

majority of the population were peasant farmers, using traditional methods to grow enough food to feed themselves and little more.

In the 11th century, Ghana was strong enough to conquer the main Berber trading town of Awdaghust, administered by the Sanhaja. They reduced it to tributary status. This had repercussions that destroyed the Ghanaian kingdom. The Almoravids, a Sanhaja sect living in the extreme west of the Sudan, near the coast of Senegal, swept into Ghana, preaching a purified religion and a holy war. They recovered Awdaghust, overthrew the royal family of Ghana and destroyed its trade. The Almoravids went on to rule Morocco and Spain. Ghana became Islamic.

The Berber nomads who now controlled Ghana were more interested in increasing their flocks and herds than in the fragile fertility of the lands or the commerce of the towns. Overgrazing started a degradation of land and vegetation. This reduced the territory of Ghana to the desert it is today.

The Soninke nation fragmented. People dispersed. Many moved south to the better-watered woodlands, where the Berber threat was lessened. The southern regions had other advantages: there were new opportunities to open the south to commerce; the goldfields of Bure were developed; new states grew up. The southern Mande, the Malinke, formed the state of Mali. From the

Above: a cemetery at Sané had a series of 12th-century royal gravestones. The Kufic script is in a style suggesting a Spanish origin. This one commemorates King Abu Bakr Ibn Abi Quhafa who died in 1110 AD.

Below: Sané, 3 miles from Gao and linked to it by the dry beds of a considerable tributary delta, has large areas of medieval habitation on the slopes of a low hill.

12th to the 16th centuries, Mali exercised authority over many different towns and peoples. The Niger river became an important commercial artery. Collecting centers along its bank were supplied by feeder routes leading southwards to the forests. Towns along the river grew wealthy. Jenne lies at the head of the inland Niger "delta," where the river breaks up into many separate streams and irrigates rich agricultural land. Here an intensive regional trade in the agricultural products of the delta developed. Jenne was also an important entrepot for North African goods, destined for the southern forests. Two hundred miles downstream, where the river tributaries again unite, stands Timbuktu. It had been founded by the desert Tuaregs but was incorporated in the kingdom of Mali in the mid-13th century. Timbuktu lay in a strategic position that joined two distinct commercial networks: those developed by the former state of Ghana and those of its eastern neighbor kingdom, Gao. Timbuktu achieved prosperity on the interchanges between the two systems.

The most northeasterly of the important Niger towns was Gao, capital of the Songhay kingdom. It stood in desert rather than farmland. From Gao, goods passed into the desert to its commercial partner, the town of Tadmekka. From Tadmekka, caravans crossed the desert to Algeria and Egypt, by-passing the territories of the Sanhaja and bringing contact with a different part of Islam. Gao built up a fleet of armed canoes on the Niger, manned by Songhay fishermen. This was one of the factors that enabled it to become independent from Mali in the 15th century.

Mali, like Ghana, had been a Mande nation state. It had the culture and institutions of a single ethnic group at its center. When the empire disintegrated, the Malinke people dispersed. Important groups became specialist traders. One, the Dyula, developed close connections with the Akan peoples to the south who were developing the gold resources of the forest of present-day Ghana.

The gold of the forest was also going south to the trading posts that had been established by the Portuguese along the shores of the Gulf of Guinea. Thus the trade of West Africa was finding a new orientation. The Mande peoples reacted and tried to retain their hold on the northern trade. These developments led to the growth of new kingdoms on the forest fringes of present-day Ghana. The Dyula guarded their own culture and identity. They lived apart from their trading partners in special towns or quarters of towns.

In the central Sudan other states grew up. Centralized administration was again needed to mobilize resistance to pressures from the peoples of the desert. People living on the edges of the desert were again in a strategic economic position to mediate between the desert traders and the forest. Kanem, like Ghana, grew to power in what is now desert country. Descriptions of Kanem, collected in the 8th century, leave no doubt that its rulers were Negroid or that its culture was Sudanic. Its population consisted of farmers of the savanna who had moved into the desert to establish or control trading outlets, not desert dwellers who had conquered the southern farmers. Kanuri power subsequently moved south of Lake Chad into the better-watered savanna of Bornu in northern Nigeria.

To the west, between Lake Chad and the Niger river, Negroid Hausa farmers established a series of kingdoms, each centered on a single walled and fortified town. Their security attracted migrants from all groups and with many different skills. They formed a heterogeneous and cosmopolitan population. In concept, scale and organization, the Hausa towns differed greatly from the nation states of the west. Their territory was less extensive. Their scale made fewer demands on administrative or military power. Their stability was threatened more by their cultural and ethnic diversity. Where Hausa cities were surrounded by fertile land, like the city of Kano, they became major centers of population.

The archaeology of the savanna kingdoms. The history of the kingdoms of the savanna rests on local traditions and the works of early Islamic travelers and scholars. These sources can never be completely reliable. The interests of the writers, the depth of their knowledge and the intimacy of their experience varied a great deal. Many scholars were forced to accept second-hand information, much of it from unreliable sources. The role of archaeology has been a subsidiary one. Although many important early towns have been partially excavated, much of this work has been limited to seeking to confirm historical evidence. Imported goods are identified. Carbon samples are dated. Building and pottery styles are compared. Changes in style are categorized. Cultural connections are traced. However, knowledge has not been advanced significantly.

There are many reasons why archaeology has not been exploited for the distinctive contributions of which it is capable. Limitations are placed on fieldwork by the arduous climate and country of many sites. There are also problems of logistics, communications and technical facilities. Nonetheless the present concentration on key city sites must be replaced by more comprehensive investigations of the other settlements of a kingdom. Systematic surface surveys of regions can contribute to an understanding of environment, subsistence economy, demography and settlement pattern. They can provide a detailed picture of the potential of a region, and show how this was exploited and how it changed through time. Excavations can be designed to investigate the nature, function, size and relative importance of different groups within a society and the relations between them. Stylistic studies can only be reliable and telling if systematic comparative analyses are made in all the areas under consideration. Their value is decreased when they are based on subjective comparisons of isolated traits, selected in a non-random way from partial and incomplete samples.

Patrick Munson's work on the early farming settlements of southern Mauritania (described in Chapter 2) indicates the value of systematic, complete and carefully planned fieldwork. It shows what is possible in the hard environment of the desert. Similar work is needed on the larger, more variable, more specialized and, therefore, more complex sites of urban society. It will of necessity be on an even wider scale.

The capital of the ancient kingdom of Ghana – known in Islam as Kumbi – was described in detail by al Bakri in the 11th century. It has been identified with the ruined town of Kumbi Saleh, in the desert of southern Mauritania. The buildings of this town covered two square miles. There are traces of occupation over a much greater area. The houses were built of stone, with two stories. The lower floor contained store rooms. They stood close together, separated by narrow alleys. A wide avenue, flanked by market places, led to the Friday Mosque, a building of imposing size. Glass, pottery and stone plaques found in some houses, closely resemble products of the Maghrib. Small glass weights, only suitable for measuring a substance as valuable as gold, were also recovered. The houses must have belonged to Maghribi merchants. A single radiocarbon sample has given a date between the end of the 11th and the late 14th centuries. This, in fact, is after the Almoravid conquest of the capital of Ghana. But a single date with a wide standard deviation is slender evidence on which to speculate. The areas investigated archaeologically must be the commercial quarter of the capital. Ruins – not of stone – ten miles away are one of the sites that may have been the traditional Soninke royal quarter. They have not been excavated.

Al Bakri described the royal tombs of Ghana. The corpse was placed in a wooden chamber, surrounded by food, drink, grave-goods and attendants. A ditch was cut around the tomb and earth piled over the burial to form a great mound. No such mounds have been found at Kumbi Saleh. However, such tombs exist in great numbers on the flat plains on the inland delta of the Niger river, the southern border of the kingdom of Ghana. Many cemeteries contain scores of mounds, several of which were excavated at the beginning of the 20th century. Frobenius also visited and described them. They contained corpses laden with ornaments, many of copper and some of gold. Copper vessels from Morocco stood among fine pottery wares. The mounds, faced in a fired clay hard enough to survive the centuries, are so large – up to 50 feet high and 200 feet across – that they stand like small hills above the flood plains.

Other monumental tombs, built by pre-Islamic peoples, have been recognized throughout the western Sudan and the southern desert. Towards the coast of Senegal, burials were surrounded by circles of sandstone monoliths, up to 10 feet high. Low mounds cover burials at the center of the circles. Those excavated have contained few grave-goods. However, their pottery was not unlike that found in the tumuli of the Niger delta. Indeed there are two cemeteries of tombs surrounded by stone circles within the delta.

A megalithic monument in Senegal has given radiocarbon dates of the 2nd and 5th centuries BC. Dates from three

Opposite: circles of low sandstone megaliths marking graves at Sine Saloum in Senegal.

Below: students of the University of Ghana excavating house mounds at Begho. Areas of treeless "elephant" grass mark early settlement sites.

other tombs suggest that they were built between the 6th and 9th centuries AD. Archaeologists have not yet found the settlements once inhabited by those buried in the tumuli and stone circles. The social and cultural context of these great tombs is therefore uncertain and almost entirely unknown.

Awdaghust was the main Berber commercial town in the desert on the northern edge of the early kingdom of Ghana. It has been identified with the present settlement of Tegdaoust, 300 miles north of Kumbi Saleh. It was excavated between 1966 and 1969. The site is large and the deposits deep and rich. It covers 25 acres and the deposits form a *tell* over 25 feet thick. Three successive towns were revealed. The first contained rectangular houses of mud brick. The main rooms of each house faced onto a private courtyard. The layout sounds reminiscent of the houses of the East African coastal cities.

The street plan of the last medieval town was realigned. The houses were built of stone. Their general plan changed. They were entered direct from the street and had their courtyards in the rear. Inside, reception rooms were decorated with recessed niches to hold lamps or display household treasures. In plan and decoration these houses resembled those of Kumbi Saleh.

Mass-produced earthenware lamps and household pottery were imported from the Maghrib. Glass weights like those found at Kumbi Saleh confirm an involvement with trade in precious metals. Copper was cast in standard ingots. So was gold. A cache of five gold ingots, of identical weight, and fragments of gold jewelry was found buried beneath the kitchen floor of a house.

The town revealed by the excavations at Tegdaoust suggests Maghrib connections. In its architecture and artifacts there are also resemblances to Kumbi Saleh. More than a dozen radiocarbon dates span a period between the 8th and 14th centuries. The correlation between Awdaghust and Tegdaoust is thus very plausible.

There is considerable controversy over the location of the capital of the empire of Mali. There are many indications that it was near Niani, on the Sankarani river, one of the tributaries of the upper Niger. Archaeological work in this area has located many ruined villages. Certainly it was once more densely populated than it is today. However, no certain evidence of the Mali capital has yet been recovered. Further down the Niger, Jenne and Timbuktu have not been investigated archaeologically. Outside the present town of Gao, large mounds of occupation debris indicate the site of the former capital of the "empire of Songhay." They have not been excavated. Material evidence of Gao's link with the Mediterranean can be seen in finds of royal grave-stones of the 12th century in a marble and style of southern Spain.

The site of Begho. The most sustained and carefully planned archaeological investigation of the capital of a West African trading state has been conducted by the

University of Ghana at Begho. Begho lies within the great northern bend of the Niger river, well south of the trading cities of the river and savanna. It is close to the Volta river, on a route through the Banda hills. The Dyula traders from the north passed this way, traveling to the Lobi goldfields of the present Republic of Ghana. Gold from the Akan fields further south was also carried through Begho on its way north. Begho stands on the edges of several different zones. Nearby, savanna is replaced by forest; Mande speakers give way to Akan; Islam meets traditional religions. An understanding of this amalgam of peoples, cultures and economies, in an urban environment, through archaeological fieldwork, is a worthwhile challenge.

There is historical evidence that, in the 14th century, Begho became the capital of one of the small Mossi kingdoms. Its closest trading relations were with the town of Jenne on the Niger. In the early 18th century it fell to the Asante kings, as they consolidated the most powerful state in the western forest. Six radiocarbon dates confirm that Begho was inhabited between these periods. Two more recent radiocarbon dates suggest that the town was founded earlier, very probably before the 13th century and possibly even at the beginning of the millennium – even before the empire of Mali grew to power. Traditions assert that the town was divided into separate quarters: the local people – the Brong; the Islamic merchants – the Kramo; and the smiths and other artisans – the Twumfour. The remains of their sun-dried mud houses can still be traced. There were several hundred in each quarter. The largest quarter was well over half a mile from side to side. The great central open area that separates the quarters was probably used for markets. Each quarter has been tested in excavation. Sadly, no significant differences between them have been discerned in the artifacts.

Pottery studies have been designed to determine the degree of continuity between the wares of the earliest town and those of the present Brong villages in the area. From this base, the aim is to identify the extent, nature and source of alien influence on ceramic style. The next step, to identify the sources, demands detailed comparative analysis of material from a wide area. This will be a difficult task and has yet to be attempted. Its lack must weaken interpretations of the Begho material. More than 90 per cent of the pottery in every area was made locally. A clear continuity of style can be traced between the earliest wares and those made by Brong potters today. Three-quarters of the pottery forms are shared with wares in current use. Foreign elements in the society can be seen in one particular painted ceramic ware. The shapes of some pottery vessels – with sharp angles and flat outturned lips – resemble forms characteristic of beaten-metal vessels. Pedestal and ring bases also seem alien. All these influences can be matched at Jenne, the traditional commercial partner of Begho.

Other artifacts – for instance, spindle-whorls and the system of measures used in weighing gold – were also of types used at Jenne. Ivory side-blown trumpets are a characteristic item of Malian regalia; pieces of two were found at Begho. Begho's houses had a series of rectangular rooms, ranged around a courtyard. They all had flat roofs. These are northern forms, suited to semi-desert conditions. Separate circular thatched huts are more practical dwellings in the forest and on its fringes. Yet they are not found at Begho. On the other hand, the walls of the houses at Begho were made of successive layers of puddled clay, poured into shuttering supports. This is not a Mande technique. They built with mud bricks.

The published reports on the Begho excavations have so far concentrated on tracing stylistic parallels, connections and influences. These suggest that the historical evidence of Begho's connection with the Niger towns, and specifically Jenne, is broadly correct. Begho, seen as a single interacting society, has yet to be investigated in any depth. Nonetheless, the potential contribution of Begho towards the clarification of the key issues in archaeological studies of early African kingdoms is considerable.

The kingdoms of the forest. Before the Portuguese landed on the Guinea coast in the late 15th century, foreigners had never entered the forest. There are no early accounts of the development of states in this great region. There is no written history. Archaeological fieldwork in the area is a difficult task. Movement is constricted. Sites are hidden by trees and undergrowth. It is impossible to get an overall view, or discern patterns in the landscape. Erosion does little to expose features in the soils. Towns have remained on the same sites for centuries. Early deposits can only be examined hurriedly and piecemeal, usually during building operations. Excavation in tropical lateritic clays and sands, in a climate with a high humidity and constant rainfall, offers its own peculiar challenges.

Despite these handicaps, West Africa, especially Nigeria, has revealed extraordinary artistic riches. Almost all of these have been found by chance. They provide vivid insights into African creativity. Still, the societies that supported and stimulated the artists remain obscure. Only in Benin do traditions of sculpting and brass work survive. Only there can a continuous historical development be traced.

The discovery of the art. For many years tin has been mined on the Jos plateau and in the Benue river valley in central Nigeria. Enormous open-cast workings extract the mineral from the bottom of thick alluvial deposits. In 1944 it was realized that the tin-bearing strata contained many pieces of sculpted figures in fired clay. Hundreds of fragments have now been recovered. They are recognized as the products of a single, prehistoric group, who once inhabited a considerable area of central and eastern Nigeria. They are named after one of the mining villages,

Nok. Two of their villages have been partially excavated. They formed simple farming communities and were among the earliest iron users in tropical Africa.

Igbo Ukwu is a village 25 miles east of the Niger river, near the head of its delta. Here, in 1922 and again in 1939, some villagers found "strange metal objects" while digging water storage cisterns beside their houses. The local district officer heard of the later finds. He managed to buy many of them and informed the Nigerian Department of Antiquities. It was to be 20 years before excavation of the site could finally be initiated.

Almost immediately a wealth of objects was revealed. Vessels cast in bronze had their surfaces covered with intricate filigree patterns of great delicacy. Staffs, swords, daggers, scabbards, fans, headdresses, bangles, pendants, jewelry and furniture were embellished in the same way. A world of animals was shown on the bronze work: beetles, grasshoppers, frogs, snakes, pangolins, monkeys, leopards and elephants.

The skill and patience of Thurstan Shaw, the excavator (and later the first Professor of Archaeology at Nigeria's senior university, Ibadan), enabled the original circumstances of the deposition of the finds to be reconstructed in some detail. One group of objects included many bronze bowls, in the form of calabashes or giant snail shells; bronze handles and strap work, that were once attached to natural calabashes; four staffs, with heads, handles and finials of bronze; pot stands, swords and a mass of jewelry. They had all been carefully placed, probably on a clay platform, in what seems to have been a shrine.

Close by, an extraordinary amount of bronze work was recovered from a grave. The corpse was arrayed in a crown, breastplate and anklets of bronze. In one hand he held the bronze handle of a fan or a staff, surmounted by the figures of a horse and rider. He was seated on a stool, bound with ornamented bronze straps. Beside him, on a woven mat, lay ivory tusks and a sculpted bronze leopard skull. His head was hidden by imported glass beads. His arms were encased in armlets of bronze and beads. Altogether, more than 100,000 glass beads adorned the corpse. The burial chamber, at the bottom of a deep shaft, was lined and roofed with timber planks. Above it, five men were sacrificed.

A third group of bronze objects had been buried in some disarray, in a shallow pit. Perhaps they were the furnishings of a shrine, abandoned when the shrine, god or religion fell into disfavor. Perhaps they were a person's ceremonial regalia, discarded by the family on his death.

As we have seen, Leo Frobenius first revealed the bronze and terracotta sculptures of Ife to the world. Since his work, similar sculptures have turned up in digging and building operations throughout the town. Down the years, fragments of terracotta sculptures have also been collected together in shrines, particularly those in forest groves just outside the town. Here they have been buried. They are dug up regularly for use in religious ceremonies.

Other sculptures have been kept by successive Onis of Ife in the royal palace. The most exciting discovery was of 17 nearly lifesize bronze heads, which turned up in building operations just outside the walls of the palace in 1938. These masterpieces have now been brought together in the town's museum.

Attempts to place chance finds of sculpture in their prehistoric context have been made in three archaeological excavations. In 1957 several small bronzes were found at Ita Yemoo, close to one of the earth walls that surround the town. Frank Willett excavated the site for the next four years. In 1969 Ekpo Eyo exposed a series of terracotta heads, placed on top of pots that were carefully arranged around a small paved courtyard. The site was close to the palace and near the spot where the bronzes were found in 1938. These excavations were halted by the Oni of Ife when he declared that the pavement covered the grave of Lafogido, a former Oni. In 1971 Margaret Garlake excavated a group of terracotta sculptures on a site that was found in gravel digging on land of the Obalara family, on the outskirts of the town. About 30 bronzes and scores of terracotta sculptures are now known. Most show a moving serenity. Grotesque deformities, hideous diseases, violent emotion and horrible deaths are also depicted.

The great treasure of bronze sculptures, looted from the palace of Benin in 1897, has already been described. The last 80 years have not added a great deal to our knowledge of them. A few more bronzes have been discovered in the royal palace. Others, that had been lost and buried nearby, have also been found. Spasmodic small-scale excavations took place near the palace in the 1950s. In 1961–64 Graham Connah initiated systematic research work. This included the extraordinary achievement of clearing lines 90 miles long, largely through virgin forest, to reveal the full extent and complexity of the earthen ramparts that surround the original town of Benin and its dependent villages.

Additional evidence. What archaeology in Nigeria has achieved is some precision in dating. Four radiocarbon dates place the Nok villages of Taruga and Samun Dukiya between the 3rd, or possibly 4th, century BC and the 5th or 6th century AD. Four radiocarbon dates have been obtained from Igbo Ukwu. Fragments of the stool on which the richly embellished corpse was seated gave a date between the 8th and 10th centuries AD. Three similar dates came from particles of charcoal in the pit containing abandoned bronzes. A fourth date, of the 14th or 15th century AD, came from the same pit. (Perhaps the earlier dates are from the original furnishings of the shrine. The later date may represent the final deposition of the goods or a subsequent disturbance.) The three dates are surprisingly early. By the 8th century, the desert trade or earliest savanna kingdoms had barely been established. It is startling to find such skilled craftsmanship in a developed and sophisticated artistic tradition, using an imported and valuable raw material, so far to the south at this period. This is particularly so at Igbo Ukwu, which is in an area that offered few rewards to northern traders. Its products – slaves, ivory and kola nuts – were all much more easily available in the north. The beads of Igbo Ukwu offer no clue to date: they do not resemble the bead assemblages of eastern Africa, which have more closely dated associations.

Twenty-five radiocarbon dates have been obtained from excavations in Ife. Five, of the 6th to 10th centuries AD, were obtained from pits said to be early graves. They contained nothing and only indicate that the area was inhabited at this stage. Thirteen radiocarbon dates are associated with the buildings and artifacts characteristic of the period when sculpture was being produced. They cluster between the late 10th century and the 14th century (with one anomalous and presumably contaminated date of the 18th century). Three earlier and three later dates have only tenuous and debatable associations with the period of the sculptures. Samples from excavations in early deposits at Benin have produced eight radiocarbon dates. The earliest goes back to the 12th or even 11th

Reconstruction of the burial at Igbo Ukwu.

century. There was certainly substantial occupation by the 14th century, and probably by the 13th century.

A series of dates has been obtained by measuring the thermoluminescence of the clay cores of bronze sculptures from Ife and Benin. This method of dating is not considered as reliable as radiocarbon dating. However, it has the advantage of dating materials whose association with the bronzes is direct. It is absolutely certain what event is being dated: the casting process itself. The cores of five Ife bronzes gave dates of between the 14th and 16th centuries. (Three thermoluminescence dates from Ife potsherds and a terracotta sculpture have given 13th- to 14th-century dates.) Four Benin bronzes were dated to the 16th and 17th centuries. These dates indicate that the bronzes of the two sites belong to distinct periods. Casting in Benin developed after the craft had died out in Ife. Two pieces that resemble the sculptures of Ife very closely have also been dated by this method. One, found in Benin, gave a 15th-century date. One from a shrine on the Niger river not far north of Ife, at Tada, gave a 14th-century date.

Art-historical analysis. With no documentary accounts and few archaeological data to work on, interpretations of the Nigerian sculptures have relied on the techniques of art historians. The immense corpus of material from Benin was first placed in a chronological order by von Luschan and Struck over 50 years ago. William Fagg took the process further in 1958. He presented his arguments before systematic excavations had taken place in Ife or Benin and before any radiocarbon dates were available. His arguments have won considerable general acceptance. Many of the bronze plaques that embellished the royal palace of Benin depict Portuguese in the dress of the 16th century. These plaques were described by European travelers in 1668 but were not mentioned by van Nyendael who visited Benin in 1702. Fagg interprets this as meaning that the plaques were completed by the late 17th century and must have been removed soon afterwards. On this evidence, Fagg places all the plaques (and heads in the same style) in the late 16th and 17th centuries. These constitute the "Middle Period" of Benin art and include the great body of Benin bronze works. Fagg assumed a continuous stylistic trend from the "sensitive naturalism" of Ife to an "empty formalism" and "fundamental pedestrianism" characteristic of Benin. The Late Period is therefore exemplified by the most highly "stylized" heads. These depict kings wearing high collars of coral bead work and, later still, horned, beaded crowns. Bronzes of the Early Period are characterized by considerably greater naturalism. Heads of this period wear bead collars that cover only the neck. The castings of the Early Period are much thinner than later works. This is attributed to the rarity and value of bronze before Portuguese imports of the metal started to reach Benin. It can also be taken as confirmatory evidence of the date of the Early Period: the 15th and early 16th centuries.

The sculptures of Ife look a great deal more realistic than those of Benin. Benin traditions insist that Ife was the source of their knowledge of bronze working. Because of the marked differences in style, Fagg allows a century for the Benin sculpture to develop its individuality. (No sculptures of this period survive. It is recognized on purely theoretical grounds.) Art-historical evidence therefore suggests that the sculptures of Ife were made in the 14th century. Their unity of style is so great that it is considered that they were not created over more than a century. This evidence is in reasonably close agreement with archaeological evidence of date. The "highly developed" art of Ife is taken to be the product of the worldly outlook of priests grown rich on the income of shrines in the mother city of all Yoruba people. A correlation is assumed between artistic and political sophistication. These serene, emotionless beings, decked in an abundance of beads and crowned with elaborate coiffures or headdresses interwoven with beads and rosettes, are interpreted as royalty or as gods treated as royalty. This equation of naturalism in the depiction of the human figure with authoritarian or aristocratic government is a consistent theme in analyses of West African art. It is untested and unproved

Bronze castings from Igbo Ukwu included a bowl, 14 inches across (*top right*), decorated with a net pattern. Its shape exactly imitates a calabash. The snail, 8 inches long (*bottom right*), is a marine Triton. It is surmounted by a leopard. The openwork cylinder, 11 inches high (*left*), depicts a woman with complex facial scarifications, flanked by snakes, frogs and spiders. These bronzes were all part of the "shrine" group.

The Nok terracottas are clearly very different in style from those of Ife. Features are sharply delineated. Forms are emphasized as geometric systems of cones and cylinders. On the other hand, the bodies of human beings, often nearly lifesize, paid little attention to detail or anatomy. The skill needed to fire hollow clay figures of this size is very great. In Ife, the treatment of the human body was very closely similar. So were the techniques of manufacture. On this evidence, Fagg recognized a stylistic relationship between Nok and Ife and thus assumed a unity of style and a cultural connection between all the main sculptural traditions of the Nigerian forest, from Nok to Ife and then Benin. His approach is cautious and closely argued. Nevertheless it seems dangerously oversimplified. It receives no support from other artifacts. It is untested. The similarities are to some extent exaggerated and based on a subjective selection of isolated traits. Many other interpretations are possible to account for those similarities that undoubtedly exist.

Scientific analysis. Other approaches to the problems of relationship have been tried. Analyses of the metal content of a casting can be misleading. So many objects are made up of fragments of earlier castings, possibly from a number of different sources. Nonetheless, analyses of a great number of Nigerian castings do show some patterning. What this means is not yet fully clear. It does indicate that there were different sources for the metal. It also indicates a wide general appreciation of the potential of different copper alloys. Copper by itself is not easily cast. If tin is added, in the proportion of about one to ten, the bronze alloy is more easily worked. Lead too can be added, giving leaded bronze: a softer metal that is more fluid in the molten state. Brass is an alloy of copper and up to 30 per cent zinc.

The castings of Igbo Ukwu are almost all bronze; most are leaded bronze. The rare objects of nearly pure copper were not cast but smithed and chased. The metal sculptures of Ife were all cast. Five are of almost pure copper. Three are of bronze. The remainder, by far the majority, are leaded brass. From Benin, only a few small objects, from deposits of the 13th century, were of bronze. These were not cast but smithed. Most Benin work is, like Ife work, of leaded brass. The zinc content of the Benin alloys increased from the Early to the Later Period. This adds validity to these stylistic categories.

Analyses of trace elements showed that Ife castings have a very low nickel content, comparable to that of European works of the 10th to 13th centuries. The Benin castings have a relatively high proportion of nickel and antimony, comparable to European works of the 15th to 17th centuries. This supports the relative dates of the Ife and Benin sculptures obtained from stylistic analyses and archaeology. It further suggests that metal came to Ife from Europe. A detailed consideration of the proportions of trace elements also suggests that some metal was traded from Ife to Benin, where European alloys were added to it. Analyses of different isotopes of lead have been obtained from a small number of castings: 14 Benin works, two from Igbo Ukwu and one from Ife. These

Left: a Nok terracotta, with obviously Negroid features, often interpreted as a trumpeter.

Below: an iron-smelting furnace at Taruga. Its contents – ore, slag and charcoal – are ranged around the edge of the excavation.

show that the Benin work is sharply distinct from the Igbo Ukwu works. Both differ from the Ife casting. A trend in the relative proportions of particular isotopes can be seen going from Benin to Ife and then to Igbo Ukwu. This is further confirmation of the results of stylistic analysis.

All West African brass workers used the "lost-wax" or "cire-perdue" method of casting. With this process, an object is modeled in wax on a clay core. It is then covered in an investment of clay. The wax includes a system of tubes or runnels. The whole complex is then heated. The wax melts and runs out through the runnels. Molten metal is then poured through the runnels to replace the wax.

In a detailed study of the process in Nigeria, Denis Williams has recognized a significant set of differences between the techniques used in Ife and Benin. In Benin (and modern Yoruba work) sheets of beeswax were used for the modeling. The clay core and investment contained a great deal of organic matter, such as fiber and straw, to make them porous and capable of absorbing the gases generated by the molten bronze. An iron armature joined core to investment and ramified throughout the core. This conducted the heat of the molten metal through the core and burned it out. It was friable and easily disintegrated. In Ife (as in prehistoric Tchad and Asante) a euphorbia latex, applied in very fine threads, was used for modeling. It often produced a very fine, filigree surface. An iron armature was not used. The clay of core and investment was made porous by the inclusion of finely ground charcoal particles, to absorb the gases. Such cores were extremely stable.

Above and below: simplified geometric forms, each sharply delineated, incised surfaces and a characteristic shape and treatment of the eyes help to give Nok sculptures their readily recognizable style. It suggests that their modeling was closely related to a tradition of carving in wood – of which no trace remains.

If these differences in technique prove to have a general validity, it will go a long way towards showing that the bronze-working skills of Ife and Benin had little connection.

Evidence from excavations. The city of Benin still has a live brass-casting industry. Its history can be traced back many generations. It is a court craft. Brasses were commissioned by the ruler, the Oba. Craftsmen worked exclusively for him. In theory, they still do. Their works reflected the history of the kingdom and the attributes of the king. Ife has no such continuity. No memory survives of a casting tradition. The wars of the late 19th century ended whatever schools of craftsmanship there may have been. Recently only one brass worker practiced his craft in Ife. His works bore no relationship to the historic works either in style or in purpose.

On the other hand, Ife has seen more excavation and produced a greater amount of material than any other important historic town in West Africa. Some of the original associations of the art works are now starting to come into focus. However, there will be no simple, single answer to the role that the sculptures played in society. Nor will the sculptures give any direct answers as to the sort of society it was. One can only be sure that it was complex and sophisticated. The works of art must have fulfilled many different purposes. They were almost certainly incorporated into the fabric of society at several different levels.

Throughout Ife, areas paved with broken potsherds have been exposed. These sherds were set on edge in the natural soil. Many had intricate and regular geometric patterns, often emphasized by the incorporation of white quartz pebbles in their surface. Such pavements have been found on prehistoric sites from Tchad in the northeast to Togo in the west.

The Ife pavements embellished small courtyards, open to the sky. It is difficult to distinguish the walls of the buildings that surrounded them. Sun-dried clay walls and beaten-earth floors are impossible to discern in excavations. They have exactly the same constituents as the soil and debris in which they lie: a much-disturbed urban situation that has seen successive rebuildings every few years for many centuries. Deep alcoves probably opened off each small courtyard and provided the living quarters. Certainly the array of domestic pots and grindstones left standing undisturbed on one pavement leaves no doubt that the courtyards were part of the living quarters of private households.

At the Lafogido site a small pavement had been cut into and 14 pots inserted around its edge. On top of each pot was a terracotta representation of the head of an animal. At Ita Yemoo shrines were built on potsherd pavements. Details of this excavation have not yet been published but preliminary reports indicate that a thatched, clay-walled shrine was built on one pavement. It held seven full-length terracotta statues, two-thirds lifesize. (These unique works have yet to be reconstructed.) Another shrine contained the pieces of two statues that were already broken when they were placed in the shrine.

Altars were generally built in each courtyard, often at both ends. (The practice of dedicating each courtyard in a house or palace to a particular god and making sacrifices to him on an altar in the courtyard is still continued by the Yoruba.) On land of the Woye Asiri family, an altar was recovered intact: a low, curved, semicircular structure, faced in sherds like the pavements. In the courtyard of a nearby building, offerings had been left stacked around an alter when the last occupants finally abandoned their home: a series of domestic pots, grindstones, a bundle of iron nails and three ground-stone axes.

At the center of almost all courtyards, pots or the necks of pots have been buried. Their exposed lips were the focus of the pavement designs. They look as if they were receptacles for libations. The pot buried in the center of a small pavement on the Obalara land has given the most certain evidence of direct association between terracotta sculptures and the construction of potsherd pavements. This pot has also provided a vivid insight into one of the uses of terracotta statuary. Around its sides were reliefs of a series of rituals and ritual objects: a drum, a flail, a torque, a dagger or cleaver, two short staffs linked by a cord, a pair of bush-cow horns similarly linked, and a human corpse placed upside-down in a basket. Most interesting was a depiction of an open, box-like container, with a roof of cloth or palm fronds suspended on a cord. In it were three terracotta heads: one of classic naturalism, the other two severely stylized cones. All can be matched in the heads that have been recovered from Ife. This is a contemporary illustration of terracotta heads in a clearly ritual context.

Within a few feet of this pavement were several separate groups of objects, each group arranged with considerable care and left undisturbed after the site was abandoned. An abundance of iron nails at the center of these groups may

Above: a reconstruction of a house in Ife, based on Obalara and Woye Asiri evidence. Terracottas stand on altars; cult objects hang above them; the recess is decorated with a mosaic of potsherd disks and a diviner's iron staff stands in it.

Opposite: pots *in situ* around the edge of the Lafogido pavement. The lids include a ram's head with a crested headdress and a hippopotamus-like creature with the same crest.

Below: a Woye Asiri pavement with a complete altar also surfaced in potsherds – a unique find. A pot neck is embedded at the center of the pavement. Scale in 10cm intervals.

indicate the position of a small timber building, all other trace of which has vanished, and which may have been a shrine. At its center lay a carefully arranged group of pieces of broken terracotta statuary. Most were heads of a graceful naturalism. Some of them were highly stylized cones and cylinders. With them were fragments of limbs and torsos. A few feet away was a group of some 40 human skulls. These were not necessarily sacrificial victims. None had articulated vertebrae. Many lacked mandibles. They were probably brought together after the corpses had decayed, perhaps in the same way that the terracotta heads from broken statues were also carefully collected and arranged within the shrine. Among the skulls stood a second ritual pot. Its neck was in the shape of an open-mouthed leopard's head. Around the shoulders was depicted a leopard in relief beside a decapitated human head. There was also a series of objects identical to those depicted on the pot buried at the center of the pavement. Elsewhere were groups of broken pots: some were household wares but the majority were special wares, designed and decorated in distinctive ways, to show their ritual purpose.

This evidence starts to show the terracottas in use. They were certainly not all royal objects. The buildings on the Obalara land are like many others. They are far from the royal palace and stand on the outskirts of the town of Ife. The terracottas were reverenced even when broken. The sculptures associated with death or sacrifice are different in style from the remainder. So sculptures must have been created for specific ritual purposes. Although the buildings on the Obalara land are certainly more than six centuries old, many of the ritual objects echo traditional Yoruba religious ritual. This correspondence is very detailed. It is likely that more excavations of this sort will extend the range of parallels and provide convincing evidence of a continuity of belief.

A continuity with the practices of Benin is also suggested. This can be seen in general terms: in the form and arrangement of altars, for instance. It is also present in human details: the vertical scarifications on the foreheads of several sculptures. It is most convincing in the same use of several motifs. Art in both towns represents the leopard in clearly ritual contexts. The pot buried in the Obalara pavement depicts a snake curled around its neck and resting its head on the roof of a shrine. We know that bronze snakes curled down the gables of important parts of the royal palace of Benin. These sorts of detailed similarity in motifs are as convincing as any stylistic analysis in suggesting a continuity between the two traditions. But they do not indicate how close or direct the affinities were, their origins or courses.

Above: cult objects depicted on the Obalara pot. Terracotta heads, bush cow horns and a manilla can be recognized.

Left: terracotta statuary in the course of excavation on Obalara's land. Many of these pieces are illustrated in the preceding visual story.

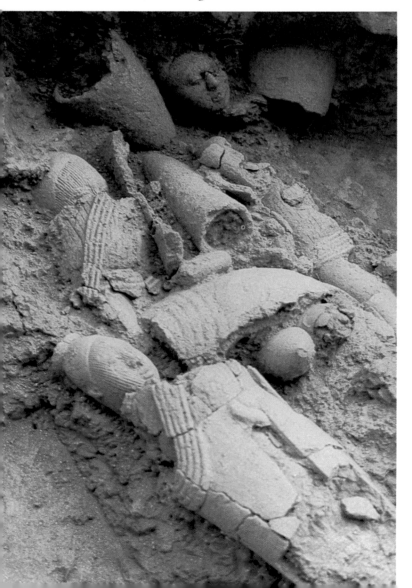

Archaeological work at Ife indicates the potential and the direction that future research will take. Still, it must be a long time before a reasonably complete and convincing picture of the context of Ife's art will be realized.

Problems of interpretation. How is one to account for the skills, artistry and wealth of the West African bronze-working centers? In particular, how did they get their copper and its alloys? These were not local. Copper, tin and lead must have been traded from the mines of the Sahara or beyond. What attracted traders to these parts of the forests? What authorities received them? Archaeological research must seek to do more than interpret the art. The prehistoric cultures of the Nigerian forests must be placed in a convincing historical context.

Igbo Ukwu is probably the most enigmatic prehistoric site in Africa. It represents an almost unparalleled concentration of wealth – in bronze and beads – in the hands of one man. It is part of a sophisticated and idiosyncratic tradition of craftsmanship and art that must have had a long history of development and is otherwise completely unknown. Yet, the present weight of the evidence indicates that it belongs to a period when the savanna states were still young. This is well before one would expect a concentration of power to have developed in forest polities. The tropical forests around Igbo Ukwu offered little produce that could be exchanged for copper or bronze. Its kola nut was inferior to varieties obtainable in the west: it did not last as long. Ivory – and slaves – were more easily obtainable to the north on the edges of the savanna. To the west, there was the additional attraction of gold. Possibly the powers at Igbo Ukwu were able to distribute salt from the coast to northern traders. But this can only have been a minor commercial item. At present, Igbo Ukwu makes no economic sense. Nothing but this one extraordinary site indicates a powerful trading authority, far beyond the economic system we know existed a millennium ago. Igbo Ukwu stands as a salutary reminder of how little we can explain the prehistory of the later Iron Age of East Africa.

The luxury and wealth of Ife can be seen in its buildings and arts and in the clothing and jewelry of a section of its populace. The equation of realistic art with a powerful, rich priesthood may not carry conviction. But the majority of the Ife sculptures also show people wearing abundant beads, including bead headdresses or crowns. Many pottery crucibles, some sherds of which were incorporated in the potsherd pavements when they were laid, show that imported glass beads were melted down and remolded to suit local tastes. This seems to have been one of the most important crafts of Ife. Elaborate

ceremonial stools of complex shapes were ground from quartz rocks. This was a task needing very great skill and effort. Beaded and jeweled human statues in bronze and terracotta are depicted seated on such stools. Beads and stools are key items in the royal regalia of the Yoruba kingdoms. Many other African kingdoms use them in the same way. So Ife too probably had centralized government and royalty.

Ife appears a wealthy state, trading in metal. How did this come about? Here Robin Horton's suggestions are illuminating and carry greater conviction than any previous studies.

Geography played a significant part in Ife's development. From Gao the Niger river flows directly southwards, until, immediately north of Ife, it turns east. The tropical forests bulge north towards this bend of the Niger. Ife is in the center of this northern extension of the forest. In the south, the Guinea coast and the network of coastal lagoons that provide sheltered waterways from the Niger delta to the Republic of Benin curve northwards towards Ife. Thus Ife is on the most direct and shortest route from the upper Niger to the tropical forest and the coast. It is ideally situated to collect forest products, for transport to the Niger river and then up the river to Gao (or across the river to the Hausa states and the northeast).

Although this route was important in the 19th century, there is no direct evidence that it was exploited earlier. But, as Horton has shown, there are hints. Just above the Niger bend, small, isolated groups of Mande peoples have lived for centuries. As we have seen, the Mande traded between the savanna and the forest. They stimulated many of the economic and political developments in West African history. These may be the relic populations of Ife's trading partners. The Nupe people have three shrines on

Below right: the walls of Ife, showing a pattern of growth and incorporation from the center. After Ozanne.

Below: Ife in relationship to trade routes and neighboring states.

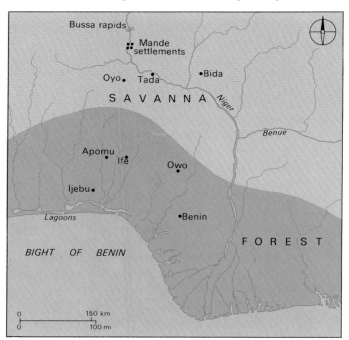

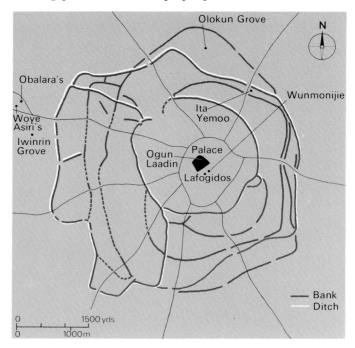

the bend of the Niger river. They contain bronzes. These are not Nupe work. One at least is identical in style to the bronzes of Ife. (Very few other bronzes are known outside the major historic cities.) Near Ife was Apomu, a very important interregional market in the 19th century. It probably originated centuries before that. Ife has given concrete evidence of a bead industry. Beads were an important item of trade for Ijebu, the town at the center of the coastal waterway trade. Significantly, Ijebu is on the lagoon closest to Ife. Thus survivors of trading communities, shrines, markets and industries, point to Ife's former commercial importance.

Ife, on archaeological evidence, ceased to be important in the 16th century. This decline can be traced, for instance, in the disappearance of the Ogane, the foreign potentate who ratified the kings of Benin, from the 16th-century Portuguese records. As the Atlantic trade with European powers was established, Ijebu and Benin grew powerful and Ife declined. Oyo, on the edge of the savanna, between Ife and the Niger river, was able to exploit both the savanna and the forest. It could, for instance, operate a cavalry army in the tsetse-free grasslands. It was also positioned to take over Ife's northern trade.

As these three new states grew, each sought to expand its frontiers outwards. This left one role for Ife: to keep the

Unlike Ife, the pattern of the banks and ditches of Benin represents the fusion of distinct, independent villages. After Connah.

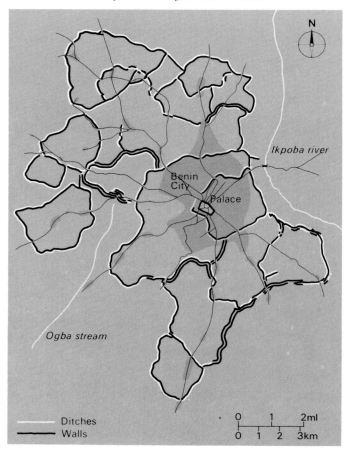

Ikpoba river

Benin City

Palace

Ogba stream

N

———— Ditches
———— Walls

0   1   2ml
0 1 2 3km

peace between the new states. Situated centrally between them, Ife could act as a buffer, a mediator and a guarantor of peace. The concept of Ife, now economically and politically weak, as a spiritual center, the mother town of the Yoruba, was created or molded to help it fulfill this new role.

When Oyo decided to break the peace and establish its supremacy, Ife was powerless to resist. Through the campaigns of Oyo in the 19th century, Ife was ruined. A few years later, Frobenius visited the wreckage of the ancient city.

This thesis offers an elegant and coherent explanation of Ife's rise and decline. But it is purely speculative. It provides a model to be tested by new archaeological work.

Benin's history, from the end of the 15th century, is readily accessible in a rich, recorded corpus of oral traditions and in the reports of many European visitors. Still, its origins, the source of its art, the skills of its craftsmen and their techniques remain primarily a field for prehistorians. Graham Connah initiated systematic fieldwork in Benin in 1961. One of the most significant parts of his work was the revelation of the intricacy of Benin's peripheral earthworks. The meandering ramparts and ditches that Connah exposed were too shallow for defense. Instead, they demarcated boundaries. They enclosed areas around separate small hamlets and their adjoining fields. Their complex plans reflect a long slow process of fusion. Over many years, distinct settlements came together politically. As they did so, their boundaries were linked by new walls, to form a single complex. This process was completed in the 15th century. Then, a massive earth rampart and ditch – over 50 feet from wall top to ditch bottom – was thrown around the royal palace at the center. It formed a true, fortified, urban center of monumental proportions. These earthworks reflect the growth of the kingdom of Benin: the slow unification of distinct village communities in an area of comparatively dense population.

In contrast, the walls of Ife have a plan that is clearly based on progressive extensions from a single center. Ife's walls were built in concentric circles. Power emanated outwards from the initial center of the town – the royal palace. As power and population grew, new areas were taken under royal protection.

The savanna states have a well-documented history. From this, their social and economic formations are comprehensible, at least in outline. One sees a coherent picture of order, progress and change. Archaeology in these areas has not yet contributed to any new understanding of these developments. In the forests, the situation is very different. With few historical aids, history presents a fragmented picture. One has vivid images of isolated items of great cultural richness. One has no deeper understanding. Yet some material is there. Horton has demonstrated its potential and how it can be used. It is now necessary to construct and test similar hypotheses.

Further reading

A great many studies in African prehistory and almost all initial excavation reports appear in periodicals, such as the *West African Journal of Archaeology, Azania: Journal of the British Institute in Eastern Africa,* the *South African Archaeological Bulletin,* the *African Archaeological Review* and the *Journal of African History,* many months, even years, before they reach book form. As a result, many of the books listed here, though more easily accessible, have been overtaken by later research.

GENERAL PREHISTORY AND ARCHAEOLOGY

Clark, J. D., and **Brandt, S. A.,** eds., *From Hunters to Farmers: the Causes and Consequences of Food Production in Africa* (Los Angeles, 1984).
Connah, G., *African Civilizations: Precolonial Cities and States in Tropical Africa – an Archaeological Perspective* (Cambridge, 1987).
Davidson, B., *Africa: History of a Continent* (London, 1966).
Oliver, R., and **Fagan, B. M.,** eds., *Africa in the Iron Age* (Cambridge, 1975).
Phillipson, D. W., *African Archaeology* (Cambridge, 1985).
Vansina, J., *Art History in Africa* (London, 1984).

PRECOLONIAL HISTORY

Ajayi, J. F. A., and **Crowder, M.,** eds., *History of West Africa,* vol. 1 (2nd ed., London, 1976).
Ogot, B. A., and **Kieran, J. A.,** *Zamani: a Survey of East African History* (2nd ed., Nairobi, 1973).
Oliver, R., ed., *Cambridge History of Africa,* vol. 3, from c. 1050 to c. 1600 (Cambridge, 1977).
Wilson, M., and **Thompson, L.,** eds., *Oxford History of South Africa,* vol. 1 (Oxford, 1969).

DOCUMENTS

Davidson, B., *The African Past* (London, 1964).
Freeman–Grenville, G. S. P., *The East African Coast: Select Documents from the First to the Earlier Nineteenth Century* (Oxford, 1962).
Theal, G. M., *Records of South-Eastern Africa,* 9 vols. (Cape Town, 1898; reprinted, 1964).

SUDAN AND ETHIOPIA

Buxton, D., *The Abyssinians* (London, 1970).
Harlan, J. L., de Wet, J. M. J., and **Stemler, A. B. L.,** *Origins of African Plant Domestication* (The Hague, 1976).
Levtzion, N., *Ancient Ghana and Mali* (London, 1973).
Lhote, H., *The Search for the Tassili Frescoes* (London, 1959).
Shinnie, P. L., *Meroë: a Civilization of the Sudan* (London, 1967).

WEST AFRICA

Connah, G., *The Archaeology of Benin* (Oxford, 1975).
Dark, P. J. C., *An Introduction to Benin Art and Technology* (Oxford, 1973).
Fagg, W., *Nigerian Images* (London, 1963).
Shaw, T., *Nigeria* (London, 1978).
—— *Unearthing Igbo Ukwu* (Ibadan, 1977).
Willett, F., *Ife in the History of West African Sculpture* (London, 1967).
Williams, D., *Icon and Image: a Study of Sacred and Secular Forms of African Classical Art* (London, 1974).

EASTERN AND SOUTHERN AFRICA

Fagan, B. M., *Southern Africa in the Iron Age* (London, 1965).
Garlake, P. S., *The Early Islamic Architecture of the East African Coast* (London, 1966).
—— *Great Zimbabwe* (London, 1973).
—— *Great Zimbabwe Described and Explained* (Harare, 1985).
Hall, M., *The Changing Past: Farmers, Kings and Traders in Southern Africa, 200–1860* (Cape Town, 1987).
Kirkman, J. S., *Men and Monuments of the East African Coast* (London, 1964).
Phillipson, D. W., *The Later Prehistory of Eastern and Southern Africa* (London, 1977).

Acknowledgments

Unless otherwise stated, all the illustrations on a given page are credited to the same source.

Bildarchiv Preussischer Kulturbesitz, Berlin (West) 39
John Brennan, Oxford 78 (bottom)
British Museum, London 35
Peter Cheze-Brown, London 79 (left), 89 (bottom left), 90 (top right)
H. N. Chittick (British Institute in Eastern Africa), Nairobi 30 (bottom), 45 (bottom), 46 (bottom), 100, 012 (bottom).
Christie's, London frontispiece, 36 (left)
J. Desmond Clark, Berkeley 53
Colorific, London 12 (bottom), 23 (bottom), 50 (botton), 91 (top)
Ekpo Eyo, Lagos 132
J. F. Eloff, by courtesy of the University of Pretoria 72 (top)
Bernard Fagg, Oxford 22 (top), 130 (right)
Federal Department of Antiquities, Nigeria 130 (left), 131
Colin Flight, Birmingham 123
Werner Forman Archive, London 25, 42 (bottom right), 98, 104 (top), 119
Peter Garlake, London 10, 14 (top), 15 (left), 17, 24 (left), 26 (top, and bottom right), 32 (bottom), 45 (top and center), 49, 51 (top), 55 (bottom right), 57 (top), 58, 64 (bottom right), 65, 67, 68 (top, and bottom right), 73, 75, 76, 79 (right), 81, 83, 86 (bottom), 87 (left), 88 (top and bottom right), 89 (top left, and bottom right), 90 (left), 91 (center and bottom), 92, 95, 97, 102 (top), 103 (top), 104 (bottom), 105 (right), 108 (bottom), 111, 112 (top and bottom right), 115 (top and bottom left), 116 (bottom), 125, 133 (bottom), 134 (bottom)
Geological Survey Department, Salisbury 71 (bottom right), 72 (bottom)
Roger Gorringe, London 50 (center), 85 (bottom right), 86 (top), 94 (bottom), 101, 105 (left), by courtesy of Caroline Sassoon 128
Robert Harding Associates, London 9, 12 (top), 13 (bottom left), 15 (right), 16 (top), 25 (top), 29, 30 (top), 31, 32 (top), 54, 63, 64 (top), 68 (center), 96, 122
Haupstadtarchiv, Stuttgart 33
Hoa-Qui, Paris 13 (bottom right), 27, 46, 50 (top), 66 (top), 69, 71 (bottom left)

Michael Holford Library, Loughton Jacket, 24 (right), 37 (top), 40, 114 (top left), 115 (bottom right), 116 (top), 117
Alan Hutchinson Library, London 16 (bottom), 26 (bottom left), 48, 55 (bottom left)
Richard Lewington, Oxford 84
Lovell Johns, Oxford 11, 52, 57 (bottom right), 60, 72 (bottom), 87 (right), 121, 135 (left)
Elizabeth McClelland 22 (bottom)
Yvonne McLean, London 20, 78 (top), 85 (top), 133 (top)
Museum für Völkerkunde, Staatliche Museen Preussischer Kulturbesitz, Berlin (West) 115 (top right)
National Archives of Rhodesia, Salisbury 34
National Monuments Commission, Livingstone 85 (bottom left)
Oxford Illustrators, Oxford 88 (top left), 99, 110 (right), 135 (right), 136
D. W. Phillipson, Nairobi 59
John Picton, London 68 (bottom right), 113 (top right)
Picturepoint, London 44, 88 (bottom left), 93, 103 (bottom)
Pitt Rivers Museum, University of Oxford 36 (right), 37 (bottom)
Leonard Pole, Saffron Walden 14 (bottom)
Popperfoto, London 38
M. Posnansky, Los Angeles 110 (left), 120, 124
P. A. Rahtz, Birmingham 56
C. Thurstan Shaw, Cambridge 129
P. L. Shinnie, Calgary 41, 42 (top and bottom left), 43
Doig Simmonds, London 66 (bottom)
Andrew B. Smith, Cape Town 55 (top)
Spectrum Colour Library, London 108 (top)
Francis E. Speed, Ile-Ife 112 (top and bottom left), 113 (top left, and bottom), 134 (top)
J. E. G. Sutton, Accra 57 (bottom left)
Frank Willett, Glasgow 114 (top right, and bottom)
Zefa, London 21, 47, 64 (bottom left), 89 (top right), 131

The Publishers have attempted to observe the legal requirements with respect to the rights of the suppliers of photographic materials. Nevertheless, persons who have claims are invited to apply to the Publishers.

Glossary

Abbasid Dynasty that ruled at Baghdad from 750 to 1258 AD. It traced its descent from Abbas, the uncle of the Prophet Muhammad. It succeeded the **Umayyad** dynasty.

Aggrey beads Cylindrical, drawn cane **beads** of glass, with snapped ends. They are often corded (showing striations caused by drawing a viscous glass) or dichroic (that is, they appear blue in direct light and yellow in transmitted light). They were traded in West Africa from early in the present millennium.

al Bakri, Abu Ubaydallah Andalusian Arab geographer of the 11th century, who lived in Cordoba. He collected oral information from traders who had visited the Sudan. From this, he described Ghana and many other states in West Africa, the goldfields, their trade with the Maghrib, and the routes and centers through which the trade passed, immediately before the **Almoravid** conquests. al Bakri's work marks a turning point in Arab historiography and allows a detailed study of economic, political and religious aspects of the early West African states.

al Fazari Arab geographer, who lived at the court of the **Abbasid** caliph in Baghdad at the end of the 8th century. His description of "Ghana, the land of gold" is the first mention of that kingdom in Arab writings.

al Omari, Ibn Fadl-Allah 14th-century Arab writer who described the kingdom of Mali from information obtained from a court functionary or the king himself, Mansa Musa, when he was in Cairo on his pilgrimage to Mecca in 1324. al Omari also got material from a learned friend who had lived in Mali for 35 years. His work complements that of his contemporary, **Ibn Battuta**.

al Yakubi Arab writer of the later 9th century.

Alluvial gold Gold, scoured from weathered or eroded ores by torrential rain or river action and carried downstream, disseminated as minute particles in suspension in river waters. It is found deposited in alluvium – the sands and silts laid down by river action. As a mining technique, the washing of alluvial gold was a relatively simple method of recovery. It probably predated the extraction of gold from **reefs** in eastern Africa.

Almoravids Religious and military movement committed to a rigorous Islamic orthodoxy, founded in the 11th century by Abdullah Ibn Yasin, among the Sanhaja nomads of the western Sudan. In their *jihad*, or holy war, they first conquered the caravan towns of the western Sahara and gained control of the Saharan caravan trade. They went on to rule much of the Maghrib, Morocco and southern Spain.

Amazonite Opaque, pale green, semiprecious stone, one of the potassium felspar group of minerals.

Assemblage Group of objects found in closed association with each other and thus used at the same time by the same group of people: objects originally and intentionally deposited together and not in accidental juxtaposition.

Atlantis Earthly paradise described by Plato in his *Timaeus*, quoting Solon and, through him, the Egyptian priests as his authorities. Many improbable interpretations, besides **Frobenius**'s, have been offered as to where it was. Most likely, Atlantis was a philosophic abstraction, like other Utopias, and was never intended to be considered as fact.

Azania Name given to the interior of eastern Africa in Greco-Roman writings, e.g. in **Ptolemy**'s *Geography* and in the **Periplus of the Erythraean Sea**.

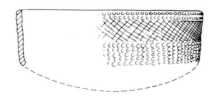

Bambata ware from Khami

Bambata ware Ware characterized by its thin body, smooth finish and the considerable decoration over most of the vessel, formed by incised lines or small punched impressions, made with a variety of pointed implements. Found in very small amounts in a few scattered rock shelters on the Zambezian plateau, it is unrelated to **Early Iron Age wares**. Its dating and associations are uncertain. Probably it was made during the first millennium AD, possibly earlier.

Beads Glass trade beads of Africa include cane beads, in which molten glass is drawn out to form a long tube which is then snapped into short lengths. Such beads were frequently reheated to round off their sharp ends. Wound beads are formed by winding a long thin thread of molten glass around a wire which is later withdrawn leaving a hole for stringing. Although glass was not manufactured in sub-Saharan Africa, glass beads were often made locally – in Ife, at Mapungubwe and elsewhere –by melting down trade beads and pouring the molten glass into a clay mold. (See also **Aggrey beads**.)

Bent, James Theodore (1852–97) English traveler and antiquarian. Bent visited the Greek islands, the coast of Asia Minor and Bahrein before excavating at Great Zimbabwe in 1891, at the invitation of the British South Africa Company, the Royal Geographic Society and the British Association for the Advancement of Science. His findings were published in *The Ruined Cities of Mashonaland* in 1893. Thereafter Bent investigated Aksum in 1893 and made seven expeditions to south Arabia.

Bog iron See **Laterite**.

Brass Alloy of copper containing up to 30 per cent zinc.

Bridewealth Traditional offering to the bride's kin before marriage, made by the bridegroom's family, in societies where marriage is seen as an exchange between kinship groups and as an ongoing transaction between the families.

Bronze Alloy of copper containing approximately 90 per cent copper and 10 per cent tin. Leaded bronze includes 10 per cent or more lead, in addition to copper and tin. Antimony and arsenic in small proportions – up to 3 per cent – serve to harden the alloy. Bronze has a lower melting point than copper and is easier to cast without flaws.

Cable pattern Form of molding based on oblique grooving, which resembles the twist of a rope or cable. It was possibly developed from herringbone patterns. This design, carved in coral, was a popular molding around the **mihrabs** of mosques on the East African coast.

Carination Angle or ridge where the profile of a vessel sharply changes direction.

Carnelian Clear red or reddish brown semiprecious stone; a form of smooth, waxy quartz with no visible crystal structure.

Caton-Thompson, Gertrude English archaeologist. Director of excavations at Great Zimbabwe and other Rhodesian sites for the British Association for the Advancement of Science in 1929. She first excavated in Egypt at Abydos in 1922 but her main interests lay in the Paleolithic and predynastic periods of North Africa and southwest Asia. In these fields she conducted excavations in the Fayum, Kharga Oasis, Badari and the Hadramaut. Her assertion that Great Zimbabwe was an indigenous African creation of comparatively recent times, and her remark that she kept local settler retorts to this interpretation filed under the heading "Insane," never endeared her to local white opinion in Rhodesia.

Celadon Chinese ceramic with a hard white or gray **stoneware** body, often carved in floral patterns, painted with a monochrome, lustrous, felspathic glaze in various shades of green, from olive to almost a pale blue. Kilns in the Lung Chuan province of China were important producers of celadon from the Sung dynasty (11th to 12th century) onwards.

Cable pattern molding

Changamire Ruling dynasty of the **Rozvi** people. Portuguese chroniclers suggested that the name incorporated the Arabic title Emir, and that this was given to the Rozvi king by coastal traders.

Chief One who has authority within a ranked society in which access to resources is unequal. A chief has no monopoly of force and lacks the power of the ruler of a **state**. Differences in status within a chieftaincy are social rather than political or economic. Control of resources is not vested in individuals. Characteristically, a chief is the agent at the center of a system of redistribution, a system that permeates his entire community.

Chikunda (Achikunda, Chicunda) Originally the slaves of the *prazos*, the early Portuguese estates in the Zambezi valley of Mozambique, the Chikunda acquired an elite status as the military arm of the *prazos*. They developed a strong sense of identity and came to look upon themselves as a nation apart. Under the leadership of their chiefs they organized

predatory bands and established their independence for nearly 30 years in the early 19th century.

Cire-perdue casting (lost wax) Technique of casting copper and its alloys, particularly useful for producing complex shapes. The object is modeled in wax over a clay core and then encased or invested in further layers of clay. The whole thing is then heated so that the wax melts and escapes or is vaporized. Molten metal is poured into the cavity formerly occupied by the wax. When the metal has cooled, the clay investment is broken open and the metal casting removed. The casting is an exact copy of the original wax model. It is also unique for there is no mold from which further castings could be obtained.

City-state Independent political unit based on a capital city. The territory of such a state may include a number of nearby rural villages or hamlets but is not extensive.

Conus shells Compact, cone-shaped shells of many different species of *Conus*, common in tropical seas, including the Indian Ocean. Disk-shaped pendants cut from the base of such shells retain a distinctive spiral pattern of grooves. They were adopted as symbols of chieftainship throughout much of central and eastern Africa. Among the Shona they are known as *ndoro*. Several, including one mounted in gold, were found with the burials of Ingombe Ilede on the Zambezi river. Others were recovered at the Manekweni **zimbabwe** in southern Mozambique. In the mid-19th century David Livingstone recorded that two conus shells were the price of a slave.

Cornice Horizontal molding running around a building or the walls of a room.

Cowries Shells of small marine gastropods, *Cypraea*, that live in shallow warm water. Small varieties, especially *Cypraea annulus*, an East African species, are found sporadically in many Early and later Iron Age deposits in eastern Africa. Often their backs were cut away so that they could be strung or used as ornaments and beads. All cowries found in West Africa were imported primarily as a currency. *C. moneta* cowries – originating in the Maldive Islands – were brought overland from North Africa from the 11th century. *C. annulus* was probably imported once sea links with East Africa were established by the Portuguese, but only in very small quantities until mass dumping in the 19th century brought swift inflation. In the late 19th century the cowrie was so devalued that the purchase of all but the most trifling commodities presented major difficulties of transportation: in 1885 a wife cost between 20,000 and 100,000 cowries.

Cucurbit Gourd.

Culture Full range of human activity, represented by objects, buildings, burials etc., and including, for example, religious practices and beliefs or social organization. In archaeological usage, culture is now a nebulous term, generally indicating artifacts made by related communities of a greater order than an **industry** and covering a greater range of human activities: i.e. a grouping of industries, considered to represent a single whole.

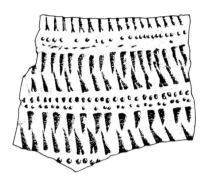

Dotted way line ware from Esh Shaheinab

Currency General-purpose money, or currency, is a widely accepted means of exchange, mode of payment, standard of value and method of storing wealth. It presupposes a developed **market** economy and exchange system and was therefore relatively rare in Iron Age Africa. Copper **ingots** may have served as a form of currency in some Iron Age societies. The circulation of special-purpose money is restricted to particular spheres of an economy.

Daga Puddled clay, often mixed with the earth from a termite mound and cattle dung, used to construct the floors and walls of houses. Wall daga is generally daubed or smeared on a framework of upright timber poles interwoven with bark bindings or lathes.

Dambo Open, grassy plain, formed in shallow depressions in the ground that have an impermeable subsoil. Dambos are waterlogged or even flooded during the wet season and retain moisture for much of the year.

de Barros, Joao The most accurate and distinguished Portuguese historian of the 16th century. Between 1522 and 1525 de Barros was captain of S. Jorge da Mina, the first Portuguese base in West Africa. Then, for many years, he was Keeper of the Indian archives in Lisbon. There he had access to all the principal documents of the early discoverers and administrators.

Divine kingship (or, in Africa, Sudanic kingship) Mystical identification of monarch and people, in which the health and well-being of king and subjects are conjoined. Some societies see such a king as a god in human form or as the living vehicle for spiritual forces, by which the king's predecessors ensure the vitality and continuity of the nation.

Dolerite Igneous rock similar to granite but darker in color, with a finer crystal structure. Hence it is more homogeneous and has no clear fracture planes. It is a fine material for chipped stone tools.

Dotted wavy line ware Pottery decorated with multiple, horizontal, grooved wavy lines, formed by fish-spines and punctate designs made by jabbing the clay with a blunt bone point. It is characteristic of the earliest villagers of the Sahara and southeastern Ethiopia. The earlier forms appear to have been decorated with grooves alone (wavy line ware – see **Khartoum Mesolithic**.)

Early Iron Age Archaeological **tradition** defined by the first appearance of iron metallurgy. Agriculture, domesticated animals, pottery, substantial semipermanent villages and houses built of poles and **daga** were introduced at the same time. The Early Iron Age started and spread over most of eastern Africa in the three or four centuries before and after the start of the Christian era.

Early Iron Age pot from Uganda

Early Iron Age wares (formerly known as "dimple based ware" in East Africa, "channeled ware" in Zambia and "stamped ware" in Rhodesia) Wares of generally thick and gritty fabric. The lip is frequently thickened and decorated by a band of oblique lines, often made by stamping the teeth of a small carved comb in the surface of the clay. The neck and upper body are usually decorated with broad, shallow, horizontal or curvilinear lines. As the original name suggests, some East African vessels had shallow indentations in the base, perhaps to make them more stable when standing or carried on the head.

Entrepreneur One who acts as an intermediary in a commercial transaction and hence the archetypal innovator. In eastern Africa the state did not provide the security and order necessary for market-oriented trade, as it did in most of West Africa. Consequently, several East African groups (see **Chikunda** and **Vashambadzi**) made their names and livings as entrepreneurs between local producers and foreign traders based on the east coast ports. Their power and influence hinged on an acute awareness of commercial forces, allied to a tough capacity to operate over enormous distances on foot. It has been claimed that "their achievements, more perhaps than any other set of facts, should effectively destroy the stereotype of a pre-colonial Africa prostrate and passive before the forces of the outside world." (See also **underdevelopment**.)

Ethnic group People who share durable ties of language, religion, kinship, clan and chieftainship.

Exfoliation Process of weathering and breakup of certain rocks, particularly granite. A granite mass develops a regular pattern of weaknesses in its initial cooling. Subsequently, rapid temperature changes – either natural, through the heat of the sun and rapid cooling under clear night skies, or artificial, from lighting fires and quenching them – cause sufficient expansion and contraction to split the rock along these natural fracture planes. This produces parallel-sided slabs of stone of uniform thickness.

Facies Distinct, contemporaneous and related cluster of artifacts occurring within a **phase** and in a comparatively limited geographical area.

Faience Ceramics or beads with a soft earthenware body covered with an opaque glass, often painted with an over-glaze design and refired.

Fairs Seasonal markets where goods are exchanged with foreign traders. They were administered and regulated by the ruler of the territory in which they were held or a central authority delegated by the foreign traders.

Ferricrete See **Laterite**.

Filigree Ornamental work in which a fine metal thread or wire is formed into delicate tracery. In West African **cire-perdue** bronze casting, patterns formed by threads of wax or latex laid on the wax surface of a sculpture are reproduced in their full refinement in the final casting.

Frobenius, Leo (1873–1935) German anthropologist who led 12 expeditions to Africa: the Congo, 1904–06; Algeria, 1910

and 1912–14; Guinea, 1907–09; Nigeria, 1910–12; four expeditions to Egypt and Sudan from 1912; Eritrea, 1915; southern Africa, 1928–30; and Libya, 1932. He was director of the Frankfurt Museum fur Volkerkunde, now the Frobenius Institute, and a leading exponent of an extreme diffusionist school of anthropology.

Glaze Glassy, vitreous surface-coating applied to pottery.

Granite Igneous rock with a visible crystalline structure, usually a light gray color, with a pepper and salt appearance. Hard, tough and with a system of parallel fracture planes, it is an ideal building material. The inland plateaus of Africa are generally the peneplains of very ancient granite batholiths or shields. Weathered granites form light, marginally fertile, sandy soils, often acid and deficient in essential basic minerals such as lime, potash and nitrate.

Grave-goods Offerings placed with the deceased on burial. They may represent personal possessions, offerings to the dead man's spirit or provisions for the afterlife.

Great Lakes Lake Victoria and the major lakes of the **rift valleys** of East Africa: Lakes Turkana (Rudolf), Albert, Edward, Kivu, Tanganyika and Malawi.

Greenstone Colloquial term for lavas or basalts that have been metamorphosed to chloritic schist. They are a component of the most ancient rocks of the Zambezian plateau, formed over 3,000,000,000 years ago and known as the "gold belts." They often contain gold-bearing quartz veins. They yield easily to pressure and faults and fractures are common.

Hamites Term used in a confusing variety of ways to denote linguistic, physical and cultural traits. Primarily, it reflects the old European assumption that light-skinned peoples are more intelligent than dark-skinned. Hamites have been envisaged as a Caucasoid ideal, the most "European-like" of Africans. To them has been attributed any remarkable technological feat, notable political organization or trace of "civilization." It is a term now almost entirely discarded.

Harpoon Carved bone point from 2 to 6 inches long, that has curved barbs down one or both sides, with a pierced or grooved base which can be attached to a wooden shaft, presumably used to spear fish. Closely similar harpoons have been found at many sites in the Sahara and Sudan, from the Niger river to Kenya, associated with intensive hunting or gathering and dated to the centuries immediately before food production developed. With **dotted wavy line pottery** such harpoons have been taken to indicate an

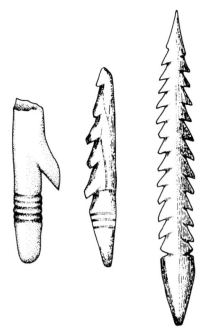

Harpoons from early fishing settlements in eastern Africa

extremely widespread and long-lived "aqualithic civilization," based on the exploitation of the resources of lakes, swamps and rivers during a period of high rainfall.

Herodotus Greek historian, born in Asia Minor about 480 BC, whose works mark the beginning of historical writing among the Greeks. He traveled in Greece, Asia Minor, Egypt and on the shores of the Black Sea and collected historical, geographical and ethnographical material. This he sifted with some critical discernment and included it in the basic theme of his writing, the struggle between the Greeks and barbarians in the three centuries before his birth.

Hoe Virtually the sole implement employed in traditional African agriculture. Made of forged iron, it generally has a shovel or leaf-shaped blade, with a heavy tang. A midrib usually reinforces the blade. The tool is hafted, often at an acute angle, in a wooden handle, that frequently has a heavy or projecting heel. The size of blade and length of handle can vary a great deal. Hoes, generally of particular shapes, are traditional **prestige goods**, used in **tribute**, as religious offerings or as **bride-wealth**.

Ibn Battuta, Mahomet Ibn Abdulla
Famous Maghribi traveler born in Tangier in 1304. His *Travels* are a prime source for Islamic and Africanist scholars. After his last journey, across the Sahara to Mali in 1352, he settled in his native Morocco and dictated this account of his journeys. Although there are indications that he kept some records, for he

mentions notes being stolen, he made many errors in place-names and became confused about dates. His accounts of his voyage down the east coast of Africa in 1331 present many problems in interpretation, so much so that J. Spencer Trimingham has questioned whether he actually went further south than Mogadishu.

Industry Objects made by a prehistoric people in one area over a defined period of time. When similar **assemblages** consistently recur within one area within a given period, they constitute an industry. An industry may include a series of successive **phases** and comprise different **facies**.

Ingots Metal cast into a particular shape, determined by custom rather than function, for trade. Copper ingots in Africa include the rods of standard lengths and weight found in the 11th- or 12th-century caravan that perished at Ma'den Ijafen in Mauritania. Large numbers of small copper ingots in crosses or "croisettes" in standard sizes, 2 and 5 inches long, were found in the **Early Irone Age** cemeteries of Sanga on the upper Lualaba river. Large, flanged, cross-shaped ingots, made for trade in the Zambezi valley and its environs, were described by an early Portuguese explorer as shaped like *aspas*, the sails of a windmill. Cross-shaped ingots or *handa* made from the copper of mines in southern Zaire were regular items of trade in central Africa into the 20th century. Bronze manillas, in the shape of a torque or bracelet, were an important form of **currency** in West Africa from at least the 15th century.

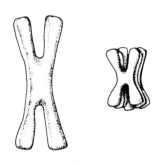

Ingots from Sanga

Interlacustrine kingdoms States in the high grasslands between Lake Victoria and the lakes of the western **Rift Valley**. These states include Ganda, Nyoro, Toro, Nkore, Karagwe, Rwanda and Rundi. All are situated on the northern periphery of Bantu settlement and were much influenced in their formative periods, early in the present millennium, by incursions of Central Sudanic, Paranilotic and, later, Nilotic pastoralists.

Iron gongs (or bells) Distinctive item of ironwork, generally made of two long

triangular sheets of iron, beaten to a concave shape and welded together around their edges. Such gongs have a thin, short, tang-like handle and are clapperless. They are often made in pairs. These large, rare and very distinctive instruments have been found in later Iron Age archaeological sites at Great Zimbabwe, the **zimbabwe** of Manekweni in southern Mozambique, the cemeteries of Ingombe Ilede, and Sanga. In the Zaire basin they are widely recognized as symbols of chieftainship.

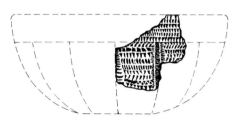

Kantsyore ware

Ironpan See **Laterite**.

Iron smelting Chemical reduction of iron ores (generally, in simple technologies, the various oxides and carbonates of iron) to iron by heating in the presence of an excess of carbon monoxide, which combines with the oxygen of the ores. The process involves charging a furnace – in Africa a domical or cylindrical structure of clay up to 6 feet high – with charcoal and ore, which is then fired. The air flow to the furnace, either natural or forced through bellows, is introduced through clay pipes – *tuyeres* or *tewels* – at the base of the furnace. At the end of the smelt, the *bloom* is separated from the viscous glassy waste material. It is then forged – a process of heating and hammering that expels waste fragments and combines carbon with the iron to make, in effect, a steel.

Kantsyore ware Ware from around Lake Victoria, though sites have been found as far south as Eyasi in northern Tanzania. It was probably made by farmers contemporary with the last pastoralists of the **Stone Bowl culture**. A poorly fired ware, with a distinctive rough surface, characterized by an overall pattern of impressions, probably made with a variety of sticks, fish spines, bones and river shells, it is similar in style to **dotted wavy line ware**.

Khartoum Mesolithic (Early Khartoum) Culture defined by A. J. Arkell from his excavations in 1949 at Khartoum, the capital of the Sudan Republic on the river Nile. He characterized it by a predominantly microlithic stone industry, bone **harpoons**, grooved and bored stones (some of them probably fishing net sinkers) and "wavy line" pottery. **Dotted wavy line wares** appear in a later phase of the culture. The economy of the Khartoum

Mesolithic villages appears to have been based on fishing.

Khartoum Neolithic Culture succeeding the **Khartoum Mesolithic**, defined by A. J. Arkell from excavations at Shaheinab on the Nile, 50 miles downstream from Khartoum. The material culture, as defined by Arkell, is very similar to that of the Khartoum Mesolithic, with the addition of pierced butts to harpoons, to attach a line. Burnished finishes are now given to the **dotted wavy line wares**, and, most importantly, sheep and cattle were domesticated. It is now evident that this culture is a manifestation of the beginning of farming, which can be traced through many areas of the Sahara and Sudan.

Kinship Blood relationship. Kin are related by descent not marriage. Such relationships must be acknowledged as significant. Recognized or *de jure* descent can be distinguished from *de facto* but unrecognized descent. Descent may become a basic principle of social organization on which many vital rights, duties and interests turn. It may be extended, by a convenient fiction, to include people who are not true kin.

Kola nut Tree crop extensively cultivated in the West African forest zone, where it has long been a significant export crop. The nuts contain caffeine and are chewed as a stimulant, particularly in the Islamic world, where alcohol is prohibited. *Cola nitida*, grown from Guinea to Ghana, lasts better than *Cola acuminata*, grown in Nigeria. It is thus more highly valued and more extensively traded.

Late Stone Age Loosely defined group of **industries** or **cultures** in which the technological emphasis is on the production of microlithic stone implements, the majority of which appear to have been set in wooden shafts to form composite arrows. On this evidence, the Late Stone Age was based on a nomadic hunting and gathering economy, in which the bow and arrow was the main weapon. It is now generally argued that the Late Stone Age represents an environmental adaptation with no specific or significant cultural or chronological content, and that the term is therefore too broadly based to be useful.

Later Iron Age Complete changes in pottery styles are evidenced throughout eastern Africa about the 11th century AD (e.g. **rouletted ware**), marking the introduction of the later Iron Age. The later Iron Age lacks the homogeneity of the **Early Iron Age** and includes several distinct cultures. In many areas the later Iron Age saw the introduction of class-based societies, centralized government, the breakdown of village self-sufficiency, production for exchange, nucleation of settlements and extensive foreign trade.

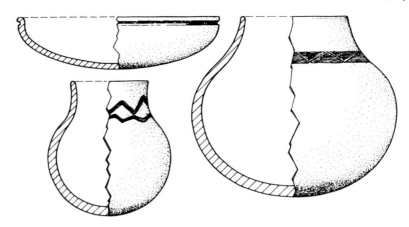

Leopard's Kopje pottery

Laterite Iron-rich residual product of climatic weathering, derived from many different rocks under strongly oxidizing and leaching conditions which have removed all other constituents of the rock. Loosely and colloquially, the heavy red clay soils of the humid tropics are called laterite. The accumulations of hydrated iron oxides – laterite in the strict sense – deposited in such soils can form nodules loosely referred to as bog iron. Bog iron in the strict sense is iron hydroxides (limonite) or carbonates (siderite) formed in the shallows of peaty lakes, largely through bacterial action. Sheets or crusts of impervious iron concretions in the subsoil or at the level of the water table are ironpan or ferricrete. These iron oxides frequently provide a useful, widespread and easily accessible source of ore for **iron smelting**.

Leakey, Louis Seymour Bazett (1903–72) Probably the best-known archaeologist to have worked in Africa. A Kenyan, he commenced his archaeological research in East Africa while a student on vacation from Cambridge in the 1920s. His absorbing interest was always early man. His many extremely important discoveries in this field, particularly at Olduvai Gorge in northern Tanzania, included a series of fossil hominids that have transformed prehistorians' perspectives of man's ancestry. With his wife Mary, and early in his career when there were no other archaeologists interested in African prehistory between the Sahara and South Africa, Leakey excavated a series of sites in the **Rift Valley** of Kenya that contained deposits that can now be identified as representing the first pastoralists in eastern Africa: the Njoro River Cave, Gamble's Cave, Hyrax Hill and others. In 1948 the Leakeys published the first description of **Early Iron Age** pottery, found around Lake Victoria and now known as Urewe ware.

Leopard's Kopje Culture of the **later Iron Age**, found in the dry, southwestern scrub and grasslands of the Zambezian plateau.

The first phase – Mambo – flourished from the 11th century AD. Its pottery had simple shapes and sparse decoration, often formed by narrow bands of incised lines or brushmarks, made by dragging a frayed stick end or bundle of grass stems over the surface. The succeeding phase – Woolandale – flourished in the 13th and 14th centuries. Its pottery is characterized by finer surface finishes, often burnished. Bands of regular, hatched, geometric patterns were incised in the dry clay. Shallow bowls and platters were given particularly fine finishes and decoration.

Long-distance trade Trade between culturally different peoples within a state or between separate states. This trade presupposes the existence of **markets** and a **market economy**. In such economies, goods are produced for exchange and not for use within the producing community. Often entire communities specialize in particular agricultural products or manufactured goods and thus lose their self-sufficiency. Long-distance trade has been seen as closely related to the growth of centralized systems, able to control or administer production, accumulation, distribution and circulation of goods, and ensure security of access to the markets and equitable transactions. Hence an intimate, usually causal connection between long-distance trade and the formation of states was once considered to be almost universal.

Lost wax See **cire-perdue casting**.

Mambo Title of the ruler or king of the **Rozvi** state.

Mansa Title of the ruler or king of Mali.

Market, Market economy A market, as a marketplace, is a site where goods may be exchanged. It connotes no particular economic regime. Such markets may have their most significant roles as places where social intercourse is stimulated, where information is readily disseminated, where different sectors of the community can be integrated and political influence or control over a population can be most easily exerted. On the other hand, a market economy is one in which goods are produced for sale and production and prices respond mainly or entirely to commercial opportunities – the law of supply and demand – and are not determined by extraneous factors such as a ruler's decrees or kin obligations.

Microliths from Lake Victoria

Mauch, Karl (1837–75) German self-taught geologist and explorer who traveled continuously in southern Africa from 1865 to 1872. He rediscovered goldfields in Shona territory in 1865. Mauch visited Great Zimbabwe in 1871, the second European to do so. He published descriptions of the ruins in A. Petermann's *Mittheilungen* in 1872 and 1874. Soon after returning to Germany, Mauch died in a fall from his bedroom window, unable to find employment save in a cement factory. His diaries were published in 1969.

Mhondoro Shona term for the spirit of a senior tribal ancestor – king, hero or founding father – who resides in the body of a lion when not communicating through a **spirit medium**. Mhondoro are ranked according to genealogical seniority.

Microlith Small stone tool, geometric in shape, made from a blade or flake. Few could have been used without hafting. Many served as barbs or tips to arrows.

Midden Heap of refuse (broken pots, ash, food remains etc.) found on the site of a settlement.

Mihrab Niche in a mosque or place of prayer, indicating the *qibla* or direction of Mecca and customarily more highly decorated than the rest of the structure.

Millet Tropical cereal grasses indigenous to Africa. Like the **sorghums**, millets are drought-resistant and have a short summer growing season. They require even less rain than sorghums: from 8 inches per annum. Types of millet include *Pennisetum* (pearl or bullrush), *Eleusine* (finger), *Digitaria* (fonio or fundi) and *Brachiaria*.

Minaret Tower from which the Muslim call to prayer is given five times a day.

Minbar Pulpit from which the Friday prayer in a mosque is led. It normally consists of a platform at the head of a straight flight of stairs and stands immediately on the right of the **mihrab**.

Monolith Single upright stone set vertically in a building or in the ground.

Monsoon Seasonal wind of south Asia and especially of the northern Indian Ocean. The monsoon blows from the northeast in winter (November to February) and from the southwest in summer (April to September). Its influence extends as far south as southern Tanzania and the northern end of the Mozambique Channel. This seasonal reversal of seaborne winds was the prime factor in stimulating seaborne traffic between Africa and Asia, in determining the maritime orientation of the East African city-states and in influencing the location of the major ports. As knowledge of local weather conditions, navigation, sailing and boatbuilding grew, so the optimum location of a trading port changed.

Moors Portuguese term used from the 16th century for Muslim traders of eastern Africa (vaMwenye, as the Africans called them). They were clearly distinguished from the Africans of the interior – "heathen kaffirs." It is also clear that they were not "Arabs," as the word is often translated. They were "dark-skinned," "dark brown" or "black," and were distinguishable from the "white Moors" who were Arabs from the Asian homelands. It is apparent that they were the indigenous Swahili people whose home was the East African coast. When the Portuguese arrived, "Moors" were settled in a series of large villages up the Zambezi river into what is now Zambia. They were also influential at the court of the **Munhu Mutapa**, though a much-quoted document of 1511, reporting 10,000 Moors in that ruler's territories, is a grotesque exaggeration.

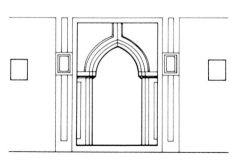

Mihrab on the East African coast

Munhu Mutapa Title of the ruler of the Shona state on the northern Zambezian plateau from the 15th century. The kingdom may have originated indirectly or directly in a secession from Great Zimbabwe. Its authority extended as far as the Indian Ocean coast in the early 16th century. It was described by many early Portuguese chroniclers. The title is variously derived from the Shona *munhu* "person," *mwene* "master, lord," or *mwana* "child," and *mutapa* "one who explores or pillages." Over 100 variant spellings exist, one of the most common being "Monomotapa." Munhu Mutapa is the current Shona preference.

Mwari Creator, High God and Supreme Being of the Shona people. In the northern Shona area he is generally considered somewhat remote from human aspirations and concerned with society as a whole rather than with individual lives. In the southwest he became a national deity with the rise of the **Rozvi** people, speaking through oracles at certain shrines. Great Zimbabwe and Khami are traditionally held to have been such shrines. The organization of the cult in the southwest is like that of a king's court, with similar officials.

Negritude Ideological movement, the expression in literature and human sciences, particularly anthropology and history, of a specifically "African personality." It was originally part of a widespread cultural revival and assertion of traditional values, beliefs and customs, led by Leopold Senghor, now president of Senegal, Aimé Césaire and, at one time, Agostinho Neto, now president of Angola. It developed during the period of struggle for African political liberty. It was then an expression of African nationalism and the antithesis of white racial supremacy. As such, it was a weapon during a temporary historical phase and has been rendered obsolete by subsequent events. It is now seen by many Africans as a hindrance to a search for unifying elements in evolving non-racial societies.

Neolithic Term invented to describe stone tools made by grinding and polishing rather than chipping or flaking. The association of such tools with farming communities in Europe led to the extension of the definition to cover the period when crops were first cultivated and animals domesticated. It has also, in Europe and southwest Asia, been correlated with the first appearance of pottery and sedentary life. As these traits are neither necessarily functionally related nor introduced at the same time, the term has now lost all precision. Application of it to African prehistory causes needless confusion.

Nok culture Prehistoric culture of central Nigeria, stretching from the Jos plateau southwards across the Benue river. It is associated with the earliest ironworking in black Africa, dated to the first few centuries BC, and produced skillfully executed terracotta sculptures of men and beasts.

Oba Ruler of a Yoruba city or of a city that has historical connections with the Yoruba. To claim the title of Oba, a ruler must be able to trace his direct descent from Oduduwa, the Creator. Obas are distinguished by their right to wear beaded crowns, a right conferred by the **Oni** of Ife. The Oba of Benin is descended from the Yoruba deity Oranmiyan, son of Oduduwa, and a local Edo (Bini) chief's daughter. Bini kingship thus has an alien origin. The present ruling dynasty of Benin can be traced back through 37 kings to about the early 14th century. The present Oba, Akenzua II, succeeded in 1933. His grandfather, Ovaramwen, was deposed by Britain in 1897 prior to the destruction of his palace and the looting of its treasures. The Oba of Benin was until recently a political authority, not simply a figurehead or constitutional monarch.

Obsidian Black natural glass formed by volcanic activity. Its fracturing properties are excellent and, where available, it was the preferred material for chipped and flaked tools. Obsidian is found in only a few places in Africa – particularly the **Rift Valley** of Kenya.

Ogane Potentate who sent symbols of authority cast in brass to the **Oba** of Benin on his accession. As the spiritual head of the Oba's dynasty, he originally exercised some sort of hegemony over Benin. It is generally accepted that traditions regarding the Ogane refer to the **Oni** of Ife. Traditionally, the Bini dynasty shares the same divine origins as the Ife dynasty and is junior to it. The powers of the Ogane were described to the first Portuguese visitors to Benin but these seem to have fallen away. The last Portuguese reference to him was by **de Barros**.

Oil palm (*Elaeis guineensis*) Palm which occurs wild and semi-wild throughout West Africa. The fruit grows in large heads and is valued principally for the oil which is extracted from the outer fleshy covering. It is used for cooking and lighting. The kernel yields a more valuable oil. The sap is tapped to produce an intoxicating wine. The oil palm also provides fiber, fuel and thatching.

Olokun Yoruba deity, owner of the sea and possessor of great wealth. One of the few inland Olokun shrines was at Ife. The evidence for a considerable glass **bead** industry there (involving the melting down of foreign trade beads) is probably not fortuitous. This indication of wealth and overseas contacts probably gave rise to the attribution of the grove to Olokun.

Oni King of the Yoruba state of Ife, a direct descendant of Odudwa, who, at Ife, created the earth and was the progenitor of the Yoruba people. In theory, the title is enjoyed by each of four lineages or branches of the royal clan in rotation. In practice, it is competed for and the most able or popular candidate is selected. The Oni's person is sacred and he is, in many respects, divine. In the past the Oni lived in complete seclusion in his palace and only came out in public for four festivals in the year.

Oral tradition Verbal testimony concerning the past. Oral traditions consist only of hearsay accounts, narrating an event which has not been witnessed or remembered by the informant. Eyewitness accounts on the one hand and rumors on the other are not traditions. Oral traditions require careful interpretation and a full knowledge of the society that holds and transmits them, because concepts of time, myth, duration, development, historical truth etc. are largely socially determined. Normally only events that influence the present are remembered. Traditions serve a primarily social purpose and are therefore continuously altered and remade to fulfill their changing functions more efficiently. They do not necessarily carry absolute or enduring elements. This does not mean their value is less than that of written historical accounts but that their analysis and interpretation require different approaches. Given its potential, oral tradition is particularly fostered and occurs almost exclusively in the courts of kingdoms, as a vehicle to support and validate authority.

Pendentive Brick or masonry triangle with a curved face (flat-faced in false pendentives) inclining inwards from each corner and converting a square bay to a circle, on which a dome can be constructed.

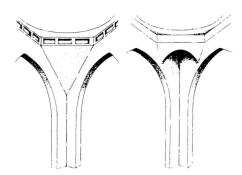

False pendentive (left) and squinch

Periplus of the Erythraean Sea Eyewitness account, written in post-Classical Greek, describing the people, ports and markets along the Red Sea and Indian Ocean coasts of Africa as far as Rhapta on the coast of Tanzania. It is thought to have been written by an agent of imperial Rome early in the 2nd century AD.

Phase Relatively brief period of time within a **tradition**.

Phoenicians Inhabitants of the narrow coastal plain of Lebanon and Syria in the early first millennium BC. After their incorporation into the Babylonian empire in 574 BC, they continued to influence events in the Mediterranean through their powerful colony of Carthage. They were the great seafarers of their time. Their role as merchants and entrepreneurs lasted until they were absorbed in the Hellenistic and Roman world.

Pilaster Rectangular pillar or column, attached to and projecting from the wall of a building.

Pliny the Elder (Gaius Plinius) Roman administrator, provincial governor and military commander in the 1st century AD. His very extensive writings include two monumental histories on the Germanic wars and his own times and *Naturalis Historia*. This encyclopedia has 20,000 entries extracted from the works of nearly 500 different writers. It is extremely uneven, with many mistakes and misunderstandings. It shows little technical knowledge or critical ability. Details that were strange and wonderful attracted Pliny more than those that were really significant.

Porcelain Chinese ceramic with a very thin, hard, white body of kaolin and felspar. Blue-and-white porcelain is painted under a transparent glaze with designs in cobalt blue, one of the very few pigments able to withstand the very high firing temperatures of porcelain. It was first manufactured in significant amounts in the mid-14th century and was exported in great quantities during the Ming dynasty (1368–1644) and the subsequent reign of Kang Hsi (1662–1722).

Prestige goods Commodities whose circulation is restricted to a particular segment of a community. Possession of them confers prestige. Their circulation creates and maintains relations of inequality. Prestige goods are not converted to ordinary use or used as **currency**.

Ptolemy, Claudius Alexandrine Greek who wrote his *Geography* in about 156 AD. In its present form, Ptolemy's *Geography* represents a compilation of the knowledge available in Byzantium about 400 AD – at least as far as East Africa is concerned.

Qibla The direction of Mecca, which is the direction in which prayers should be said by a Muslim worshiper.

Quern Stone on which cereal grains are ground. In black Africa this is traditionally a saddle quern. Saddle querns have a concave or trough-shaped upper surface. Grain is ground in this by means of a backwards and forwards motion of a rubbing stone or *muller*, held in both hands.

Radiocarbon dating Method of obtaining, in theory, an absolute date in terms of calendar years for organic material, by measuring its carbon-14 (C-14) content. This radioactive isotope is formed in the atmosphere and passes with normal carbon (C-12) into all living organisms. When the organism dies, its C-14 breaks down into C-12 at a steady known rate. The longer the organism has been dead, the lower the proportion of C-14 relative to C-12. This proportion is measurable in the laboratory within certain statistical limits represented by the standard deviation (± a certain number of years) quoted with all radiocarbon dates. As the amount of C-14 in the atmosphere has varied over the centuries, it is now apparent that radiocarbon dates cannot be considered as calendar dates. The calibration of the two forms of dates has still to be fully worked out. However, the differences in the last three millennia are not great.

Randall-MacIver, David (1873–1945) British archaeologist, Laycock Student of Egyptology at Worcester College, Oxford. He excavated at Great Zimbabwe in 1905, at the invitation of the Rhodes Trustees and the British Association for the Advancement of Science. His *Mediaeval Rhodesia* was published in 1906. He directed fieldwork in Egypt and the Sudan for several years for the University of Philadelphia, before settling in Rome in 1921 and devoting the remainder of his life to Etruscan studies.

Reef gold Gold in undisturbed mineralized ore bodies, as opposed to **alluvial** or eluvial (hillwash) gold, where the metal has been eroded from the weathered reef, transported and redeposited. Reef gold has to be mined, which means excavating to uncover the reef; breaking it up by fire or other means and extracting the ore it contains; crushing, milling or grinding the ore to a fine dust; and, in the absence of modern chemical processes, washing the waste, i.e. panning it to separate and remove waste soil or dust, leaving the metal as a residue. Mining is generally a more dangerous, arduous and laborious process than recovering redeposited gold from the soil or from alluvial deposits.

Rhodes, Cecil John (1853–1902) British financier and diamond magnate; prime minister of the Cape Colony (1890–96); donor of the Rhodes scholarships at Oxford. Rhodes obtained a Royal Charter for his company to govern the country north of the Transvaal in 1889. He inspired and financed the consequent occupation of what became Northern and Southern Rhodesia in 1890. He showed an early and continuing interest in Great Zimbabwe, purchased relics from the ruins prior to the occupation and retained a personal right to purchase all finds from all ruins in the territory thereafter. He quickly recognized Great Zimbabwe's value as a dramatic symbol

of the success, virtue and appropriateness of the foreign colonization and exploitation of the territory. He sponsored the first investigations of the ruins by **Bent**.

Rift Valley Two valley systems in East Africa that are part of a line of weakness in the earth's crust stretching from the Dead Sea through the Red Sea, the Awash valley of Ethiopia, Lake Turkana (Rudolf) to Lake Malawi and its river outlet to the Zambezi river. In East Africa the line bifurcates. The western Rift Valley passes along the borders of Zaire, Rwanda and Burundi to Tanzania. Branches contain the Lakes Albert, Edward, Kivu and Tanganyika. The eastern rift passes through central Kenya. It is between 20 and 40 miles wide and over 1,000 feet deep. Its length is studded with a number of small saline lakes. The area was one of tectonic and volcanic activity and the valley floors contain visible evidence of successive faults. Many extinct volcanic cones and caldera occur in and near the valley.

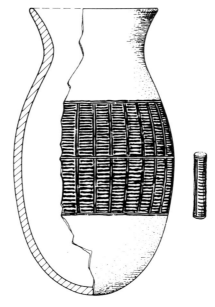

Rouletted ware and (right) roulette

Rouletted wares Pottery decorated by rolling a small cylinder of carved wood or a short length of twisted or plaited material (string, raffia, palm fronds), held in the palm of the hand, over the damp clay of the vessel's surface. The technique can generally be associated with the **later Iron Age** and some of the forest kingdoms of West Africa.

Rozvi Section of the Shona people who rose to prominence in the late 17th century. The Rozvi **Mambo**, Dombo, drove the Portuguese from the plateau in 1693. Rozvi territorial power ended in defeat at the hands of Nguni invaders in the 1830s. During their

expansion, the Rozvi incorporated many Shona groups. Now only those who share the royal totem are considered Rozvi.

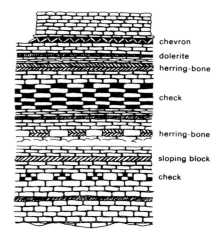

Decorative walling on the facade of Nalatali from the Rozvi period

Sasanian-Islamic ware Ceramic with a soft, buff body and a deep blue alkaline glaze, over an incised zigzag decoration or applied strips or blobs of clay. A very common ware at Siraf, in southern Iran, where it is dated to the 7th–10th centuries AD.

Seljuk Turkish dynasty that controlled most of Central Asia and Iraq in the 11th–13th centuries. The Seljuks of Rum left most striking monuments in what is now modern Turkey.

Selous, Frederick Courtenay (1851–1916) British hunter, naturalist and explorer. Selous entered Matabeleland in 1872 and thereafter, with the Ndebele king's permission, hunted over the Zambezian plateau for many years and acquired, for a foreigner, an unrivaled knowledge of it and its peoples. He acted as guide to **Rhodes**'s British South Africa Company force when it occupied the territory in 1890, under a British royal charter. Selous left the country finally in 1896, disillusioned by the Company's conduct of military campaigns against the local people. He was killed serving in the British Army in Tanganyika in World War I. A man of exceptional kindness and gentleness, his many books reveal his cultured personality and wide interests. He is believed to have been the model of Rider Haggard's *Alan Quatermain*.

Serology Aspect of human biology and biochemistry concerned with the study of blood types and groups. Human blood-group substances show variation between individuals. Different individuals in the same population will have different types but a population as a whole can be characterized by the proportions of different types present. Populations can be distinguished by statistical analysis and, ideally, their relationships to other populations, the sequence of these relationships and hence their history and origins can be discerned.

Sheba (Sheba is the Biblical spelling; Saba is more correct.) The Sabaeans were, throughout the first millennium BC, the **Phoenicians** of the "southern seas" beyond the Mediterranean: the Red Sea and the northwest Indian Ocean. They monopolized the trade of these regions. Their home was the southern tip of the Arabian peninsula in what is now Yemen. It was fertile and well watered and produced aromatic spices – including myrrh and frankincense. These were carried by caravans north, along the "Sabaean route" that followed the Red Sea coast of Arabia to Syria and the Mediterranean. The biblical Queen of Sheba, Bilqis in Arabic, probably had her headquarters at one of the northern Sabaean towns on the caravan route. She took characteristic Sabaean gifts to Solomon, king of Israel, in the 10th century BC. Solomon had his fleet in the Gulf of Akaba and was the largest trader in goods from Ophir, now a synonym for a gold-producing land, probably in Oman. The Sabaean capital was at Marib, 60 miles west of Sana'a, the capital of present Yemen. Remains at Marib include a massive masonry dam to control the wadi floodwaters for irrigation and a great stone elliptical temple of similar dimensions to Great Zimbabwe, built in the 8th–6th centuries BC and known as the Harem of Bilqis. Sabaean emigrants crossed the Red Sea and settled in the northern extremity of the Ethiopian plateau about the 6th century BC. They exerted great political and cultural influence on the foundations of the Ethiopian kingdom (the recently ousted imperial dynasty traced its descent to Menelik, offspring of Solomon's seduction of the Queen of Sheba). Ge'ez, the literary and liturgical language of Ethiopia, is a modified form of Sabaean and written in a Sabaean syllabary. Ports and trade that were originally Sabaean are described in the **Periplus of the Erythraean Sea**.

Shrine Object or place hallowed by its associations with a holy person or divinity. In Africa shrines are by no means all monumental structures or buildings. Stones, caves, groves of trees or other natural features may be treated as shrines. In Ife the find spots of concentrations of prehistoric terracotta sculptures or other artifacts are now shrines, although the original purpose of these sculptures is quite unknown.

Smithing Fashioning metal by repeated hammering and annealing (reheating the metal to produce a new crystalline structure) as opposed to casting molten metal.

Soapstone Stone very rich in talc and thus extremely soft and easily carved and worked.

Its color ranges through various shades of green to yellow.

Sorghum Staple grain crop of the African savanna. With wheat, barley and rice, it is one of the world's four main cereals. Sorghum requires more than 15 inches of rainfall p.a. It has a short summer growing season, needs little attention, is drought-resistant and can be easily stored. The five basic races of sorghum (*Sorghum bicolor*) are *bicolor*, *caudatum*, *durra* (which was introduced from East Africa to India and thence to the rest of Asia), *guinea* (dominant in the West African forests and able to grow where the rainfall is up to 120 inches p.a.) and *kafir* (kaffir corn – the dominant race in southern Africa).

Spandrel Space between the curves of an arch and its surrounding rectangular moldings or framework.

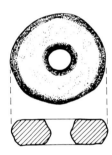

Spindle whorl from Nhunguza

Spindle whorl Circular object with a central perforation intended to act as the flywheel on a spindle, giving momentum to its rotation. They provide valuable evidence for spinning and weaving, for the thread and fabric, and the components of looms (particularly in Africa, where loom weights were not used) rarely survive in archaeological deposits. In much of Africa during the **later Iron Age** spindle whorls were disks cut from sherds of pottery. In eastern Africa their dates and distribution suggest that spinning and weaving were introduced by early Arab immigrants to the east coast cities and the interior.

Spirit medium (Shona: **mhondoro**) One who, during a ritually induced trance, is possessed by the spirit of a former king, hero or ancestor of the community. He acts as an intermediary between spirits and men. He is often the preeminent repository of the group's law, precedents, traditions and history. The basic function of some mediums is divining. Others are essentially public figures who play important political roles.

Squinch Arch placed across each corner of a square bay to reduce it to an octagon, and forming the springing on which a dome can be constructed.

States of modern Africa

State In Europe a state is defined in terms of centralized authority with territorial sovereignty, a monopoly of physical, military or coercive force and specialized office holders. It is the product of a society based on class, where access to certain resources is the prerogative of certain groups. In precolonial Africa the distinctions were by no means so clear-cut and the European criteria are much less significant. States and stateless societies formed a continuum. Subjects of African states retained the lineage-based loyalties characteristic of stateless societies but, in addition, they had a number of cross-cutting institutions, such as age grades, hunting societies or initiation groups. These could attract and retain the loyalties of the disparate groups within the state and so integrate them in a single wider political community.

Stela Upright stone, often carved, decorated or inscribed.

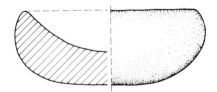

Stone bowl from Prospect Farm

Stone Bowl culture Name given by **Louis Leakey** to a series of "Neolithic" industries found by him and Mary Leakey in the **Rift Valley** of Kenya, characterized by small thick-walled dishes and platters pecked and chiseled from volcanic tuffs and lavas. These sites are now seen to have belonged to pastoralists in the first millennium BC, the first food producers in East Africa.

Stoneware Ceramics intermediate between terracotta and porcelain. They have a hard body that fires a pale buff, light brown or gray. They are most commonly made of a mixture of china (kaolin) and siliceous clays (containing a high proportion of sand). Stoneware is fired at a temperature between 1200 and 1300°C. Stoneware glazes commonly consist of ground felspar, a very common mineral (as in **celadon**). At these temperatures a glaze can also be produced by throwing salt in the fire, which vaporizes and combines with elements in the ceramic body to give a salt glaze. Such glazes are generally monochrome blacks, browns and greens.

Stratigraphy One of the major tools of archaeological interpretation based on the recognition and description of superimposed archaeological or geological layers or strata. With successive deposits, the upper must have accumulated later than the lower. Rare exceptions to this law (e.g. from slipping, burrowing or other disturbance) do exist. These can, with careful excavation, be identified and accounted for.

Subsistence economy System of production that provides only for the immediate sustenance and needs of the producers and generates no surplus for development, investment or administrative costs. In a subsistence economy communities are self-sufficient and exchange transactions are dependent on social status and kinship relations. Goods have a social or use value rather than an exchange value.

Sudanic kingship See **Divine kingship**.

Swidden Agricultural system in which land lies fallow for longer than it is cropped. This allows the vegetation time to regenerate to bush and often eventually to woodland or forest. The shifting of fields is prompted by declining soil fertility, weed invasion or erosion. Swidden is the dominant agricultural system of the savanna. It is land-extensive and inhibits large, concentrated or nucleated settlement. It does not necessarily imply that smaller settlements have to be moved.

Terracotta Clay fired at a low temperature, equivalent to that of an open fire. The fabric remains porous and is not vitrified.

Territorial cult Religious institution related to a land area and not to a kinship grouping. Territorial spirits are considered to be the owners of a particular area. The main function of a territorial cult is to ensure the material and moral well-being of the entire population of the area. It provides such a population, which may be otherwise heterogeneous, with a group identity. It is especially concerned with such things as fertility of the land, rain making and success in hunting.

Thermoluminescence Method of dating baked clay, terracotta or pottery directly. It is

based on the principle that certain particles, produced at a regular rate through radioactive decay, are trapped in the lattice structure of any crystal (including those in all clays). They are only released on heating the crystal. The time that has elapsed since the crystal was last heated (i.e. the time since the clay was fired) can be calculated by measuring the number of particles originally trapped in the material (measured by light emission) and comparing this with those trapped in it after exposure to a radioactive source of known strength.

Tradition In archaeological usage, persistent configurations of artifacts, products of simple technologies made over a relatively long period of time; a sequence of **industries** or a succession of **phases** of industries, which develop out of each other and form a continuum in time.

Principal ethnic groups in Africa

Tribe Confusing and emotive term covering a shifting kaleidoscope of traits, defining groups of people in many different senses: subjects of a particular king; speakers of the same language or dialect; inhabitants of a particular area; those who share a particular awareness and state of mind. It is a term often applied only by outsiders or officials for what they envisage as a group. The people themselves may share no sense of identity. It is a term now best discarded.

Tribute Symbolic statement, expressed in tangible terms of goods or services, of loyalty and submission, made by a subordinate to a superior or by a subject to his king or protector. Tribute sets up a relationship of mutual dependence and binds the two parties. A ruler is expected to provide protection and largesse. Hence, a large proportion of tribute is

redistributed and an extremely important function of a chief's court is as a center for redistributing the products of the chiefdom. In Africa, where a ruler's strength is generally measured almost entirely in the numbers of his followers, tribute is rarely onerous and its symbolic significance frequently outweighs its economic value.

Trypanosomiasis Disease caused by a microscopic parasite transmitted by biting flies of the *Glossina* genus, the **tsetse fly**. Trypanosomiasis is known as "sleeping sickness" in man, because of the lethargy produced in the last stages of infection. It causes no ill effects in its main hosts, savanna antelope, but is deadly for most domesticated animals.

Tsetse fly Biting fly belonging to various species of the *Glossina* genus, transmitters of **trypanosomiasis**. *Glossina* live mainly on wild game. Their habitat is open woodland, thicket savanna or tropical forest, where the winter temperature is not below 16°C or the summer temperature over 32°C. Human settlement tends to deplete or drive away game and thus the tsetse fly, enabling cattle to be introduced. Tsetse-infested areas are an important determinant of settlement for cattle-owning groups.

Tumulus Mound covering a burial.

Umayyad Muslim dynasty that reigned from 661 to 750 AD, based principally in Syria, Palestine and Egypt. The Umayyads expanded the Muslim territories enormously. On their downfall, a refugee Umayyad caliphate was established in Cordoba, Spain.

Underdevelopment Process by which a surplus is transferred from one state to another; it obtains where the two states are joined in an exploitative relationship and form the two poles, satellite and metropolis, or core and periphery, of a single economic system. Underdevelopment of African states by their foreign trading partners extends back at least to the start of the Atlantic slave trade. Elements of it can be discerned even earlier. Underdevelopment implies loss of productive forces, lack of proportional growth, loss of development opportunities and the creation of a relationship of dependence.

Unequal exchange Primary means by which a surplus is appropriated from the periphery by the metropolis in the process of **underdevelopment**. For some scholars, if between two trading partners wages are unequal but profits equal, surplus passes from the country paying the lower wages to that paying the higher wages. Others see unequal exchange in the export of raw materials that are precious or wasting assets in exchange for manufactured goods.

van Nyendael, David Dutch merchant who visited Benin in 1699 and 1702, had an audience of the **Oba** and has left the most lengthy and detailed description of the city and its trade. This was published in W. Bosman's *A New and Accurate Description of the Coast of Guinea* (Utrecht, 1704; London, 1705).

Vashambadzi (Mushambadzi, sing.; Mussambazes in Portuguese writings) Name, said to be derived from *sambazar*, to trade or mine gold, denoting a class of specialized, professional African traders. In the 18th century they were based on the Portuguese headquarters at Zumbo on the middle Zambezi river and operated in groups throughout the **Rozvi** territories, bartering for gold from village to village, as well as visiting the Rozvi court and **fairs**. They traded in cattle as well as gold. Trade was a seasonal occupation and some were farmers for the remainder of the year. Although they were agents for the Portuguese, who were banned from Rozvi territory, they were certainly not slaves – as the Portuguese described them – but operated largely independently. They also engaged in commerce for themselves.

Yam (*Dioscorea*) Large tubers, produce of a twining vine. Pounded to a meal and cooked as a stiff porridge, they are the staple food of a large part of tropical Africa from the Ivory Coast to Cameroun. They are propagated by cuttings. Yam festivals, celebrating the first harvest with considerable ritual, occur in many parts of West Africa. They indicate the high antiquity and significance of the crop and provide a means of regulating the time of harvest and thus prevent the wasteful gathering of immature tubers. The indigenous African yams are *Dioscorea cayenensis* and *D. rotundata*. Much confusion has been caused by suggestions that yams or their cultivation were first introduced to Africa from Southeast Asia. In fact, Asian forms were introduced to Africa only in the last 500 years.

Zanj Arab term used by people of the Persian Gulf to denote the inhabitants of the East African coast between Cape Guardafui and the Equator, usually considered to be Bantu-speaking Negroids. The name first came to prominence in connection with the revolt, in 868 AD, of Zanj slaves engaged in draining the marshlands of southern Iraq.

Zimba Notorious horde of cannibals who, according to Portuguese chroniclers, caused terror along the East African coast in the 1580s, killing and eating their victims in every town they conquered north of Mozambique Island. They besieged and laid waste to Kilwa and Mombasa before they were all but annihilated as they stormed Malindi in Kenya. Less luridly, they were probably warriors from the Lundu kingdom, between Lake Malawi and the Zambezi river. In their military campaigns, they extended their hegemony to the coast in a bid to win control of the ivory trade with the Portuguese.

Zimbabwe Shona word, sometimes considered a contraction of *dzimba dza mabwe*, "houses of stone," but probably better derived from *dzimba woye*, "venerated houses," and hence "chiefs' houses or graves." It is particularly applied to a great stone-built ruin on the southeast edge of the Zambezian plateau. It is more correctly applicable to all structures of similar style that were also courts or centers of government. Southern Rhodesia will, on independence, adopt this as the name of the new nation.

Index